Social Movements in Karnataka

A Study of Kudremukh Region in the Western Ghats

V.K. Sridhar

AAKAR

Social Movements in Karnataka: A Study of Kudremukh Region in the Western Ghats

V.K. Sridhar

First Published 2019

ISBN 978-93-5002-593-2

Published by
AAKAR BOOKS
28 E Pocket IV, Mayur Vihar Phase I
Delhi 110 091 India
aakarbooks@gmail.com

Laser Typeset at
Arpit Printographers, Delhi

Printed at
D.K. Fine Art Press, Delhi

Content

Acknowledgements

Studies undertaken by social movements on collective action can be defined as collective efforts of a section of people to pursue certain shared objectives, goals, and values even in the face of opposition and conflict which are seen in an isolated form rather than interconnectedness. Collective conflicts may assume various forms of actions ranging from organized modes of protest such as *dharnas* (sit-ins), boycotts, *hartals* (strikes), picketing and peaceful sloganeering and protest marches to active and violent outbursts of people by the non-institutional means of resistance through 'revolution' in a social movement. But many forms of interpersonal, dispersed and unshared conflicts, even when involving groups do not lead to collective action. The social structures are described by more than one variant like caste, class, religious groups, stratification in terms of education, wealth and so on. Thus scholars have drawn an actor-oriented approach which seeks to understand conflicts as outcomes of the interaction of different actors pursuing often quite distinctive aims and interests. The major works were influenced by everyday resistance with the critique of structural variants of Marxist theories which widen the spectrum of social movements opposing hegemony of productive resources to include culture, ideology and their way of life.

The major divide which differentiates mobilizations of

different types directed towards change with reference to a social system is based on the question of whether the collective mobilizations are seeking to bargain for a greater share of the rewards and facilities by the existing system or alter the system itself. The works of M.S.A. Rao and Ghanshyam Shah were the first in the systematic attempts to comprehend contemporary social movements. They could be classified as revolutionary (radical movements that sought to transform all society such as the Naxalite struggle) reformist (movements for limited change for all society, such as the backward class movement) and redemptive (radical change for specific social groups such as sectarian movements). Shah categorized social movements such as revolt, rebellion, reform and revolution in terms of their objectives or the nature of change in the political system they sought to achieve. The most important factor for social movements to emerge is to challenge hegemonic ideas in society and to activate public debates that were previously taken for granted. Social movements are also classified on the basis of issues around which participants get mobilized. The movements are classified on the basis of the participants, such as peasants, tribals, students, women, Dalits, etc. In a democratic society social movement represents an important challenge that leads to the building of equality. They arise out of the tensions and imperfections of the society, very often representing the oppressed groups specifically with egalitarian structures. The role of social movements has been documented in numerous individual case studies relating to ethnic, language, gender, environmental and other movements. The present study of social movements where different scholars have carried out research in an isolated manner. However, there is a need for interlinkages of social movement which served the constituent of the disadvantaged people whom the movement represents which is complex and manifold.

I would like to thank Vijay Rajan Singh (DCF) Karkalla, Vittal Hedge, Muniyappa, G.V. Kempe Gowda, Jagdish, Periyaswamy, S.Venkataraya, T. Veerana, Kulkarni, Shubhas Kharbare, Rajan Yedoor, Somantha Nayak, B.G. Kushalappa, K.S. Kashinath, K.G. Sridhar, Praveen Bhargava, Girja Shankar,

Vittal Rao, D.V. Girish, Gunashekaran, K.M. Abdul Jabber, Ramesh, Direck Anil, Srikant, Vasu, Ashish Kothari, Rajeev Sanial, Bharath D. Malai and B.P. Ravi.

I thank the University Grants Commission for providing financial assistance which helped me to conduct interviews and discussions with representatives of different organizations leading the movement, Trade Union Organizations, Peasant Organizations, Coffee Boards, Small Growers Federation, trade unions & NGOs, Karnataka Vimochana Ranga, Karnataka Forest Department, Wild Organizations and Human Rights activists. I thank the staff of several libraries and archives in India, the Chikmagalur District Library, Karnataka Planters Association, Coffee Yatra, Plantation Workers Union. The Karnataka State Archives, Institute for Social and Economic Change, Coffee Board Library, Centre for Wildlife Studies, Kudremukh Iron Ore Company Limited, Indian Institute of Science, Aryana Bhavan and United Planters Association of India (Coonoor). In Delhi I would like to thank the libraries of Centre for Political Studies, JNU, Teen Murti, World Wild Fund Library and Centre for Science and Environment. Further, I wish to thank the Bombay Natural History Society (Mumbai), and Kalpavriksh (Pune). I am indebted to all my friends in JNU and the enriching experience of being affiliated to student politics which gave me the privilege of discussing political issues around movements with the party cadres, leaders and activists of different organizations who provided vital support during the course of the work. I am thankful to all my colleagues in the Motilal Nehru College and the library staff for issuing books and last but not the least, I wish to record my special thanks to my family.

V.K. Sridhar

Introduction

The study of social movement has assumed a central place in contemporary social science research. The term 'social movement' refers to associations, groups and individuals that are allied with each other through sharing a particular programme of action or sense of identity. It is large, more extensive, and more diverse and is termed as "movement" to emphasize its involvement in action. It does not have a precise definition accepted by scholars of different disciplines or even within the discipline of political science. Some scholars use the term 'movement' interchangeably with organization or union. Others may use it to mean a historical trend or tendency such as renaissance, etc.[1] The terms such as democracy, masses, popular, equality, etc. are often used differently by different social activists, political leaders and scholars who have written on movements. These terms were concerned with the emancipation of the exploited classes and the creation of a new society by changing property relationships.

The social movement saw collective mobilization from the perspective of class drawing on the classical Marxist approaches, neo-Marxist and functionalist traditions like trade union politics, peasant, tribal, and other movements. Social movement relates to the long-term goal of democratizing development and transforming society. It helps us to understand what is wrong with the present and what needs to be done in the future. The orientation of a social movement to bring about or prevent changes is not constant and may change according to the course of time. The major components of social movement are objectives, ideology, programmes, leadership, and organization, which are interdependent and influence each other. Social movements are also classified on the basis of issues around which participants get mobilized. Some others classify movements on the basis of the participants such as peasants, tribals, anti-untouchability, linguistic, nationalist, etc. In many cases the participants and issues go together.

The classification of movements is difficult as the objectives of the social movement change from narrow specific local issues to broad aims for social transformation or may refer to one or two particular issues. According to M.S.A. Rao, social movements are reformist, transformatory and revolutionary. They essentially involve sustained collective mobilization through either informal or formal organization and are generally oriented towards bringing about change in the existing system of relationships. T.K. Oommen's typology is based on the process of movement crystallization, the life-cycle and the phases of social movements, which are charismatic, ideological and organizational. These typologies though useful, do not explain the dynamics of the movements which undergo change in the course of time.[2] The traditional social movements were primarily class-based with reorganization of power as a central goal, which functioned within the framework of political parties.

The new social movements as a contrast were not about changing distribution of power, but often about quality-of-life issues. The latter tend to have organizational structures, stress decentralization and participatory decision-making and have also developed new forms of political activism such as clean environment and expressions of cultural identities. In India the most important factor for social movements to emerge is to challenge hegemonic ideas in society and to make public debates that were previously taken for granted. For example, Ramachandra Guha's work on the Chipko movement marked the beginning of a public debate on the environment with emphasis on everyday resistance inspired by Antonio Gramsci's writings on hegemony and consciousness. Ranjit Guha's, *Elementary Aspects of Peasant Insurgency* (1982) has influenced the subaltern studies 'history from below' and has inspired extensive work with the label of new social movements. The traditional Marxist scholars have been criticized by 'Subaltern Studies' for ignoring the history of the masses, as if the subaltern classes do not make history on their own, depending solely on the advanced classes or the elite for organization and guidance.[3] It is argued that the traditional Marxists have undermined cultural factors and viewed a linear development of class consciousness. On the other hand the subaltern studies' historians are criticized by other Marxist scholars for ignoring structural factors and viewing consciousness as independent of structural contradictions. In India under the rubric of new social movements like civil rights, farmers, and environment movements have been taken up by civil society against the state which is seen as oppressive and unable to solve the problems of exploitation, poverty, and uneven development.[4]

New Social Movements

In the 1980s, European and American societies witnessed the emergence of large-scale movements around issues which were basically humanist, cultural and non-materialistic in nature and have been referred to as "new social movements."[5] The issue-based politics of movements based on shared identities and common characteristics of not only class, but also gender, race, ethnicity, religion, and other cultural criteria have developed "new oppositional counter-discursive forms of consciousness and action".[6] In India according to Fuentes and Frank these NSMs are popular social movements and expressions of people's struggles against exploitation and oppression in a complex dependent society.[7] Gail Omvedt classifies the struggles into old and new, the former as peasants and the latter as farmers' movements.[8] These movements have sought to act more as pressure groups, periodically staging huge demonstrations and intense campaigns, but not directly identifying with any political party. They demand remunerative prices for their produce, concessions and subsidies in the prices of agricultural inputs, electricity charges, irrigation charges and betterment levies. The new social movements seek to go beyond the

Marxist political economy stressing capitalism at the cost of the state and civil society and the realm of culture as a means of collective action. The NSO theories stress post-materialist values like quality-of-life, aesthetics, freedom, gender equality, sexuality, ecology, etc. in collective action as opposed to conflict over materialist values and resources.[9]

These 'new' social movements claim to use politics amounting to social change without state power. The claim to achieve empowerment by NGOs at the grassroots by using non-party/'a-political' has led to de-politicized mobilization towards the existing class structure and diverting mobilization from each other. This has also resulted in the emergence of varied NGOs like Green Peace, Friends of the Earth, the Sierra Club, Earth First, World Wild Fund for Nature and various less formal organizations and groups. They received substantial funding from International Financial Institutions despite their occasional outbursts against neoliberalism. These associations with globally-based networks are allied with each other through their overlapping membership, frequent communication and joint campaigns with one another and form coalitions and seek to establish claims on national and global civil society. The focus on the local-global nexus has become more compelling given the interconnections between environmental issues and those pertaining to rights. The transformative edges of new social movements in the forefront of the alternative development movement in the West as well as globally have made the issues of poverty and social deprivation less relevant in the global discourse.[10]

The social movements took some time to recover from the onslaught of neoliberalism.[11] They were largely fragmented with each group fighting its own little battle independently. Margaret Thatcher proclaimed that "(t)here is 'no other alternative' (TINA) to the neoliberal alliance between the corporate open free market and the state; to growth rates; biotechnological advances, information revolution, infrastructure development, growing purchasing power of people, inflation, indebtedness, etc.[12] The retreat of the state has led to the commercial interests of private actors who have taken precedence over the conservation, protection, access and sustainability of the earth's fragile natural resources.[13]

A detailed discussion of this rich body of literature is beyond the scope of this introductory chapter. We have used the term social movements since the claims of the new social movements may be contested. However the question of land continues to be relevant in different forms and the counter-hegemonic force is still weak. The study will focus on the Kudremukh region which illustrates the conflicting claims of small coffee growers rights of the workers, rights of the local tribals and environment concerns which involve a conflict of interests, can be negotiated through peaceful means. But these conflicts are increasingly leading to hostile camps with allegations and counter-allegations. These involves however, did not contribute to the growth of a broad bared social movement by involving different ideological streams, discourses and categories. This urges us to rethink class-based politics, which fail to explain social movements.

Coffee Crisis and Small Growers Around the Kudremukh Region

The coffee plantation crop occupies an important space in the economy of Chikmagalur district, which was earlier a part of the erstwhile princely state of Mysore[14] has a distinct physical character of the region. The land systems, investment patterns, historical origins and political ethos vary quite sharply across different regions.

The unprecedented coffee crisis due to the continuous fall in coffee prices since 1998 reached the lowest prices in 2002. The price of Arabica, which averaged ₹ 90 a kg in 1999, dropped to ₹ 63 a kg in the last quarter of 2001 and in the same period Robusta fell from ₹ 68 a kg to ₹ 33 a kg. This coincided with the dismantling of the Indian Coffee Board adding to the belief that the coffee board was the reason for the crisis. The Coffee Board which acted as a monopoly has been taken over by private business companies and is feeling the impact of a steep decline in prices by the vagaries of free trade that govern the industry internationally. The price crash coincided with drought for three consecutive years (2002-04) resulting in a severe outbreak of the dreaded pest white stem borer and leaf rust disease in Arabica coffee. During the crisis the small coffee growers which was fragmented and led by many associations did not come together to discuss the global crisis. Instead the issue was to focus on various cuts in salaries of the labourers.

The bigger organizations like Karnataka Planters' Association affiliated to United Planters' Association of India (UPASI) have opposed militant mass protest by coffee growers. The KPA, for instance, was on its toes to condemn a spontaneous gherao of the chairperson of the Coffee Board and believes in peaceful negotiation and settlement for resolving issues. It has been successful in lobbying and meeting the Union Commerce Minister, Finance Minister and Prime Minister to express their anxiety with respect to the coffee price situation and other related aspects.[15] The more balanced approach of these associations has been respected by the respective state governments and centre.[16] The chairman of the Karnataka Planters' Association A.S. Muthanna affirmed that between 1998 and 2002 the coffee industry had lost up to ₹ 2,000 crore. He warned that the coffee industry was "on the verge of collapse".[17] In view of this crucial contribution, the government should protect and promote the cash crop growers of this region as its responsibility. This sort of severe crash of prices has drained the farmers of their earnings and the steep hike in the input costs due to withdrawal of subsidies, hike in the price of fertilizers, electricity, water, diesel, seeds and plants has made agriculture too expensive.[18]

The Ministry of Commerce concerned with the problems of the coffee growers implemented a special package in 2002 called Special Coffee Term Loan (SCTL) for the coffee growers announced by the Reserve Bank of India. The major criticism against the "Special Coffee Term Loan" (SCTL)[19] was that it remained unpaid. The first relief came by a waiver of interest on SCTL from 2002 to 2005 wherein growers had to pay one-third and the remaining two-third was shared by the bank and the government of India. The Government announced the Vidarbaha Package in 2006 which included waiver of interest on all over due loans in 25 districts of the country where suicides were high owing to debts. The three districts of Chikmagalur, Hassan and Kodagu were included and this package considerably reduced the interest burden of the growers who had not opted for the SCTL package.[20]

The response of the trade unions and peasant organizations to the crisis has been sedate as different organizations came together to form a Joint Action Committee and submitted a memorandum to the Government of India. It organized a strike by workers on December 11, 2000 demanding various tax concessions to "save the plantation industry and its workmen".[21] There are 15 lakh workers employed directly and indirectly and most of the labourers are categorized as permanent, temporary and migratory. In recent years the shortage of labour has been filled by migratory labourers from Odisha, Bengal and Assam.[22] Thus Indian coffee farmers is characterized by inter-regional variations and is different across the coffee regions. The small growers are the majority of the coffee planters in Chikmagalur district and require a region-specific policy for the survival of coffee plantations.

In this background the protest against Kudremukh Iron Ore Company (KIOCL 1969-99) which wanted an extension of contract was coming to an end and the company wanted an extension of the contract for another twenty years. Initially the permission was extended till 2002 under a "temporary working permission" granted by the Ministry of Environment and Forests (MoEF). The main argument against the company was raised by Karnataka Vimochana Ranga, a CPI (ML) organization, which stated that KIOCL was export-oriented and the pollution caused to river Bhadra might also affect the Tunga river. The campaign was joined by different organizations and amongst them the coffee planters also protested against the KIOCL for closing the company because of shortage of labourers in coffee estates. The villagers who worked in the company if closed would become destitute and be compelled to work in the neighbouring coffee estates. The issue was also linked with the local people in the nearby villages of Jamble, Neelibedu, and Samse[23] whe were dependent on the company for their livelihood either as permanent employees of the company or as contract labourers. They had their own grievances against the company regarding employment opportunities for their families or relatives.

Mining and Kudremukh Iron Ore Company Limited

Kudremukh is situated at 1,894.3 metres above the sea level, and is rich in iron ore deposits. The Kudremukh Iron Ore Company (KIOCL)[24] conducted mining operations, benefaction and transportation of the ore as slurry through pipelines to the Mangalore port. Kudremukh Iron Ore Company (KIOCL) was granted a 30-year mining lease in 1969 and allotted 3,203.55 hectares of reserve forest land in Kudremukh. In 1987, the first notification declaring Kudremukh as a national park brought the mining area under the purview of the Wildlife Protection Act 1972, which does not allow non-forest operations, including mining within a protected area.

Though the mining lease ended, the central government extended it initially for one year by giving a Temporary Working Permission under Section 2 of the Forest Conservation Act. The Forest Conservation Act lays down an elaborate process for clearing projects with tracts over 40 ha. The project proposal is sent to the centre while the state can grant approvals for diversion of tracts up to 5 ha. The Forest Conservation Act mandates the Union Government's approval for diversion of forest land for non-forestry uses. It does not ban such conversion with the condition for several regulatory measures.

The Forest Conservation Act 1980 was an attempt by the centre to introduce some long-term thinking into otherwise short-sighted conversion of forests to other uses. The Forest Conservation Act of 1980, enacted after forests have moved from the state to the concurrent list in 1976, made central government permission mandatory for diverting forest land to non-forest uses across the entire country. This powerful legislation has, to a large extent, curtailed the indiscriminate logging and release of forest land for non-forestry purposes by state governments. The Supreme Court's intervention on forests has undergone a change with enlarging the scope of existing conservation laws particularly the Forest Conservation Act

1980 leading to negative social, ecological and administrative effects.[25]

The genesis of the Godavarman case was the reluctance of the central as well as the state governments to take tough decisions relating to environment in general and forests in particular. This powerful legislation has, to a large extent, curtailed the indiscriminate logging and release of forest land for non-forestry purposes by state governments. Initially the definition of "forest land" was assumed to be only that land which has been legally notified as forest as per the Indian Forest Act or Reserved or Protected Forest.[26] Over time its mandate has been extended even to lands with preliminary notifications where rights are still to be settled, in addition to "any area recorded as forest in the government records". Although the FCA has nothing to do with the settlement of rights, it brought even the slow and inefficient forest survey and settlement process in different states to a near halt. Thus FCA effectively converted several million long-standing forest dwellers as illegal "encroachers" on their ancestral lands.

The Forest Conservation Act was enacted to check the widespread felling of trees on developmental projects site. But the Act's stringent provisions are supported by environmentalists because the state governments are complaining about the project delays through the Forest Conservation Act. The social movements have also protested against the diversion of forest land on mining that has led to protests from various individuals and movements. The management of KIOCL defended the mining on the plank that check-dams such as Lakya dam were constructed before the commencement of the project operations to store tailings and allow clean water to the plant for recycling. The campaign was also joined by Bangalore-based Non-Government Organizations like Wildlife First, which initially filed Public Interest Litigation (PIL) in the High Court but later filed a petition under the Forest Conservation Act 1980 before the Supreme Court in 2001. The case was heard through Interloculatory Application in the IA 670 case where the Supreme Court was assisted by the Central Empowered Committee (CEC) which decided its own procedures, and was not bound to follow the procedure laid down in the Civil Procedure Code or any of the state forest laws when dealing with applications.

The closure of the company has attracted criticism from workers' unions as it did not hear all the affected workmen before passing the order. The KIOCL was a bustling mining camp housing nearly 2,279 employees consisting of 468 executives and 1811 non-executives and their families with a total strength of 10,000 staying in the camp area. The three unions which were recognized by the company were Kudremukh Shram Shakti Shangathan, affiliated to (Hind Mazdoor Sangh), Kudremukh Employees' Union affiliated to (Indian National Trade Union Congress) and Kudremukh Mazdoor Sangh affiliated to (Bharitya Mazdoor Sangh). The workers' union raised the issue of livelihood, but received compensation from the management. On the other hand, daily wage workers affiliated to (AITUC) were deprived of rehabilitation and compensation on grounds that they were only contract workers. The Wildlife First demanded the closure of the company which led to the final notification of the Kudremukh National Park which is spread over an area of 563 sq. kms and falls in three districts namely, Dakshina Kannada district (158 sq. kms), Udupi district (89 sq. kms) and Chikmagalur district (316 sq. kms.). The conventional approaches to Protected Areas, National Parks and Wildlife Sanctuaries are at the forefront of modern efforts to conserve biological diversity which is in a state of crisis.

Biodiversity Conservation

The dominant conservation paradigm which has been a 'fortress' approach gained legibility after the enactment of the Wildlife Protection Act in 1972. The Wildlife Protection Act 1972 has given enormous powers to declare "any area considered necessary" as a protected area which includes both national parks and sanctuaries without consulting the affected communities. This act also prohibited hunting[27] of wild animals and birds scheduled in the Act and the areas led to declaring as National Park and Wildlife sanctuaries, which are dedicated habitat for wildlife and no activities, in these areas. The Project Tiger was established in 1972 to protect and increase tiger numbers in selected forest areas. The Census of Tigers estimated during 1972 was 1,827 to 4,334 in 1989 have been seen as the success of the project. The emergence of the Wildlife Act of 1972 and Forest Conservation Act 1980 has led to the changing nature of forests as wildlife sanctuaries and national parks.[28]

Protected areas have been designed on the basis of a particular set of scientific principles that focus on standard criteria such as requisite size and shape of the area; landscape fragmentation, the creation of 'breeding nuclei' within 'inviolate' core zones, and assigning of ecological values to large mammals, described as 'umbrella species', against which human actions are to be judged. Biologists have identified several proximate causes for the tiger's dramatic decline due to loss of habitat to conflicting land-use, over hunting of the tigers' prey species by people, and killing of tigers to protect livestock or to meet commercial demand of their body parts.

The conservation programme in India can be divided into three main areas: creation and management of protected areas, protection of wildlife in protected forests and control and management of wildlife trade. Traditionally the role of the forest department under which the reserve forests are under its control while the district forests may fall under legal categories other than those defined in the Karnataka Forests Act are under the Revenue Departments. The conservation of animals gained impetus for setting up parks came from a class of ex-hunters turned conservationist belonging to the erstwhile princely states. With the increase in the number of national parks and sanctuaries the focus was on charismatic animals like tigers, rhinoceros, Asiatic lions, and others. More recently the Indian elephant and the snow leopard have also been the beneficiaries of conservation projects. The national parks and wildlife sanctuaries form only 3% of our country's land area. Within these areas we have human habitations, roads, dams, mines, power plants and other activities which have been the biggest threats to forests and wildlife and have caused habitat fragmentation.

The human settlements inside the forests with agricultural fields has fragmented the habitat for wildlife, especially for large fauna such as tigers, hornbills, and lion-tailed macaques that are habitat specialists requiring vast stretches of undistributed forests for their survival in terms of dietary habits and home ranges. The tribals, namely Gowdlus in the Chikmagalur district and Malekudiyas in the Dakishna Kannada district do not have title deeds or *pattas* for their lands and are labelled as 'encroachers' by the forest department. Their rights were not enquired into and protected due to a faulty settlement process. Around the country there are a number of cases where *pattas*/ grants leases have been issued to people by the Revenue Department. But the 'status' of these lands are under major discrepancies between the forest department and the tillers of the land who have not been consulted or informed.

The wildlife protection through giving incentives to relocate human population to less ecologically sensitive areas is seen as a magic solution which benefits both human and wildlife and a new paradigm of site-specific, incentive-driven through participatory voluntary settlement. The decade -long struggle by various organizations against the eviction of tribal people from the national parks taken by the Naxalites under the banner of "Maoist" when the forest department served eviction notices to them. The land question has once again emerged in rural India and especially among the tribal population of India since it ensures a sense of ownership of land and a sense of psychological security for the tribal population.

Outline of the Book

I. Land Revenue and Commercialization of Coffee Cultivation in the Princely Mysore State 1800-1881

The chapter analyses the specific features of the role played by the state in a colonial set up and the following questions are posed. What kind of land revenue system was imposed by the British in the princely Mysore state? Did the land policies of the colonial power lead to the establishment of isolated clusters of commercialization at the cost of the stagnation of the traditional agricultural economy and integrated to global commodity networks? Did the labour policies lead to the creation of social enclaves of people de-linked from the surrounding communities? What was the impact of the plantation on the patterns of trade of the region? Was the transport network that was developed in response to the requirements of coffee plantations dysfunctional vis-à-vis the needs of regional development? The transition of the princely Mysore state[29] included both continuity and change as the British continued the pre-colonial land revenue which was carried out by the active intervention of intermediatory classes and groups.

II. Global Coffee Crisis and its Effects on Small Growers from Chikmagalur District of Karnataka

In the context of the coffee crisis during the 1990s, Chapter 2 examines the problems of price crash; rescheduling packages announced by the Government of India and the future of coffee plantations with its effect on small growers. The following questions are posed here. What are the demands of different organizations representing the coffee industry such as the United Planters Association of India, Karnataka Planters' Association, and Karnataka Growers' Federation? What were the dividing lines between different coffee plantation unions? Finally why did the movement fail to become a comprehensive movement of small growers in the politics of Chikmagalur district?

III. Forest Conservation Act 1980 and Supreme Court Intervention

The close link of forests, wildlife and environment are interconnected, but the regulatory system treats them as largely independent from each other.[30] The Ministry of Environment and Forests (MoEF) is primarily concerned with the planning, promotion and coordination of the implementation of India's environmental and forestry policies and programmes. The third chapter deals with the Forest Conservation Act (FCA) in relation to conversion or diversion of forests to non-forest purposes like coffee plantation and mining in the name of development. The negligence on part of the state government led to the Supreme Court reinterpreting the meaning of "forest" in the FCA of 1980. The chapter argues that the forest case or Godavarman case which was assumed to apply only to reserve forest has been applied to all areas that are forests irrespective of the nature of ownership and classification. The chapter deals with the contestation with the physical status of these lands as grazing lands which has been encroached for personal gains and also been seen as a vote bank by the state politicians.

IV. Mining, Pollution and Workers' Rights with Reference to Kudremukh Iron Ore Company Limited

The Supreme Court has questioned the right to a healthy environment as part of the fundamental right of life, directing polluters to follow environmental norms and regulations. This chapter explores the role played by different kinds of protests in the case of the Kudremukh Iron Company Limited, a public sector company, closed in 2005. This chapter poses the following questions: What are the shifts in the approach of the state with regard to mining? Why has pollution continued unabated in private sectors? What are the limits of judicial intervention with regard to mining? Why were the priorities of workers not considered due to the closure of mining? Why couldn't the trade unions dictate the central content of bargaining policy for themselves?

V. Biodiversity Conservation and Rehabilitation from Kudremukh National Park

The chapter analyses the contestation with regard to the formation of Kudremukh National Park. It attempts to highlight what sustainability really means. What are its nuances, underlying assumptions, strengths and limitations? How sensitive are the country's development policies to biodiversity concerns? Do current conservation attempts adequately cover the entire range of life forms? Who can effectively conserve biodiversity by local traditional communities or by governments? How can conservation, sustainability and equity be achieved in the use of biological resources? Can human habitations be relocated or not? Is movement towards thoughtful conservation and development possible?

VI. Naxalite Movement, Democracy and Development

The relocation of tribals has been taken up by the Maoist movement with a singular focus on armed struggle. What is the specific socio-economic context leading to the emergence of a Maoist movement in a particular area? What is the role of intellectuals, human rights' organizations and media mediating between the state and Maoist organization? What are the factors which have led to the emergence of ideological and political influence of the Hindu Sangh Parivar? The chapter further discusses the demand to democratize forest governance addressing the socio-ecological context which enables the participation of weaker sections of the society.

The book is an attempt to make a reassertion of class in political analysis, drawing on the classical Marxist, neo-Marxist and functionalist traditions like trade union politics, peasant, tribal, and other movements.[31] Even though movements involving women, peasants, dalits and adivasis can be understood as new social movements. The importance of class dynamics in NSMs and emphasis and concerns about class inequality and unequal distribution of resources continue to be relevant because we live in a class society. The concept of class remains significant in political analysis since it takes into account different dimensions of social life.

References

1. Ghanshyam Shah (2002): *Social Movements and the State,* Sage Publications, New Delhi, p. 15.
2. M.S.A. Rao (1984): *Social Movements in India,* Manohar Publications, New Delhi.
3. The approach has influenced the subalterns who appreciate the contradictions that are part of the subaltern consciousness. Collective action has been popularized by E.P. Thompson (1966) who studied 'history from below'. James Scot in his book *Weapons of the Weak* has inspired extensive work with the label of new social movements.
4. James Petras (2000): "The Third Way: Myth and Reality", *Monthly Review,* Vol. 51, No. 10, March, pp. 19-35.
5. Social movements may be expressions of cultural struggles

over meaning, but the meanings for which they fight are not always clear when we consider the material struggles alongside these cultural contestations. See Anthony, Bebbington, (2007): "Social Movements and the Politicization of Chronic Poverty", *Development and Change*, Vol. 38, No. 5, p. 740.

6. Ponna Wignaraja, (1993): *New Social Movements in the South: Empowering the People* (ed), New Delhi, Vistaar Publications.
7. M. Fuentes, and A.G. Frank (1989): "Ten Theses on Social Movements", *World Development*, Vol. 17, No. 2.
8. Gail Omvedt (1993): *Reinventing Revolution: New Social Movements and the Socialist Tradition in India*, East Gate Books, London, pp. 127-153.
9. Maitrayee Chaudhuri (2014): What is 'New' in the New Social Movements? Rethinking Some Old Categories, in *Social Movements: Transformative Shifts and Turning Points* (ed) by Savyasaachi and Ravi Kumar, Routledge, pp. 159-186.
10. Janaki Srinivasan (2010): 'The WSF and the Debate on Alternative Development in India', *Critical Engagement*, CACIM Occasional Publications Programme, p. 14.
11. The word 'Neoliberalism' used interchangeably with capitalism is concerned with economic policy. The neoliberal reform is commonly perceived as referring only to the realm of the economy but also requires an appropriate restructuring of the polity. The short-term stabilization measures include cut-backs in government expenditure; high interest rates and currency devaluation. The long-term measures include deregulating the economy, liberalizing trade and investment and privatizing state enterprises. The major difference however, while the other elements of the neoliberal agenda are compatible with globalization, they are not necessarily part of it.
12. Savyasaachi and Ravi Kumar (2014): *Social Movements: Transformative, Shifts and Turning Points* (ed), Routledge, Taylor and Francis Group, New Delhi, p. 1.
13. Michael Watts and Richard Peet (1996): *Liberation Ecologies* (ed), Routledge Publications, New York, p. 8.
14. The four different administrations during the British period: Bombay Presidency (in Uttara Kannada), Madras Presidency (in Dakshina Kannada), and Coorg Princely State (Kodagu). The state of Mysore after the reorganization of the state in 1956 (now called Karnataka since November 1, 1973) was brought together after the amalgamation of four different administrations of the British period.
15. D.C. Srikantappa (2002): Crisis in Coffee and Relief Sought by

Growers, Letter to Mr. Jaswant Singh, the then Honourable Minister for Finance by Coffee Growers' and Employees Convention, 16th October. Also see Memorandum of Crisis in Coffee and Relief Sought, submitted to Honourable Minister, Mr. Vidya Sagar Rao, the then Minister of State for Commerce and Industry, on behalf of the Coffee Growers of Karnataka, Kerala and Tamil Nadu, Government of India, July 2, 2003.

16. Lakshmi Venkatachalm (2004): Opening Remarks of Chairperson, Coffee Board at the 174th meeting of the Coffee Board on 6th December.
17. "Coffee Industry on Verge of Collapse", *Deccan Herald*, November 11, 2002.
18. Interview with Mr. Prasanna, Gram Panchayat Member, Shirivase village, Chikmagalur Taluk on June 21, 2015.
19. Minutes of the meeting held under the chairmanship of the Ministry of Commerce and Industry, Department of Commerce, to consider the progress of implementation of SCTL package for coffee growers and other financial problems of the coffee sector, July 7, 2003, New Delhi.
20. Karntaka Growers' Federation (2013): Annual Report From the President's Desk.
21. Plantation Workers May Strike on December 11, *Financial Express*.
22. Interview with George Austin, Communist Party of India, Taluk Secretary of Coffee Labour Union on June 20, 2015.
23. The rehabilitation of 63 families who gave up their lands to the company has been rehabilitated in Jamble, Nellibeedu and Samse villages and given alternative land of 2 ½ acres of alternative land and one person in each such family has been given a suitable job in the company. The company has constructed a 5-bedded and well-equipped hospital for its employees and primary health facilities at Nellibeedu and Vinoba Nagar. More than 3,000 children from Malleswara and nearby villages receive quality education in the Kendriya Vidyalaya, Junior College and primary schools run with the assistance of the company.
24. KIOCL was started for mining of iron ore at Aroli-Gangamoola range of hills of Western Ghats which is also the birthplace of three rivers Tunga, Bhadra and Nethravathi in Chikmagalur district of Karnataka in 1976 by the Ministry of Steel.
25. A.K. Roy (1997): "Can Courts Run the Country", *Economic and Political Weekly*, October 11, pp. 2579-81.
26. Sharachchandra Lele (2007): "A Defining Moment for Forests?" *Economic and Political Weekly*, Vol. 42, No. 25, June 23, pp. 2379-

2383.

27. The conservation of forests, grasslands, and wetlands, in India which have become national parks and sanctuaries after independence were also the old hunting grounds of Indian princes, which were developed under the British colonial rule. Hunting was also an important pasttime and the integral life of the princely states and wild animals like tigers, lions, and leopards were not protected and their hunting was a valued sport. See Divyabhanusinh (1998): "A Princely Bequest", *Seminar* 466, June, p. 42.
28. Ibid.
29. "Princely states" were kingdoms, many of ancient lineage, and with a long history of exercising political power. It was British colonial terminology that referred to rulers as "princes". The quasi-independent status they enjoyed under British rule made them hostile to the anti-imperialist nationalist movement.
30. Geetanjoy Sahu (2014): *Environmental Jurisprudence and the Supreme Court: Litigation, Interpretation, Implementation*, Orient Blackswan, New Delhi, pp. 12-33.
31. Glyan, Williams and Emma Mawdsley (2006): "India's Evolving Political Ecologies" in *Colonial and Post-Colonial Geographies of India* (ed) by Saraswati Raju, M. Satish Kumar and Stuart Corbridge, Sage Publications, pp. 261-78.

Geography and Area of Study

Karnataka state is situated in the west-central part of the Deccan peninsular India with a coast line of 300 kms. on the west bordering the Arabian Sea. To the north-west and north are the states of Goa and Maharashtra, to the east is Andhra Pradesh and to the south and south-east are the states of Kerala and Tamil Nadu. Each region of Karnataka has its own historical significance, political dynamics, caste equations and local socio-cultural specificities.

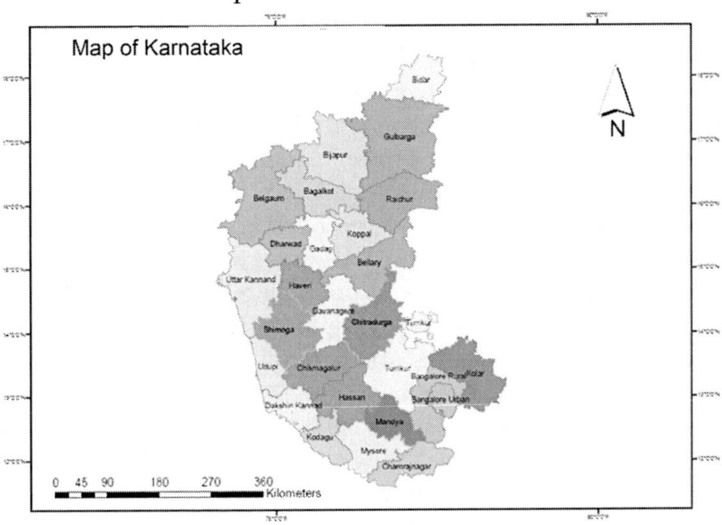

The state of New Mysore after the reorganization of the state in 1956 (now called Karnataka since November 1, 1973) was brought together after the amalgamation of four different administrations of the British period. The state of New Mysore was divided into four different administrations during the

British period: Bombay Presidency (in Uttara Kannada), Madras Presidency (in Dakshina Kannada), and Coorg princely state (Kodagu). The different forms of tenure were governed by a complex set of acts, rules, executive orders, administrative practices and customs. The government followed its own style and speed in enacting the land reforms.[1] The challenge before the new state was to formulate an essentially uniform law that would accommodate local problems and variations to the greatest degree possible.[2] The state is divided into three well marked physiographic regions. These are the coastal plains, the Malnad and the eastern Maidan region or Bayaluseeme.

Western Ghats Regional Specificity

The Western Ghats covers 22.81 per cent of Karnataka's geographical area (11 districts and 40 taluks). The site of the Western Ghats falls under different agro-climatic zones, namely the southern transition and dry zone, coastal, hilly, northern transition and dry zones of Karnataka. Coffee is grown on highly productive well drained soils with many species of plants crowding each other and creating sustainable for the human-rich soils and these areas are subjected to heavy rainfall. Plantations are generally established on the sides of valleys and on the spurs of the Western Ghats and the other important feature is the uniformity of temperature. The Chikmagalur district which is part of the Western Ghats is characterized by coffee plantations, areca nuts, betel leaves, cardamom, pepper, cashew and paddy. The plantation economy in India is developed as a source of supply to Western markets.[3] The Western Ghats regions of Karnataka have two distinct physiographical components: Coastal Plain and Malnad. The Malnad region popularly known as 'Sahyadri Hills' is a hilly tract lying between the western narrow coastal plain and the far stretching eastern maidan region has a complex relief structure with elevation ranging from 300-2,000 metres from the mean sea level with higher elevation on the southern part of the region.

Malnad is adorned with some well known peaks– Mullayanagiri (1,913m), Kudremukh or Chandradrona

Parvata (1,892m) and Kodachadri (1,343m). Malnad is the rainiest region having a reliable mean annual rainfall of about 3,000 mm. Places like Bagamandala, Agumbi, Sringeri, Koppa and Thirthahalli receive more than 4,000 mm rainfall annually. Malnad is rich in forest wealth and the tropical evergreen forest cover is dense in the western slope of the ghat which receives heavy rainfall. The main soil types found in the region are medium, red, mixed block, and red and laterite.

Karnataka is the largest producer of coffee in India. It accounts for nearly 50 per cent of area under coffee cultivation and contributes about 70 per cent of coffee output in the country. Coffee is cultivated in Chikmagalur district in an area of around 85,465 hectares with Arabica being the dominant variety grown in the upper hills and Robusta being the major variety in the low level hills. There are around 15,000 coffee growers in this district with 96 per cent of them being small growers with holdings of less than or equal to four hectares. The average production is 55,000 MT: 35,000 MT of Arabica and 20,000 MT of Robusta. The average productivity per hectare is 810 kilograms for Arabica and 1110 kilograms of Robusta, which are higher than the national average.

The two important varieties of coffee grown on a commercial scale are Arabica and Robusta where Arabica are grown at high attitudes ranging from 3,500-4,500 feet above sea level where the annual rainfall is 200 cm, whereas Robusta are grown at lower altitudes of 1,500-2,500 feet above sea level. The area under coffee cultivation in Karnataka indicates that Kodagu district has the largest area under Robusta. Chikmagalur accounts for the largest area under Arabica. There are around 6 varieties of Arabica coffee grown: S.795, Selection 5B, Selection 6, Selection 9, Cauvery/Catimore and Chandragiri. There are variations across states in relation to coffee seeds like S.795 is largely grown in Karnataka (about 72%), Selection 9 variety in Kerala (about 87%) and Tamil Nadu (about 80%).[4] The other important feature of coffee plantations is grown under shade trees unlike countries like Brazil, Vietnam wherein it is grown in open conditions.[5] It accounts for nearly 50 per cent of area under coffee cultivation and contributes about 70 per cent of coffee output in the country. The Western Ghats region has been identified as one of the twelve biodiversity hot spots of the world.

Chikmagalur District

The Chikmagalur district is a fantastic dividing line between the Malnad and Maidan regions of the district. The district offers a wide variety of places of tourist interest like lofty hills, swift flowing and meandering rivers and brooks, pilgrim centres of various faiths, evergreen forests, a wide variety of bird life, a variety of crops ranging from plantations to dry crops and folk traditions.

The district borders Shimoga district to the north, Davangere district to the north-east, Chitradurga and Tumkur districts to the east, Hassan district to the south, Dakshina Kannada district to the south-west and Udupi district to the west. The rivers Bhadra Tunga, Hemavathi, Netravati, and Vedavathi flow all year round. The district is rich in iron, magnetite and granite deposits. Black soil is found around Baba Budan Giri Hills, whereas red and gravel soil are found in the southern parts of the district.

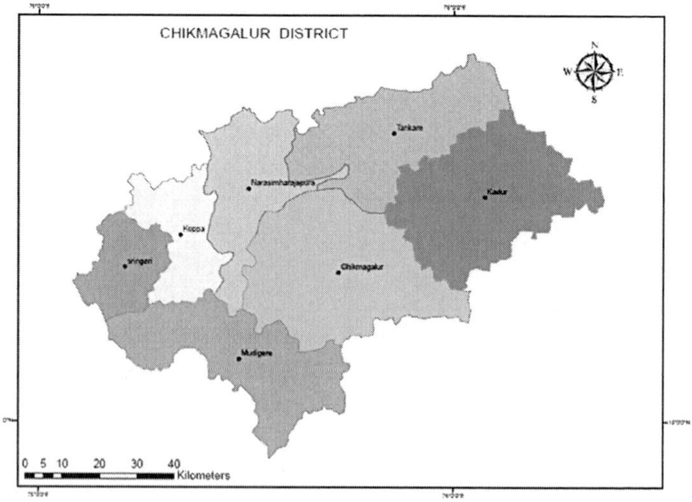

Administration

Chikmagalur district comes under Mysore Division. The district is divided into seven taluks and the headquarters of the taluks are located at Chikmagalur, Kadur, Tarikere, Mudigere, Koppa, N.R. Pura and Sringeri. These taluks are grouped into two Revenue Sub-Divisions, viz. Chikmagalur Revenue sub-division and Tarikere Revenue sub-division. Chikmagalur Revenue Sub-Division comprises of the taluks of Chikmagalur, Mudigere, Koppa and Sringeri, while Tarikere sub-division has jurisdiction over the taluks of Kadur, Tarikere and Narisimharajapura.

Economy

Agriculture is the economical backbone of the Chikmagalur district with coffee cultivation forming the major part of it. Agricultural production in the district is spread over three seasons—namely Kharif, Rabi and summer. Important crops grown are cereals, i.e. rice, ragi, jowar, maize and minor millets, pulses like red gram, horse gram, green gram, avrekai (hyacinth beans), black gram and Bengal gram. The Coffee Board located in Chikmagalur town is the government authority that oversees the production and marketing of coffee cultivated in the district. Coffee is cultivated in Chikmagalur district in an area of around 85,465 hectares with Arabica being the dominant variety grown in upper hills and Robusta being the major variety in the low level hills. There are around 15,000 coffee growers in this district with 96% of them being small growers with holdings of less than or equal to 4 hectares.

Industries

Kudremukh Iron Ore Company Ltd. (KIOCL) in Kudremukh area of Mudigere taluk. KIOCL was established in 1976 to develop the Kudremukh mine and to produce 7.5 million tonnes of concentrate per year. The facilities were commissioned in 1980 and the first shipment of concentrate was made in October 1981. A pelletization plant with a capacity of 3 million tonnes per year was commissioned in 1987 for production of high quality blast furnace and direct reduction grade pellets

Location of Kudremukh

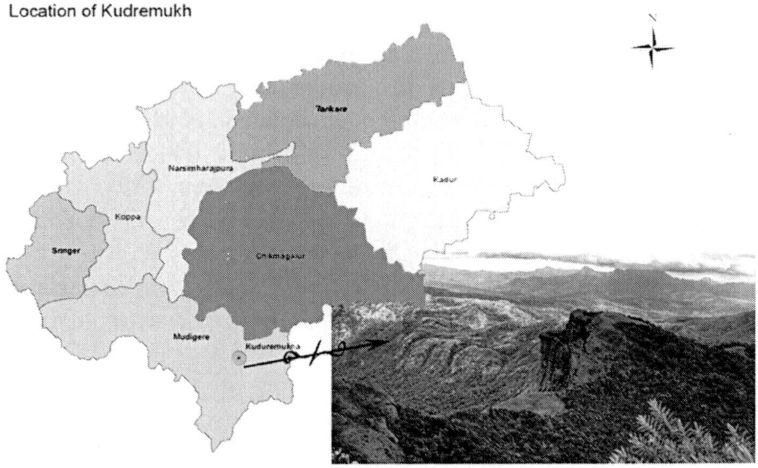

for export. KIOCL received a massive setback when its mining license expired and operations were stopped by the Supreme Court with effect from December 31, 2005. With many of the employees losing their jobs and the social backlash that may result thereof, efforts are being made to generate jobs for these workers in other areas. Kudremukh and Kudremukh National Park: Kudremukh range (in Kannada *Kudure* means horse and *mukha* means face, Horse face), so named because of the unique shape of the Kudremukh peak. Overlooking the Arabian Sea, the broad hills are chained to one another with deep valleys and steep precipices. Situated at 1,894.3 metres above sea level, Kudremukh is rich in iron ore deposits.

References

1. Murahari D. Naik (1989): *Agrarian Unrest in Karnataka*, Reliance Publishing House, New Delhi, p. 20.
2. A.S. Shrinidhi and Sharachchandra Lele (2001): "Forest Tenure Regimes in the Karnataka Western Ghats: A Compendium", Working Paper No. 90, Institute for Social and Economic Change, Bangalore, p. 2.
3. C.B. Damle (1993): *Land Reforms and Changing Agrarian Relations*, Rawat Publications, New Delhi, p. 16.
4. M.S. Narayana (2014): "Size Distribution of Estates, Inequality and Poverty: Evidence for India's Household Coffee Farmers",

Journal of Asian Policy, Vol. 7, No. 1, Routledge, Taylor and Francis' Group, pp. 18-40.

5. R.C. Keshavamurthy (2005): "Shade: A Vital Factor in Coffee Growing in South India", Vol. LXIX, No. 2, *Indian Coffee*, Bangalore, pp. 35-38.

1

Land Revenue and Commericalization of Coffee Cultivation in the Princely Mysore State 1800-81

Introduction

The study makes an attempt taking into consideration the power and authority that were forged in a princely Mysore state, under colonial rule from 1800-1881. The scholarship on the 18th century has given rise to a lively debate among historians whether the century represented a rupture from the past as a result of the decline of the central Mughal authority.[1] The East India Company has been viewed as a determining and defining disjunction with regional studies based on land records. In recent times scholars such as Washbrook, Peril, and Bayly have stressed the pre-colonial phase which continued the processes where the tax farmers and lease arrangements under the Company permitted wealthy, influential groups to expropriate public funds under the canopy of the English agents.[2] The princely Mysore state the transition included both continuity and change as the British continued the pre-colonial land revenue which was carried out by the active intervention of intermediatory classes and groups.

Pre-Colonial Regime on Land Revenue

The land revenue system that prevailed under the Vijayanagar rule did not undergo any serious change during the early days of Mysore's history. It was during the reign of Chikkadevaraja Wodeyar (1672-1704) who started off the centralized and militarized administration[4] to increase revenue collected by the state officials and simultaneously exempting lands held by his soldiers from revenue demands. This resulted in large territories being auctioned off to ambitious warriors- mostly Hindus who as tax farmers called *Amildars* (local officials) pressed the accumulation of wealth.[5] The sovereignty claims of the most aggressive of such chiefs who were called *palegars*[6] became powerful in their respective regions and subsequently emerged as landed aristocracy of the state. Some of them had attained certain legitimacy due to their support to temples, Brahmins and other religious leaders (namely *jangama* preceptors of *lingayats*).

The state of Mysore under Hyder and Tipu (1761-99) was built meticulously on the might of the army and the civil bureaucracy, which comprised around one-lakh employees, knitted the kingdom and contributed to its unification and consolidation. In the revenue administration, Haider Ali subjugated several of the *palegars*, and restored some of them on the condition of paying tribute and rendering military service when called on.[7] The main objectives of the Tipu administration were to strengthen the military which was brought to its highest point from 1783-1799[8] against the East India Company. The regime of Hyder and Tipu Sultan was strong primarily because they were partially able to suppress the *palegars* and thereby directing a larger part of the economic surplus taken from the villages to the state machinery.[9] But the *palegars* were waiting for an opportunity to re-establish their local power-positions, and when the British army attacked Tipu Sultan such an opportunity arose. The British encouraged this local upsurge, to get control over the countryside. In some districts *palegars* were under favourable conditions and the majority of them chose to resist and rebel against the British.[10] The capture of Serirangapatam and Bangalore, the principal centres, and the region falling to the south of Mysore were taken by the British but the resistance did not automatically stop. The central and northern parts remained in the possession of Dhondia Waugh and the allied Maratha army.[11] He played an important role by building an army and a political confederation of all those *palegars* from Tamil Nadu, Kerala, and Maharashtra who sought to overthrow the British. The rebellious spirit affected the whole of south India, except a small part of the Nizam of Hyderabad. Under Thomas Munro 80 *palegars* were eliminated by a combination of force and pension-bribery, which Frykenberg calls the 'silent settlement'.[12] The property rights before the arrival of the British were held by groups like *palegars* who were the local chiefs or elites and belonged to dominant castes in alliance with the Brahmins. They were considered significant intermediaries for transmitting revenue and maintaining rule[13] in ryotwari areas. The ryots were small 'managerial castes' who were in fact landlords.[14]

Colonial Phase

The East India Company had to bear a severe financial crunch due to the Anglo-Mysore War 1798-99 and the second Maratha War in 1803-05, which had strained the internal financial structure of EIC.[15] The heirs of Haider Ali and Tipu Sultan were pensioned off and the old Hindu dynasty of Wodeyar was restored to the throne which created the new state of Mysore under a Hindu Maharaja in subordinate alliance with the Company. According to this treaty the British undertook the defence of Mysore in return for a subsidy amounting to seven lakhs of star *pagodas*.[16] From 1800-1811 the administration of Mysore was guided by Dewan Purniah, who acted as a Regent for the minor King Krishnaraja Wordeyar III. During his tenure the office of Asophs was abolished but that of the *Fouzdar*[17] who already had the control of police also took control of the revenue. He tried to restore the lands back to Brahmin *inamdars* by bringing back most of the landholders who had fled the country and restored *inam* lands and cash allowances to temples and mutts of worship.[18]

Under Purnaiya for the much-reduced state increased substantially and in many years exceeded 30 lakhs, in this way a large surplus was created. The bulk of the revenue was the land revenue, which in 1799 made up to 88% of the total income of the state and the other items included the *sayer* (excise duties on the sale of various goods, revenues from liquor, tobacco and sandalwood). The increase in revenue was mainly due to increase in land revenue, which in turn was due to extended cultivation made possible after 1799. The first conditions that the British exerted on the kingdom by signing the Subsidiary Treaty were the annual contribution in monthly instalments and a tribute to the crown. In areas that came under its direct rule, it extracted this amount through its own revenue collection, machinery by setting targets for bureaucrats.[19] There was certainly a decline in the number of soldiers, which fluctuated sharply with the state of peace.[20]

The Mysore territory after the boundaries were fixed in 1799 consisted of three divisions—Patna, Ashtagram, Chitradurg and Nagar. These divisions included 115 to 120 *taluks* or subdivisions being in charge of an officer called *amil* or a*mildar*. The *amildar*'s assessment of a village was made according to his own idea of his ability to pay and compelled the patel or collector to collect the amount. According to Stein, the king did not collect the regular taxes, but it was accepted as tributes. The basic unit of political organization was not the kingdom but a small region controlled by an assembly of dominant cultivators or Brahmins or chieftains who paid a tribute to the king in recognition of his over lordship but managed affairs with their localities.[21] The *Sharat* system was a contract made by the *amildar* that he would guarantee a certain amount of revenue to the government and if the collection fell short of that amount he would make up the deficiency, and if it exceeded the surplus should be paid to the government. The amount, which the *amildar* thus engaged to realize, was generally on the increase in the early years. But later heavy arrears began to accumulate and the system virtually transformed into the annual auction of high offices that were sold to the highest bidder. This led to the introduction of friends or relatives into the service of the government and led to malpractices and the greatest beneficiary was the *amildar* because the amount of recoveries was being carried to his own credit.[22] The *sharat* system emerged and prevailed because of the elaborate mechanism from Raja to Dewan, and the Dewan had commission agents in the *foujdars*. They in turn had the *amildars* as their agents and ultimately the *patel* and *shanbhoga* were the agents who exploited the peasants.[23]

The British did not develop alternative tax farming till the establishment of the ryotwari system in the 1820s when Thomas Munro the chief architect of the system, claimed that the ryotwari system as the indigenous system because it was based on historical relations of a village and also the basic unit of agrarian relations on which the primary unit of a society, culture and economy were linked to each other. Munro's proposal was termed as a pragmatic and cunning proposal: "If we are to have corruption, it is better that it should be among the natives than ourselves, because the natives will throw the blame of evil upon their countrymen, they will retail their high opinion of our superior integrity, and our character, which is one of the strongest supporters of our power".[24]

The ryotwari system meant that the government made a deal not only with the peasant that tilled the land, but also made the 'settlement' with whoever owned the land.[25] The *Mysore Gazetteer* gives details of the confusing state of affairs in the state during this period, where *inam* grants like *sanads* (that is documents conveying emoluments, titles, etc under the seal of the ruling authority),[26] were hereditary titles without restrictions to the heirs and powers of alienating the land were distinctly added in the *sanads* for a long period.[27]

The question of land revenue varied enormously from district to district, and indeed from village to village, since the revenue administration was still badly organized and often arbitrary and the cultivator was thus often left with very little of the crop.[28] The economic system did not penetrate deep inside the countryside, but compromised with the pre-capitalist relations and the burden was totally shifted to the peasants of Nagar who owned revenue dues worth ₹ 13 lakhs to the government. The deep financial crisis erupted and the princely Mysore state also witnessed widespread peasant insurrections in several parts popularly known as the Nagar Peasant Rebellion since it was more intense in the Nagar province. The partial elimination of feudal warlords called "*Palegaras*" by Hyder and Tipu Sultan took refuge under colonialism and subverted its overthrow by implanting pre-capitalist landed property and converted themselves into a class of intermediaries largely belonging to castes as Brahmins, Bunts and Jains. They were used in the bureaucracy because of the educational qualifications that filled the structural requirements and further acted as the influential mediator between the Company and the peasantry. The introduction of land tenures created a class of landed interests which were exclusively drawn from the upper castes. The elaborate system of collecting taxes was done by *shanbhags* (usually Brahmins) who were responsible for keeping village accounts. The Patil/ Patel belonged to the Vokkaliga or Lingayat communities and was responsible for revenue collection and maintenance of law and order in the village.

Thus the pauperization of the peasantry by continued or often dependent debt to landlords who in the eyes of the East India Company failed to act as agricultural capitalists and lacked entrepreneurial ability, or the capital for extending cultivation and increased the revenue to the state.[29] The pre-capitalist mode of production was essentially a self-sufficient condition that has been referred as 'natural economy', which is geared to the production of 'use values', instead of commodities for exchange. The East India Company with its relentless spirit of exploration for harnessing commercial avenues in India discovered a gold mine in coffee cultivation and developed it into a viable plantation crop for commercialization of coffee and subordinated it to the world market.

Genesis of Coffee Cultivation

The decisive act of the East India Company after the takeover of Mysore realized that the whole physical basis of governance depended on geographical, geological and botanical knowledge of the region. This was promoted by the need to obtain information on the land, its people and resources. Accordingly Col. Mackenzie agreed to survey Mysore in 1800 with the main objective of commercial views[30] but in larger advantage to the Company in the improvement of scientific knowledge.[31] The reference to 'scientific knowledge' elucidates the superiority of the colonial explorer as a state enterprise. But along with this he also collected 1,700 epigraphs, 600 old manuscripts, local histories and myths where the colonizer used them to his advantage. After Mackenzie it was the turn of Dr. Francis Buchanan for the task of undertaking an extensive survey of the natural, industrial and agricultural resources and products of Mysore.[32] The travel also gave a detailed description of the general conditions of the country with emphasis on its agriculture, arts, commerce, religion, customs, manufactures and industries, its population and a few other matters relating to the territory.[33] The country came to have several types of plantation exhibiting great diversity over space and time like indigo, tea, coffee and rubber came up in different parts of India. The cultivation of opium and indigo in Bengal and Bihar in the early 19th century was dominated by about half a dozen giant European houses. In India the major plantation crops were indigo in Bihar, tea in Assam, Nilgiri and Wyanad, jute in West Bengal, cotton in Maharashtra, coffee in Karnataka, Tamil Nadu and rubber in Kerala, tobacco in Andhra Pradesh. The earliest plantations in Mysore were in the present day Chikmagular district (earlier known as Kadur district) was the first to grow coffee in India. The province of Koffa, a district of Abyssinia is considered to be the original habitat of Arabica coffee beans. The Arabs also grew it under irrigation in the province of Yemen over a number of years. The coffee seed made its appearance in India in the 16th century from the Yemeni port of Mocha, carried by the Sufi saint Hazrat Shaik Jamer Allah Mazarabi arrived from Yemen in the 17th century called Baba Budan Giri (Giri Meaning Mountain, hills) Sufi saint on the way from Mecca picked seven fertile coffee beans from the port of Al-Makha, Yemen, and wrapped them around his belly and smuggled it out in the hills of Mullayyana Giri of the Western Ghats. After the demise of the Baba Budan, his cave was sanctified and emerged as a sacred pilgrimage. There is an annual fair where thousands of Muslims gather to worship. The cave-shrine is also a sacred place for Hindus as the believers of Hindu legend claim it a seat of Dattatreya, an incarnation of Vishnu and son of Atreya Rishi, one of the Sapta Rishis (seven sages).

The coffee cultivation before 1830 was entirely by local

population in their houses known as *Hittalu* coffee (backyard of the house). In the *Hittlus,* coffee was grown along with a variety of other products like lime, plantains, ginger and mangoes.[34] It was listed among the 'Jungle produce' of Mysore and was on sale in the markets of Bangalore and Srirangapatam.[35] The forests belonging to the Chikmagalur district had a different history because of remoteness and fewer demands being made on them. In this district virgin forest lands were available in Mudigere and Koppa taluks and therefore much of the focus to use forest lands for coffee cultivation remained confined to these areas. Coffee cultivators had all the encouragement and free access to forests to develop estate, which they did utilize and enjoyed great privileges and therefore were the main reason for overrunning the forests.[36] Subsequently the coffee plantation spread to Hassan district, near Manjarabad and Sakaleshpur. Kadur was in those days considered North Mysore and Manjarabad was considered South Mysore. The change from a crop to estate was a consequence of the decision taken by Maharaja Krishna Raja Wodeyar III of Mysore in the early 19th century. The Maharaja of Mysore in order to encourage coffee cultivation offered land to the peasantry under the *Batayi* land, which is held for payment of a share of the produce to the government. It led to the large tracts of forest land obtained both by the native Indians and Europeans were left unplanted because in turn there was nothing to pay to the government. The government made a rule before making the grants that unplanted coffee cultivation was liable to forfeiture of 500 plants per acre if they were not planted within 5 years.

Several jungles were cleared for coffee, but when the Maharaja's collectors found it difficult in getting the peasants for coffee cultivation led to leasing out of its share of the Baba Budan produce to Thomas Parry of Parry, Dare and Company of Madras[37] who used to sell 'Mocha' coffee imported from Muscat, Basra and Bushire for ten years in 1823-1833. This marked the entry of organized metropolitan capital into the planting sector in southern India. With the growers compelled to sell their produce to Parry's, the government was assured an annual share of ₹ 4,270 and this was renewed after the first decade for five years at ₹ 7,422 a year.[38] The practice of sharing half the produce with the ryot and the other half to the crown, commonly known as *vara* or *warung* indicates that coffee gardens on the Baba Budan Hills were a monopoly of the Mysore Darbar that shared the crop with the cultivator on this basis. The Parry Company had a complete monopoly on Mysore coffee as the agreement permitted them to purchase the cultivators coffee at a price set by them and at the same time would have to seek approval for any export of coffee.

Traditional Coffee Growing Areas

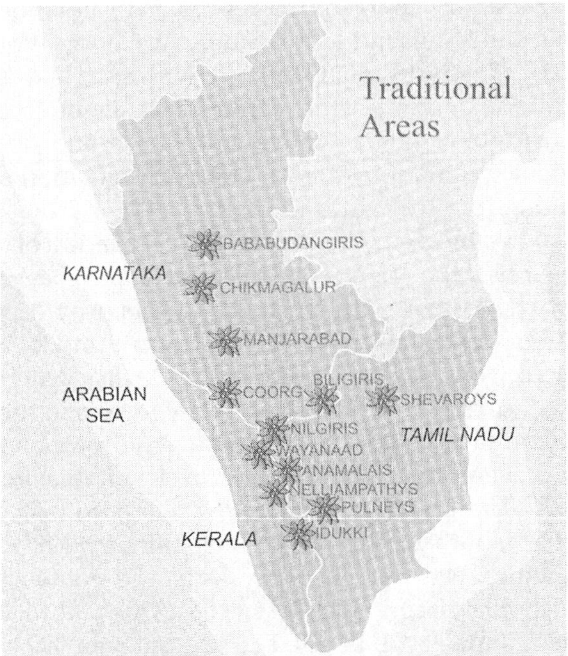

Source: Coffee Board, Bangalore

Cash Crop to Commercial Enterprise during Commissioners Rule: 1831-81

In 1831-81, the British took over the administration of Mysore state from Krishnaraja Wodeyar III on the pretext of misrule. In 1838, the Superintendent of the Nagar Division H. Strokes, considered the extension of coffee cultivation as paramount importance. The significant change came from commissioner Mark Cubbon (1834-61) who abolished Parry's contract because coffee cultivation was spread out and measuring it was a major problem. The contract system was replaced by an excise duty of ₹ 1 gave way to export duty on coffee and threw open the coffee cultivation to free competition.[39] Soon coffee growing hills which have also lent their names to the growth of Indian coffee are the Bababudans in Mysore, Nilgiris, Wynaad, Shevaroys, Anamallais and Palnis in Madras State, the Coorgs (both north and south).[40] The East India Company with its relentless spirit of exploration for harnessing commercial avenues in India discovered a gold mine in coffee cultivation and developed it into a viable plantation crop for commercialization of coffee subordinating it to the world market.

The geographical area helped for the cultivation of coffee in Mysore regions—the *Malnad* or hill country and the *Maidan* or the plains. The former, with extensive forests providing shade and a number of streams was extremely fertile and suitable for coffee. There were five types of land in *Malnad* where coffee was planted; *kans* or forest, *male* or heavy forests in the passes and slopes; village jungles termed *uduve* with a rich deposit of manures were considered as the best suitable for coffee cultivation.[41] The first European coffee plantations in Mysore were opened south of the Bababudan hills by Mr. Cannon. Thomas Cannon was the most successful and notable pioneer of large-scale plantation of coffee in the 1830s and his famous Mylemoney estate is still in good condition even today. In the 1840s he had extended his holdings to about 500 acres and was shipping out the best known coffee as "*Cannon's Mark One*" named over Cannon's Nose Peak in the Bababudan. The next pioneer was Fredrick Green who opened an estate at "Aigur" in Manjarabad in 1843. Soon after Aigur was opened he was joined by Mocketts in Saklespur.[42] The indigenous farmers also followed in the footprints of the English planters in this regard and grew coffee mostly in the forest land where cultivation of coffee was optional and with a small portion of their farm was under coffee, they were growing betel nut, ginger, plantations and other fruits, turmeric and vegetables at the same time.[43] The peasants and local entrepreneurs often planted coffee in between other crops and they were not dependent on only crop and failure of the crop meant comparatively little loss.

Land Under Coffee Cultivation in Mysore in the Early 1960s

District	*Total amount of acres under Europeans*	*Total amount of acres under Indians*	*Total*
Bangalore	15	—	15
Kolar	45	59	104
Mysore	764	1,082	1,846
Hassan	21,017	24,708	45,725
Shimoga	142	2,034	2,176
Kadur	4,028	12,647	16,675
Total	26,011	40,530	66,541

Source: Bhaswati, Bhattacharya (2014): "Local History of a Global Commodity: Production of Coffee in Mysore and Coorg in the Nineteenth Century", *Indian Historical Review,* 41 (1), Sage Publications, p. 71.

The indigenous farmers were benefited from the economic conditions created by the colonial power, even though these conditions were meant to favour the development of European capitalist enterprise and not that of the small holder production.[44] The prosperity generated by the profit from coffee may have led to the acquiring lands. But on the other hand the yield of coffee varied with one acre of coffee land under indigenous farmers yielded five *maunds* of coffee with the same measurement of land under Europeans yielded at least twenty-five *maunds* of coffee. The Europeans realized that the native did not do his best to grow coffee, and the situation has been described by D.P. Mackenzie while expressing his opinion:

The natives, so far as I can gather, would prefer the *halat* system;

> it is more consonant with their ideas; it allows them to cultivate as they like, that is, in most instances, not cultivate at all; and it enables them to take up large tracts of land, stick in a few plants here and there for the name of the thing, and thus hold jungle, in the hopes of some day selling it at a profit, and causing in the meantime, a loss to the Sircar, by keeping bona fide planters from entering on the cultivation. It is also so far the benefit of the poorer ryot as, save the expense of planting, he pays nothing to the state until his trees bear. But…this is not cultivation, and as a dose of medicine is given for its good to a child against its will, so I believe that a moderate assessment of say, ₹ 1 an acre for four years and ₹ 2 afterwards in perpetuity would make the ryot exert himself, and force himself, and force him to exhibit, for they well know the profits of the cultivation, an energy of which he has not little idea...

The native growers dominated the coffee cultivation in Mysore and continued as the data shows that the number of holdings under European planters increased from 153 (25,244 acres) to 865 (61,955 acres) and the number of those under Indian planters rose from 12,285 (34,470 acres) to 28,116 (102,779 acres) during this period. The data is incomplete in the sense that although Indians were buying up large tracts for coffee cultivation, we do not have the actual landholding owned by the small growers.

Golden Era of Coffee Cultivation

The attitude of the government in favoring European planters was basically a reflection of its subordinate status to colonial power in British India.[45] In 1862 the Commissioner of Mysore Lord Bowring succeeded Mark Cubbon and once again the reorganization took place.[46] Bowring in his book expressed the situation about coffee plantations as the European planters conferred an immense benefit on Manjarabad and the adjoining sub divisions where they had established themselves. "The native holders averse to the curtailment of their own feudal powers and fearing the consequences of the labourers quitting their employ frequently regard with a jealous eye the colonization of their country by the interlopers".[47]

The export of coffee occurred from 1863 onwards and

the increase in the *halat* can be seen from the year 1863-69. The major source of income to the government was through the excise duty levied on areca-nut, cardamom, pepper and tobacco on removal from the place of the production and export duty levied on coffee. This also resulted in the growth of banking in the coastal region which was introduced in 1868 when the Presidency Bank of Madras opened a branch to cater to the needs of British firms involved in exporting plantation produce. The growth of banks was largely due to the Western Ghats and the Arabian Sea; the region remained inaccessible for long and was not conducive for the setting up of industries. Early entrepreneurs, therefore, took successfully to selling financial services. Even today coastal districts maintain a strong banking culture with almost every other household having at least one member employed in the banking sector.[48]

Coffee *Halat* from 1831-81

Year	*Halat Rs.*	*Year*	*Halat Rs.*	*Year*	*Halat Rs.*
1831-32	4,270	1848-49	33,349	1865-66	1,02,781
1832-33	7,472	1849-50	27,509	1866-67	43,199
1833-34	7,472	1850-51	32,300	1867-68	1,06,357
1834-35	7,476	1851-52	25,952	1868-69	1,04,407
1835-36	7,476	1852-53	35,952	1869-70	66,978
1836-37	7,476	1853-54	31,327	1870-71	69,775
1837-38	6,262	1854-55	50,204	1871-72	74,948
1838-39	21,011	1855-56	32,229 42,711	1872-73	79,161
1839-40	14,811	1856-57	34,065	1873-74	54,978
1840-41	21,943	1857-58	43,234	1874-75	66,335
1841-42	15,205	1858-59	44,456	1875-76	74,573
—	—	—	—	—	—
1842-43	21,720	1859-60	76,469	1876-77	52,816

1843-44	19,779	1860-61	79,091	1877-78	38,108
1844-45	23,256	1861-62	68,113	1878-79	33,453
1845-46	23,006	1862-63	93,393	1879-80	36,712
1846-47	27,320	1863-64	1,09,463	1880-81	33,661
1847-48	30,059	1864-65	92,791		

Source: Hayavadana, C. Rao (1927): History of Mysore (1399-1799) compiled for *Mysore Gazetteer*, Vol. V, new edition, Bangalore 1927, p. 155.

The coffee cultivation soon established itself as an outstanding quality in the world market. In earlier days there was no direct service of steamers to take away the crop. The coffee was cured and transported to market centres on their own account by the large growers. Many of them were keen to test the market with their produce and if possible establish a reputation for their quality. Many estate or production centres became well-recognized premium coffee markets in Mangalore, Bombay, London and other buying centres. This led to the increase in transport agents, curers, attended to many of the chores needed to get the coffee across to a favourable market, get shipping intelligence, cash and dispatch cheques from coastal banks.[49] The producers received about 66 to 70 per cent of the sale of coffee at Mangalore and 60 per cent of the value in London. The retailer's share was the largest at 13 to 14 per cent of the retail price of coffee. The wholesaler's margin was about 5.9 per cent, the curing and grading charges about 6 per cent. The brokers charged the equivalent of 25 paisa for every ₹ 100 worth of sale.[50] The enlargement of the coffee production unit from a cash crop to an estate enterprise involved the employment of hired labour. The two major coffee beans grown are Arabica and Robusta is highly seasonal. Almost the entire Arabica crop is harvested from December to the middle of February.

The geographical distraction of Arabica coffee is largely concentrated in the northern producing area of Chikmagalur, Manjarabad, north Coorg and Billigiris. The southern Kodagu areas and Wynaad is largely Robusta crop and the harvest begins in January or February and continues to about two to three months. The labour needs of the coffee industry vary considerably depending on the nature of the season.[51] The caste identities constituted the largest group belonged to the lower castes or 'untouchable' castes, namely Hasalaru, Mundala, Koraga, Bant from Belgaum, Bijapur, Dharwar and North Kanara Districts, Banjara or Lambani and Adi Karnataka from the Tumkur district.[52] The shortage of labour was also felt in the tea producing districts of Assam where emigration of labour came mostly from Chottanagpur, Ghazipur, Benaras, Santhal Paraganas, Bihar etc. The initial success of growing "chick coffee" crumbled to the outbreak of pests and diseases, like white stem borer (*Xylotrechyus quadripes*), leaf rust (*Hamileia Vastatrix*)[53], which probably entered India along with the seedlings brought from Ceylon. The area under coffee reached its peak in the 1870s and thereafter began a steady decline and this replaced coffee with tea in many districts as they were not profitable to operate.

The coffee industry was laid waste by the attack of these diseases. There would have been an end to coffee planting in Mysore except in the case of a few elevated tracts on the Bababudan range of hills. But, most fortunately for the planters, the government, and the people of Mysore, Mr. Stanley Jupp—a South Mysore planter—took a trip to Coorg in 1870, which lies on the south-west of Mysore, and was impressed with the variety of coffee grown there and recommended that experiments[54] in Chikmagalur were made with carefully selected seed which was obtained from Coorg. Although coffee remained the dominant crop of the district but with the introduction and rapid expansion of tea cultivation in 1860 was instrumental in shifting from coffee to tea plantation.

Caste and Coffee Labourers

In the initial year the contractors called *maistries*[55] who went around different districts of the state in search of labourers by giving advance money to labourers for purposes such as birth ceremony, marriage, death and in turn got *bhakshis* (commission).[56] The plight of the labourers is explained in Shivaram Karanths novel *Choma's Drum* where the lead role was an untouchable whose dream to cultivate his own land as he worked in the fields of landlords along with his children. Choma drowned his sorrows in alcohol and playing his drum with the monotonous sound. The story highlights the plight of the plantation labour with irony. "The hut was his own-but not claimed by rains and storms and the dinner would be before dark, for no lamp had been lit in Choma's hut. What precious thing did they have to do at night to need a lamp? Plantations debts are like plantation malaria: once in their grip no release till death".[57] Most of the landless labourers went to coffee estates due to poverty or due to the crop failure or due to drought went to work in the coffee estates. The British culpability in legalizing the debt-bondage system through the indentured labour is exemplified in the various measures they took to protect mass recruitments to their plantations in India. The abolition of the slavery law in 1843[58] also led to the release of workers aimed at promoting the basic capitalist ideas of free labour and free market. The Workmen's Breach of Contract Act of 1859[59] which made violation of contract terms legally punishable and thus made it impossible for bonded labour to escape slavery unless the entire loan was paid.[60]

The vocabulary of caste supplemented notions of organic social relations and indigenous law to form a compelling view of servile labour as a customary practice. The labourers were reduced to a state of total dependence on their masters for their basic needs for survival and the planter's response to workers' helplessness often turned out to be ruthlessly exploitative and inhuman. The Mysore territory once supplied labour to Ceylon and Wynaad[61] but owing to famine the attached household's labourers were only paid in kind by way of food grains and other essentials and cash payments were almost unknown for farm labour.[62] The indirect colonial rule in the princely states of Mysore, Travancore and Cochin had an important bearing on the formation of labour force, particularly its recruitment and disciplining them. The debt bondage enforced by the planters through the *maistries* played a major role in mobilization and disciplining of labour.[63] The famine was also responsible for the general shortage of labour for coffee work which varied more sharply, as the harvesting operations lasted only about two or three months in the year, unlike tea which was cropped most of the year. Large gangs of Moplahs (Muslims) from Kerala came to Chikmagalur to work in the estates on a contract basis. Migrant workers are loyal to their employees however when the employer fails to provide continuous work or adequate wages, they either return to their home village or did work with other employer. This does not result in any kind of upward mobility because when the wage work becomes scarcer, the migrant manages to create a job for himself in the city's informal sector as a hawker or domestic servant which provides him no more than a subsistence income. The indirect colonial rule in the princely states of Mysore, Travancore and Cochin had an important bearing on the formation of labour force, particularly its recruitment and disciplining them. The debt bondage enforced by the planters through the *maistries* played a major role in mobilization and disciplining of labour. The serious labour issues induced the different coffee planters to form associations to discuss various issues related to the plantation industry.

Coffee Association

The planting association in an isolated environment of Malnad region forms an important phase in the early development and the exchange of views on common problems and the sharing of experience led to the conditions for a joint action through different associations.[64] The different regional associations like Mysore Planters Association in 1864, North Mysore Planters Association in 1881 and the Southern Mysore Planters Association in 1880 and a Bababuddin Mysore Planters Association in 1911. Then the earlier one in Wynaad in 1857, the Shevaroys Planters Association in 1871, the Coorg Planters Association in 1878 pointed to the emergence of a sufficiently large number of planters association in each district[65]. The different Mysore planters association was brought together to form a single association from 1924 to represent Mysore planting interests except those in the former Chief Commissioners State of Coorg. The subsequent change from MPA into Karnataka Planters Association was only when state assumed the name of Karnataka.[66]

The Mysore Planters Association faced greater problems and the associations were confronted by sudden decisions that affected them. They reacted vigorously with protests and petitions. The southern Mysore plantations complained of the unsatisfactory working of the *anche* (post office), shortage of silver and copper coins and they were surprised at the *amildar* ordering the forest officials to enter the estates for the inspection of trees in the field. The planters complained vigorously to get labourers because of the new place, dense forest, and heavy rainfall and diseases like malaria continued to be a major problem. They affected the plantation population both labourers and planters alike. The coffee planters' representing landed interests, raised many issues during the colonial period.

The questions led to the emergence of the central organization called the United Planters Association of South India (UPASI in 1893) organized to tackle the various problems of the industry.[67] The major grievance of the planters of the South Indian Association 13 in number had signed a memorandum with the Government of India in 1892 to black list defaulting labour contractors and suggested amendments to the Act XIII of 1859. The KPA represented the planting community to cope with their common problems and worked towards reaching a consensus on major issues faced by the planters. Militant demonstrations were not in the tradition of these associations, but believed in dignified language and conduct. The planters therefore created the institutional framework to reflect their common interests and to give form and shape to them through mutual discussion of community problems, the search for a broad measure of common agreement and the sharpening of community responsibility.[68] The concluding years of the colonial rule in Mysore was hit by a disastrous famine. The Dewan of Mysore had to resurrect the economy where the famine policy was subordinated to development works initiated by the Famine Commission of 1880. The post famine relief works were concentrated on modernization programmes like more rail networks and industrialization works were started in famine-prone areas.[69] The emphasis was to transport the food grains from the ports to interior districts affected by the famine and to cover the gap between the surplus and deficit areas by minimizing price differentiation.

Conclusion

Since the 1880s, the princely state of Mysore experienced a reasonably enlightened government. The princely state of Mysore after the British rule in 1881 was under double slavery of the Wodeyars and the British through the medium of representative assemblies for greater peace and containment. In the early 1890s a standing committee was constituted by the government to consult them in taking vital decisions. The princely rulers had no connections to the dominant caste on the land. They were thus unable to anchor their power in kinship ties to the rural elite. They needed a different strategy to establish their legitimacy which led to political accommodation, enlightened governance, and reform to anticipate and defuse conflict.[70] The colonial rule expanded with the sole purpose of raising new revenue in the local arenas to meet the increasing demands for funds, which the Government of India placed upon the province as the result of mounting costs of the imperial system. The Mysore land revenue system provided the government as the main source of income between the state and local political systems. The ryotwari system reinforced the landlords while with the tenants nothing was settled because the land was principally associated with the social status and historically remained in the control of land associated groups. The high level taxation pushed the peasants into arrears and land fell into the hands of usurers. The ryotwari settlements put more profits in the hands of the landowners with commercial assets to invest, which enabled them to dominate the rural agrarian economy in the 19th century.[71] It was in settling the land tenures that the British divided the society into compartments where they could develop their personal and group interests and never any common interests.

The significant fact of the land revenue code there was no fresh laws to regulate the tenancy problems in the state. The concentration of land fell gradually into the hands of landlords, moneylenders and traders, these three categories often indistinguishable in the countryside.[72] The settlement was uneven across the state with disrupting the local economic and social structure as there were eleven modes of land tenures in south India besides the numerous other tenures which cannot be defined. The colonial conquest of Mysore generated vast changes with cash crop economy, as separate clusters in isolation from the rest of the region in which it operates may be described as an "enclave economy". It created a lopsided development in the region and the plantation constitutes one such case,[73] flourished for a while and was devastated by lead rust diseases caused by the fungus, left the Arabica coffee plantation of South East Asia (including India).

The commissioner's rule ended in 1881 and the patronage to the coffee industry where a planter had the provision of choosing either a 30 year settlement at one rupee per acre or a permanent settlement at 1½ rupees. The commercial crops like coffee reduced between 1881 and 1911 particularly due to failure of rainfall successively from 1883 and 1885 and 1904 and 1909. The industry was clearly stagnant which was an all-India phenomenon and to some extent explained by the rise of the coffee industry in Brazil and the coffee industry remained stagnant up to 1947.

References

1. The 18th century as a century characterized by 'change' has been described by Irfan Habib in his studies focused on Mughal political collapse as an inevitable consequence of endemic structural faults rooted in the very conception of empire: high land revenue rates demanded by Delhi caused large-scale rural exploitation, leading to peasant migration and rebellion. This created an agrarian crisis that resulted in the weakening of the empire's political edifice. Irfan Habib (2003): 'The Eighteenth Century in the Indian Economic History', in Seema Alavi

(ed) *The Eighteenth Century in India*, Oxford University Press, pp. 57-84.

2. It is indicated that the proponents of the 'continuity' thesis are often labelled as 'revisionists' because their views have considerably revised the notions of looking at the colonial political economy. The major works are by C.A. Bayly, D.A. Washbrook, and F. Perlin consider the 18th century as a time of economic vigour, even development and rejects the conventional characterization of chaos and economic decline. The recent studies have begun to probe the complex pre-colonial regimes of South Asia and have rejected the conventional characterization of chaos and economic decline, and stress the continuations of prior centralized indigenous regimes of the subcontinent regarding revenue collection which Bayly rejects and what he calls the 'Black Century' conception of the 18th century. Burton Stein stresses the continuity of rule from the pre-colonial rule of Mysore to British governance, which probes the pre-colonial formations of centralized military, civil administration, commercial regulations that justified the formation of the British colonial state. See Bayly (1983): *Townsmen and Bazaars: North Indian Society in the Age of British Expansion, 1770-1870*, Cambridge University Press, F. Perlin (1978): "Of White Whales and Countrymen in the Eighteenth Century Maratha Deccan", *Journal of Peasant Studies*, Vol. 5, pp. 172-237. Burton Stein (1989): 'Eighteenth-Century India: Another View', *Studies in History*, pp. 1-26.
3. "Princely states" were kingdoms, many of ancient lineage, and with a long history of exercising political power. It was British colonial terminology that referred to rulers as "princes". While the quasi-independent status they enjoyed under British rule made them hostile to the anti-imperialist nationalist movement.
4. Sanjay Subrahmanyam (1989): 'Welfare and State Finance in Wodeyar Mysore, 1724-25: A Missionary Perspective', *IESHR*, Vol. 26, No. 2, pp. 204-27.
5. The *lingayat* peasantry in Mysore, for example, rebelled against attempts by Chikkadevaraya Wodeyar to raise the land revenue. See Burton Stein (1985): 'State Formation and Economy Reconsidered', *Modern Asian Studies*, 19, pp. 400-01.
6. The *palegars* were appointed persons of trust and integrity by the king, in different parts of the country. They were expected to clear the jungles and bring the wasteland under cultivation. The *palegars* became powerful in their respective regions and

subsequently emerged as landed aristocracy of the state. Besides these *palegars* there were a number of offices in all the villages and towns.

7. Under Haider, the *palegar* chiefs (hereditary chieftains who possessed armed retainers) remained semi-autonomous. In 1780 during Haider's Carnatic expedition, the *palegars* provided 10,000 irregular cavalry and infantry. See Nikhiles, Guha (1997): "Tipu Sultan's Quest for Legitimacy and His Commercial Measures" in Irfan Habib: *State and Diplomacy Under Tipu Sultan* (ed), p. 114.
8. Tipu's annual revenue until 1792 was over two crores of rupees or 69 lakhs of pagodas. However, the Treaty of Srirangapatnam in 1792 reduced his kingdom by half which was estimated at 40 lakhs of pagodas. To make up for the loss in revenue, in 1795 he increased the assessment by 37.5% (30% on produce and 7% excise duty). See Kaushik Roy (2004): "A Military Revolution in Mysore? Technological Changes, Social Transformation and Military Modernization under Haidar Ali and Tipu Sultan between 1752-99", *Contemporary India,* Vol. 3, No. 4, July-September, p. 26.
9. Tipu introduced new forms in the administrative system and the cultural life for his subjects. He considered his government as *Sarkar-i-Khudabad* (government given by god). He introduced *Hukmanama* which contained 128 articles laid down about the administration, mainly the duties of administrative officers which were addressed to Chief Officers, present and future, namely the amils (the Executive), the sirastedars (the chief accountant) and the shanbhogs (village accountant) and punishments accorded if they failed to perform them, the measures adopted for promoting agricultural productivity which was the principal revenue of the state came from agriculture, inducements for cultivation of crops and plantation, treatment to be accorded to Muslims, Christians, orphans, standards of morality to be maintained by prohibiting the manufacture of tobacco, drugs and liquor. See A.R. Kulkarni (2006): 'Explorations in the Deccan History', *Indian Council of Historical Research*, pp. 68-78.
10. In 1782, many *palegars* deserted to the Company's side as Haider resumed their role as tax collectors and the power to maintain law and order was taken away during the reign of Tipu Sultan and the state took over the duty of enforcing civil authority. Bjorn Hettne (1978): *Political Economy of Indirect Rule: Mysore 1881-1947,* Curzon Press, London, p. 30.
11. G.S. Halappa and M.V. Krishna Rao (1962): *History of Freedom*

Movement, Vol. I (ed), Bangalore.

12. Robert Frykenberg has focused on the relationship between the state and society and in his view the strength of the local influences and traditional political process, which the British confronted with relation to local power, organized around family, caste, kingship and village. The traditional social order was too strong to be ignored and consciously or unconsciously the Company succumbed to its influence. Robert E. Frykenberg (1977): "The Silent Settlement in South India, 1739-1853: An Analysis of the Role of the Inams in the Rise of the Indian Imperial System", in *Land Tenure and Peasants in South Asia*, Orient Longman, pp. 37-54.
13. The Permanent Settlement of 1793 reforms in Bengal Presidency was entailed setting a fixed revenue demand and encouraged the maintenance of large estates with tenure relations and agrarian management under the centralized control of estate managers.
14. Gail Omvedt (1980): "Migration in Colonial India: The Articulation of Feudalism and Capitalism by the Colonial State", *The Journal of Peasant Studies*, p. 202.
15. Michael Mann (1995): "A Permanent Settlement for the Ceded and Conquered Provinces: Revenue Administration in North India, 1801-1833", *The Indian Economic and Social History Review*, 32, 2, Sage Publications, London, p. 250.
16. M.H. Gopal (1960): *The Finances of Mysore State 1799-1831*, p. 2.
17. *Fouzdar*–Chief military administrator in the district of a region.
18. Shama Rao (1936): *Modern Mysore from the Beginning to 1868*, Printed by Higginbothams, South Parade, Bangalore, p. 343.
19. The tribute imposed was 24.5 lakh Rupees imposed on Mysore under Article II of the Subsidiary Treaty of 1799 and at the later stage in 1881 this was increased by 10½ lakh rupees and the enhanced payment of 35 lakhs were made regularly for a period of 32 years from 1896 to 1928. Although in 1928 it was again reduced to 24.5 lakhs as fixed in the treaty, the absolute practice continued. Mysore tribute formed almost 50% of the total contributions of all the 198 tribute-paying states to the imperial exchequer[19]. The enormity of the tribute can be assessed by the net revenue collections of the kingdom in 1809-10. The net revenue receipts were Rs. 28,24,646, peaking at 37,18,633 in 1811-12 and gradually falling to Rs. 28,64,950 in 1825-26. Joseph, Sebastian (1979): 'Mysore's Tribute to the Imperial Treasury: A Classical Example of Economic Exploitation', *Quarterly Journal*

of Mythic Society, Vol. 70, No. 3 July-September 1979, p. 154.

20. M.H. Gopal (1960): *The Finances of Mysore State 1799-1831*, pp. 30-45.
21. Burton Stein (1975): *The State and the Agrarian Order: Essays on South India*, Honolulu, pp. 76-78.
22. Shama Rao (1936): *Modern Mysore From the Beginning to 1868*, Printed by Higginbothams, Bangalore, pp. 411-415.
23. From 1799-1831 there was a British resident in Mysore, who sent his letters and reports to his intermediate supervisors at the government at St. George (Madras), which in turn submitted the information to the Governor-General in Council at Fort William (Calcutta) who forwarded the correspondence to the Court of Directors in London. See M.H. Gopal (1993): *British Sources of the Economic, Political and Social History of Mysore State*, Vol. I, Popular Prakashan, Bombay.
24. Nilmani Mukherjee and Robert E. Frykenberg (1962): "The Ryotwari System and Social Organization in the Madras Presidency", in Frykenberg: *Land Control and Social Structure in Indian History* (ed), p. 238.
25. Siddalinga Swamy (1997): *Agrarian Relations in Mysore, 1799-1881*, Nation Builders Booksellers, Bangalore, p. 52.
26. *Mysore Gazetteer*, (1929), Vol. IV, pp. 156-157.
27. The British contemplated the investigation of inam tenures in the state by setting the inam commission in 1864. It consisted of an Inam commissioner, a special assistant and three assistants. In the first instance all of them were invested with judicial powers, these powers were taken way in 1872 when the commission was reorganized See *Mysore Revenue Manual* (1931): Vol. I, p. 220.
28. Dharma, Kumar (ed), (1982): *The Cambridge Economic History of India, 1757-1970*, Vol. II, Cambridge University Press, pp. 183-184.
29. Mohammed, Mustafa (2007): 'The Shaping of Land Revenue Policy in Madras Presidency: Revenue Experiments—The Case of Chittor District', *The Indian Economic and Social History Review*, 44, 2, p. 221.
30. Tipu Sultan had created a monopoly on teak and sandalwood and it was constituted as a 'royal' tree. The felling and sale of trees were in his hands, and constituted a monopoly of the rulers because of the property rights over certain varieties of trees. The commercial regulations issued to the commercial department (*Mulikut tujar*) of his government wanted to prevent the enemy

to access such commodities, and also to prevent spying under the guise of trading more because of its strategic rather than its commercial importance. The state monopolies also included gold, betel nut, pepper, cardamom and silk. The state controlled the trade centres and competed with indigenous and foreign merchants. They were well aware of the plans of the East India Company's strategy of trade expansion and political control over India. His revenue regulation did not exclude the sphere of trade and industry. Bjorn Hettne, (1978): *Political Economy of Indirect Rule: Mysore 1881-1947,* Curzon Press, London.

31. Deepak Kumar (1995): *Science and the Raj: A Study of British India,* Oxford University Press, pp. 32-33.
32. The surveyors and geographers have been regarded as agents of imperialism rather than mere data collectors. The British representation of Indian society was derived from the perspective of an Indian society, which is hieratically organized, by degree of purity and pollution. Marika Vicziany (1986): 'Imperialism, Botany and Statistics in Early Nineteenth Century India: The Surveys of Francis Buchanan (1762-1829)', *Modern Asian Studies,* Vol. 20, pp. 625-660.
33. Francis Buchanan (1807): *Journey from Madras, Through the Countries of Mysore, Malabar and Canara,* London, Vol. I, p. 51 and Vol. II, p. 135.
34. D.S. Somashekar (2002): *'From Lab to Cup-Stages in Coffee Research, A Study of the CCRI at Balehonnur, from 1915-1947'*, p. 1.
35. M.M. Appaiya (1993): *Coffee: The Consolidated Story,* United Planters Association of India, Connore.
36. G.L. Beckford (1972): *Persistent Poverty: Underdevelopment in Plantation Economies of the Third World,* Oxford university Press, London, p. 167.
37. Parry Dare and Co founded in Madras by Thomas Parry in 1788 and the second oldest surviving business house in India today.
38. S. Muthiah (1993): *A Planting Century: The First Hundred Years of the United Planters Association of South India 1883-1993,* Bangalore, p. 111.
39. In the ryotwari areas, particularly in the case of large holdings, tenants under different terms cultivated lands. The terms were as follows: (a) Vara system the produce was equally shared between the landlord and tenant and the landlord paid the assessment on land to the government. (b) Mukuppa under which 2/3 of the produce went to the tenant and 1/3

to the landlord who was to pay the assessment on land to the government. c) Under the Chaturbhaga system the landlord obtained the 1/4 of the produce and paid half of the assessment on land, the tenant got 3/4 of the produce and paid the other half of the assessment. Selections from the records of the Mysore government No. 15 –papers regarding the abolition of *Halat* on coffee etc., Chikmagalur District Office Library.

40. Velayutham Saravanan (2004): 'Colonialism and Coffee Plantations: Decline of Environment and Tribals in Madras Presidency During the 19th Century', *The Indian Economic and Social History Review,* 41, 4, Sage Publications, p. 449.
41. Bhaswati, Bhattacharya (2014): 'Local History of a Global Commodity: Production of Coffee in Mysore and Coorg in the Nineteenth Century', *Indian Historical Review,* 41 (1), Sage Publications, p. 71.
42. Karnataka State Gazetteer (1927): *Chikmagalur District,* Government of Karnataka, Publication by Government Press, Bangalore, p. 135.
43. In 1856 Elliot who started his own plantation at Bartchinhulla, Saklaspur, Mysore State says in his account that "when I entered the province in 1855, anyone who desired to have a given tract of forest land for coffee planting sent an application to the government for it. An inquiry was then made, and if no objection existed to the land being made over to the intending settler or applicant, a *puttah* or grant, free of charge for the land was made a which mentioned the name of the land and the boundaries of it, and stated that the land was to be planted within three years time, and it if not planted, it was laiable to be resumed by the state." Elliot, H. (1894): *Gold, Sport and Coffee Planting in Mysore,* London, pp. 140-160.
44. Dick, Kooiman (1992): 'Plantations in Southern Asia: Indigenous Plants and Foreign Implantations', *South Asia,* Vol. XV, No. 1, p. 75.
45. Ibid., pp. 59-73.
46. The stern rule of Mark Cubbon as Chief Commissioner gave immediate returns in terms of revenue stood at 58 lakhs of rupees, and when he left in 1861 it had reached 100 lakhs.
47. Shama Rao (1936): Modern Mysore from the Beginning to 1868, Printed by Higginbothams, Bangalore, pp. 534-55.
48. Ravi Sharma (2005): 'Building on a Strong Base', *Frontline,* October 21, pp. 92-94.

49. S.G. Speer (1953): *UPASI 1853-1953,* published by United Planters Association of South India, Coonor, p. 196.
50. Hayavadana C. Rao (1927): *History of Mysore (1399-1799)* compiled for Mysore Gazetteer, Vol. I, new edition, Bangalore 1927.
51. Ibid., p. 39.
52. H.L. Nage Gowda (1969): *Bettadinda Battalige or the Story of Coffee,* Published by Sahitya Sadana, Arasikere, Manipal (in Kannada), p. 175.
53. Leaf-rust is a fungus which rises during the post monsoon period. When it affects the plants, yellow spots appear on the leaves and coffee plants become completely defoliated with dry twigs and completely debilitated.
54. The experiments turned out to be a remarkable success, the young plants raised from the imported seed grew with extraordinary vigour, and it was soon found that the new variety would help to grow well, and even on land on which all attempts to reproduce the "Chick" variety had utterly failed. Then this sinking industry rose almost as suddenly as it had fallen; old and abandoned estates, and every available acre of forest, and even scrub, were planted up, and land which used to change hands from 5 to 10 rupees an acre was eagerly bought at twelve times these amounts.
55. Although the term *maistri* is commonly translated as labour contractor, this definition is far too narrow. Aside from recruiting labour, it was usual for a *maistri* to assume responsibility for both the supervision of his workers on an estate and for their welfare needs. Planters made a clear distinction between *maistries* and professional labour contracts who merely delivered workers to estates. In Assam they were known by different names like Arakatis, Sardars, or Kanganies and had to resort to various types of fraud and coercion to get them to work on the plantations.
56. Tanika Sarkar has argued that slavery and bondage are two separate forms theoretically but in practice it would be extremely difficult to distinguish one from the other with absolute certainty, for during most of our period, the two constantly overlapped and merged into each other. The British colonizers while addressing the issue of slavery in India followed a policy of non-interference in the earlier years allowing the natives to administer their own laws in matters of property, inheritance and contract. Later under pressure it paved the way for a new

form of labour control and exploitation globally. See Utsa Patnaik and Manjari Dingwaney (1985): *Chains of Servitude: Bondage and Slavery in India* (ed), Sangam Books, Madras, pp. 97-126.

57. Ramachandra, Guha (2003): *The Last Liberal and Other Essays*, Permanent Black, New Delhi, pp. 200-13.
58. Nancy, Cassels (1988): 'Social Legislation Under the Company Raj: The Abolition of Slavery Act of 1843', *South Asia*, 1, pp. 59-87.
59. Ibid., pp. 32-44.
60. Ibid., pp. 22-32.
61. By 1865 the collector of the Nilgiris reported that approximately 80 per cent of the estate labour in the district came from Mysore. See *Report of the South Indian Planters Enquiry Committee*, Madras, 1896, p. 10.
62. Ibid., p. 186.
63. The spread of destitution among the peasants has led many thousands to seek work in the industrial areas or plantations. The plantations lie mainly in the forest tracts, cleared by the planters, where the local population was extremely sparse and labour recruited from the villages or from adjoining villages. George K. Tharian and P.K. Michael Tharakan (1986): 'Penetration of Capital into a Traditional Economy: The Case of Tea Plantations in Kerala, 1880-1950', *Studies in History*, Vol. 2, No. 2, pp. 199-228.
64. The British planters of Chikmagalur felt the need and were granted a piece of land by the Maharaja of Mysore for building a club house in 1883. It was at the bar of these clubs that the Planting Association was formed both at the district and state level to have their voices heard by influential planters. As a result of these deliberations on planting affairs, various planting associations were founded. A committee was formed under the Chairperson of Mr. W.A. Allardice, the owner of Mylermoney estate.
65. H.L. Nage Gowda (1969): *Bettadinda Battalige or the Story of Coffee*, Published by Sahitya Sadana Arasikere, Manipal (in Kannada).
66. S. Muthiah (1993): *A Planting Century: The First Hundred Years of the United Planters Association of South India 1883-1993*, Bangalore, p. 92.
67. The United Planters Association of Southern India was founded in 1893 and is the apex organization of the producers of tea, coffee, rubber and other species in the southern stares of Karnataka, Kerala and Tamil Nadu affiliated to the UPASI are

the three state Planters Associations in Tamil Nadu, Kerala, and Karnataka and about 25 district and other associations in these states. The UPASI is an important link between the government and the industry and plays a key role in the formulation policy for the industry.

68. Karnataka Planters Association (1980): "The Development of Malanad," Plantation Industry in Perspective, p. 26.
69. Ira, Klein (1984): 'When the Rains Failed: Famine, Relief and Mortality in British India', *The Indian Economic and Social History Review,* 21, 2, pp. 199-201.
70. E. Raghavan and James Manor (2009): *Broadening and Deepening Democracy: Political Innovation in Karnataka,* Routledge, New Delhi, p. 5.
71. During this period the Land Revenue Code underwent a number of amendments but only those of 1912, 1928, 1939 and 1940. Even these amendments did not seriously affect the provisions regarding the superior and inferior landholders were ameliorative measures and no comprehensive steps were taken to protect the tenants, whether in respect of security to tenure or fixity of rent, because in spite of recommendations of the *Inam* committee the demand between the cultivators or *jodi* was left vague and open to manipulations by the *inamdars*. The significant fact of the land revenue code there was no fresh laws to regulate the tenurial or tenancy problems in the state. See P.T. George (1970): 'Land System and Laws in Mysore State', March-June Vol. 12, No 1 & 2, *Artha Vijana,* Poona, p. 127.
72. C.B. Damle (1993): *Land Reforms and Changing Agrarian Relations,* Rawat Publications, New Delhi, pp. 4-5.
73. Keya, Deb (1979): 'Tea Plantations in the Brahmaputra Valley (1839-1914): A Case Study in the Colonial Set Up', Centre for the Study of Regional Development, Jawaharlal Nehru University (unpublished thesis), p. 4.

2

Coffee Board, Global Coffee Crisis and its Effects on Small Growers from Chikmagalur District of Karnataka

Introduction

The princely state of Mysore after the British rule in 1881 was under double slavery of the Wodeyars and British through the medium of representative assemblies for greater peace and containment and ignoring the wishes of the people. The patronage to the coffee industry was when a planter had the provision of choosing either a 30 year settlement at one rupee per acre or a permanent settlement at 1½ rupees. The major issue for the progress of coffee cultivation was the outbreak of pests and diseases. The coffee cultivation was reduced between 1881 and 1911 owing to the failure of rainfall successively from 1883 and 1885 and 1904 and 1909. Coffee cultivation continued in Chikmagalur due to the untiring efforts of Dr. Leslie. Coleman[1] and led to the establishment of a coffee experimental station at Balehonnur in Chikmagalur district. In India efforts were made by the enterprising planters to evolve disease resistant plant material through selection and also by crossing Arabica with other rust-hardy species like Liberica which were introduced to tide over the situation. In this context, hybrids like 'Hamiltons', 'Jacksons', Netra Konda and selections like 'Coorgs', 'Chicks' and Kents were important. 'Kents' was a proven selection that was the predominant planting material during the 1920s. Further because of its superior bean, kents was exclusively used in breeding programmes taken up after the ignition of organized research work from 1925 onwards by the Central Coffee Research Institute. The success of any breeding progamme depends on the proper evaluation and exploitation of the available gene pool. Hence, a massive gene bank was established at CCRI with collections from both indigenous and exotic sources.

The technological advances achieved as mentioned below, enabled a sustainable growth of the coffee industry in the subsequent decades.

- Discovery of physiological traces of coffee leaf rust and rationalization of Bordeaux mixture spray
- Formulation of fertilizer dosages and the role of shade in coffee cultivation
- Studies on life cycle of coffee white stem borer, cockchafer, nematodes, scale insects like green bug, mealy big and their control methods.
- Technology for preparation of quality coffee.

The indigenous collections were made between 1925 and 1940 by surveying the existing plantations for vigorous, disease-resistant Arabica and Robusta plants and over 250 collections were established at CCRI. The pioneering work of Walter Mayne, the first Coffee Scientific Officer on the existence of physiologic specialization of leaf rust opens the chapter of coffee research and experimental work, while at the same time the coffee industry in Sri Lanka perished on account of pests and diseases.[2] The rise of Brazil as the dominant supplier and the huge crops which accumulated in the 1930s, led to the disastrous fall in prices which affected Indian coffee as well. Even by destroying 68 million bags of coffee between 1931 and 1942, Brazil could not stem the fall in prices. Despite the technological breakthrough the productivity of coffee continued to be at a low level. The Indian growers were heavily in debt and had to abandon their estates and this led the Government of India to introduce a statutory organization to cope with the problems of coffee cultivation.

Coffee Board

The coffee industry in India was in a desperate state due to the Second World War resulting in very low prices and ravages of pests and diseases. The 1930s saw the gradual decline of the area under coffee until the lowest point. The growers with the support of the Mysore State Government pressed the Central Government to set up a body to promote local consumption. The Indian Coffee Cess Act was passed in 1935 and a committee to administer the Cess Fund was set up under the Act. The beginning of the Second World War and allied reverses in Europe added to the problems of Indian coffee like shipping became scarce as well as the exports highly vulnerable on the high seas. Suddenly the exportable surplus had no outlet and threatened internal coffee prices. The situation called for quick action and the producers petitioned which led to the creation of the Coffee Board which was set up by an ordinance in early 1941. The eventual enactment of the Coffee (Marketing and Expansion) Act, 1942 by the Central Assembly and its post-war succession by the permanent measure of India were the producer-inspired steps that the government took to cope with the problems of coffee. The Coffee Board followed the procedure of convening a formal conference of coffee growers before legislation was to seek public comment and was proposed in the Assembly. The tradition of democratic practices and the Act itself ensured that the Board's autonomy was real and respected. The Indian Coffee Board is the sole authority of marketing of coffee both in the internal and the international markets. The Coffee Board comprises 33 members including the chairman who is the chief executive and appointed by the Government of India.[3] Under the Act, the Chief Executive was the Chief Coffee Marketing Officer who reserved the power to withhold action on any decision of the Board on which he considered it for or necessary to consult the government before action was taken. In 1952, the government did not follow the customary practice of convening a grower's conference before proposing the changes. The most important change proposed was the sweeping powers taken by the government to appoint producers and trade members on the Board, the abrogation of the Boards autonomous character. The Coffee Market Expansion Act was introduced in Parliament in 1953 and one of its features ensured that the government did not propose to export any part of the coffee crop in 1952-52. The planter community was against fixing the price of coffee below the existing level as it adversely affected growers interests. The Coffee Board became liable to the discretion of government, as the powers of the government exercised through a body of executives appointed by it.

The remaining 32 members represented the various interests such as the members of Parliament (3), representatives of the government of principal coffee growing states (4), representatives of large coffee growers (3), representatives of small growers (7), representatives of coffee trade interests (3), representatives of curing establishment (2), representatives of labour interests (4), representatives of coffee growing states other than principal coffee growing states (2), representatives of consumer interests (2), representatives of instant coffee manufacturers (1), and eminent personalities in the field of research marketing/management/promotion of coffee (1). The state has protected the coffee plantation and has given concessions by giving lands for coffee cultivation and also because of the foremost export earners for the country and a source of valuable foreign exchange. This has been a reason for the government to protect the industry and so the Coffee Board was founded.[4]

Extension and Development Activities of the Coffee Board

The forerunner of the Indian Coffee Board has been the Indian Coffee Market Expansion Board, to stabilize prices at reasonable levels by collecting surplus coffee produced in the country and marketing it in planned stages to prevent a glut in the internal market. The extension service of the Indian Coffee Market Expansion Board was started during 1948 when coffee growers were yet to understand the significance of coffee cultivation practices, to be a vital link between the coffee growing community and the research department. The principal activity of the extension wing of the Coffee Board is transfer of technologies standardized by the research department to the coffee growers for achieving better production, productivity and improving the quality of coffee. Thus, it is helping to bridge the gap between coffee growers and research scientists in adoption of coffee technology in the coffee estates.[5] With the expansion of coffee in the traditional coffee growing states of Karnataka, Kerala and Tamil Nadu with one liaison officer has grown into a vast network and also expansion of coffee in the non-traditional areas of Andhra Pradesh, Odisha and the North-Eastern region. The extension network has been expanded vertically and horizontally to meet the requirements of coffee growers in different parts of the coffee growing areas.

The Coffee Board's functions are carried out under various departments like Administration/Secretariat, Research Department, Central Coffee Research Institute, network of research stations, promotion department, market research and intelligence unit and accounts and finance. The broad functions of the extension wing are transfer of technology from lab-to-land through various extension methodologies, demonstration of promising technologies through Technology Evaluation Centres (TECs) in different regions and organizing training programmes for capacity building of all the stakeholders of the coffee industry. It also helps in improving production, productivity and quality of coffee, estimating crop production, monitoring of weather, pests and diseases, implementing labour welfare measures, procurement and supply distribution of improved seeds and inputs for pest control, providing feedback about field problems to the scientists of research departments.

The different schemes announced by the Government of India for the further development of the coffee industry in the post-1950s are as follows:

(i) The Coffee Development Plan was launched in 1956-96 with gradual expansion of extension network to cater to the technology needs as well as short-term and long-term credits. The different types of loans operated under the coffee development plan includes (i) intensive cultivation loan, (ii) replanting loan (iii) extensive cultivation loan, (iv) special purpose loan, (v) crop hypothecation loan and (vi) hire purchase term loan.

(ii) The replanting loan cum subsidy of the Coffee Board was commenced during 1973-74 to encourage small coffee growers for replanting of old, uneconomic coffee plantations with high yielding, disease-resistant plant material for improving production and productivity.

(iii) Interest subsidy scheme during 1977-78 to provide interest subsidy to small coffee growers on term loans availed from nationalized banks and cooperative institutions.

(iv) Expansion Subsidy Scheme commenced during 1979-80 to provide incentives to coffee growers for bringing new areas under coffee cultivation and the scheme was discontinued from 1990.

The Coffee Board effectively conducted and controlled the pooling system where all producers, small and large, had to surrender their entire produce to the pool of the Coffee Board or approved agencies of the Coffee Board. Private dealers who did not have a dealership agreement with the Coffee Board were not allowed in the market.[6] The restrictions imposed by the Coffee Board in the movement of coffee nuts, strict quality management, stagnation in the price level for a long time made the farmers to go against the pooling system. In the light of resentment among the coffee growers some relaxations to the pooling system were introduced.[7]

Restructuring of Coffee Board

The structural adjustment programme sponsored by the World Bank has suggested abandoning the objective of food self-sufficiency and relying on international trade to obtain food grains, more so if we do not have a comparative advantage. The comparative advantage is a rather nebulous concept (more so its indicator, that is the border prices) there is ample evidence to show that international prices are more volatile. It is being argued that, in today's world, it is possible to bridge the gap between domestic demand and supply by way of food import. However, a large and poor country, such as India cannot afford to take the issue of sizeable quantities of food imports lightly. The policy of food self-sufficiency, which has remained the cornerstone of our agricultural policy, paid us rich dividends. The new export oriented agricultural policies that are part of agricultural globalization have led to a shift from the production of food crops to commodities for exports, such as cotton, horticulture, sunflower, orchards and eucalyptus. This was particularly noticeable in the southern states of Andhra Pradesh, Karnataka, Tamil Nadu and Kerala.[8] The financial stress has caused epidemic suicides in the Warangal district of Andhra Pradesh. The shift from the welfare state to a new system of free-market economy had led to the widening of the gap between the privileged few and the large mass of the marginalized sections of society, Dalit labourers, daily wage workers, and workers in the informal sector thus widening the gap of inequality in society. In 1992-93 the Coffee Board of India amended the Coffee Act of 1942 and announced that 30% of their produce was in the open market. As the Internal Sale Quota (ISQ) proved to be a success, a Free Sale Quota (FSQ) system was introduced during 1995. Under this system, small farmers were allowed to sell 100 per cent of their product in the open market while large farmers were allowed to sell 70 per cent. Big farmers had to pool 30 per cent of their produce with the Coffee Board. Through FSQ, an open market system came into existence for coffee in India. The following reasons for the rejection of the pooling system are as follows:

(i) Stagnant prices
(ii) Mounting marketing cost
(iii) Delay in payments
(iv) Minimum Release Price and Bonus
(v) Excessive emphasis upon quality
(vi) Strict restrictions
(vii) Curbs on transportation

The marketing of the beans had been under the monopolistic control of the Coffee Board, an autonomous body functioning under the Union Ministry of Commerce and Industry. The centralized pooled system made it obligatory on the part of the coffee growers to surrender all his produce to the pool and used to receive his returns on the basis of quality and quantity of the produce.

Global Coffee Crisis

The coffee crisis is due to a complex web of factors is due to oversupply that took place in global markets for agricultural commodities in the last two decades. In 1955 due to the instability of prices the United States government showed initiative in the creation of an International Coffee Agreement (ICA) where a target price for coffee was set, and export quotas were allocated to each producer. When the indicator price calculated by the International Commodity Agreements (ICO) rose over the set price, quotas were relaxed when it fell below the set price, quotas were tightened. The ICA agreement was relatively a success for each country based on estimates of the global coffee market which resulted in stabilizing coffee prices.

The end of the ICA regime in 1989 followed by lower and volatile prices, which was accompanied by a high proportion of the income generated in the consuming countries and a declining level of producer held stocks.[9] In order to reduce the effect of World Trade Organization intervention in global agriculture in India, the Association of Coffee Producing Countries (ACPC) has initiated the coffee retention scheme under which 20 per cent of the produce will be hoarded until the price touches a specified and profitable level.

The import of cheap Robusta coffee from Vietnam and Indonesia should be reduced by imposing non-trade barriers. Vietnam was a country, which grew little coffee, but it was encouraged by countries like France and USA, Coffee Trans National Corporation such as Nestle and multilateral banks such as the World Bank, the French Development Fund (FDF) and Asian Development Bank (ADB) which led to a rapid expansion of coffee. The FDF issued a 40 million loan to Vietnam as late as 1998 to create 40,000 acres of coffee plantation by stripping pristine forests. Vietnam became the second largest producer of coffee in the world and the largest producer of the cheaper Robusta variety. The harvest areas expanded from 1.5 lakh hectares in 1995 to 5.5 lakh hectares in 2001 and exports rose in this period from 4 million to 14 million bags of coffee.[10]

Coffee in Global Output

Country	Percentage
Brazil	31.70
Columbia	14.10
Vietnam	11.90
Ivory Cost	9.90
El Salvador	5.70
Zimbabwe	5.70
India	3.20
Guatemala	3.10
Angola	3.00
Kenya	2.10
Costa Rica	2.00
Uganda	1.00
Indonesia	1.00
Tanzania	0.90
Ethiopia	0.70
Ecuador	0.60

Source: Coffee Board, Bangalore

The coffee sector is one of the main victims of the fall in the prices of its products. With the establishment of the World Trade Organization in 1995, trade in agricultural commodities was brought under the multilateral trading process. Earlier, agricultural trade used to be done through bilateral agreements and countries were free to favour countries to impose quotas, as they wished. The Most Favoured Nation (MFN) clause implies that any concession granted to one member automatically applies to all members of the WTO. The principal of non-discrimination is carried into the domestic realm through the application of the national treatment clause, which implies that any concession granted to a domestic product should also be granted to the imported product.[11] The removal of quantitative restrictions is one of the conditions that have become obligatory by India's entering into agreement on agriculture with WTO. This has specific implications for the coffee economy of the country and naturally therefore for the coffee growers of Chikmagalur.

Coffee in Chikmagalur District

Chikamagalur district has a population of 11,39,104 as per the 2001 Census and has seven taluks: Sringeri, Koppa, N.R. Pura, Tarikere, Kadur, Chikmagalur and Mudigere The commercial agricultural setting of the Chikmagalur district is dominated by coffee cultivation, are extensively marketed. The coffee plantation crops are cultivated mainly in the hill tracts or *Malanad* of South India especially in Karnataka, Kerala and Tamil Nadu. The other states of India in which coffee is grown on a limited scale are Andhra Pradesh, Maharashtra, West Bengal, Assam, Andaman and Nicobar islands and Madhya Pradesh. India is the sixth largest coffee producer in the world. It is grown in the southern states of Karnataka (70 per cent), Kerala (20 per cent), and Tamil Nadu (7 per cent). The area under coffee cultivation in Karnataka indicates that Chikmagalur accounts for the largest area under Arabica (*Coffee Arabica*) about 40 per cent, Kodagu, about 22 per cent and Hassan, about 18 per cent and Kodagu district has the largest area under Robusta (*Coffee Canephora*). The two important varieties of coffee grown on a commercial scale are Arabica and Robusta.

Planted Area of Coffee in Karnataka State

There are around 300 surviving collections of Arabica and 73 types of Robusta and 17 different species of coffee. The Central Coffee Research Institute (CCRI) has developed 13 Arabica selections for commercial cultivation of which, seven selections are popular among the growers and cultivated on a commercial scale. There are around six varieties of Arabica coffee which are grown in Chikmagalur: S.795, Selection 5B, Selection 6, Selection 9, Cauvery/Catimore and Chandragiri. There are variations across states and districts. For example, S795 is largely grown in Karnataka (about 72 per cent), Selection 9 variety in Kerala (about 87 per cent) and Tamil Nadu (about 80 per cent).[12] Arbaica coffee has more beverage value and hence fetches a higher price in the international market, when

S.No.	State/ District	2001-2002		
		Arabica	Robusta	Total
1.	Chikmagalur	58,330	28,225	86,555
2.	Kodagu	26,110	56,250	82,360
3.	Hassan	25,030	7,040	32,070
4.	Mysore and Others	800	0	800
	Total	1,10,270	91,515	2,01,785

Database on Coffee (2003): Market Intelligence Unit, Coffee Board, Bangalore.

compared to the Robusta variety of coffee.

In Karnataka coffee is grown as an intercropping, multi-storeyed cropping, diversification, etc means cultivation of two or more compatible crops for better utilization of available land and resources to the best advantage of growers. This situation paves the way for bringing about an association of several economic species together. The shade grown conditions in coffee holding trees provide revenue to the coffee growers in the form of timber, firewood and edible fruits. Along with this the traditional cultivators also grew a wide variety of species and fruit as auxiliary crops such as pepper, cardamom, vanilla, oranges, bananas and areca nuts intertwined in the shade canopy. The shade cultivation has been adopted due to the peculiar agro-climatic conditions prevailing in the Western Ghats such as the wide range of fluctuations in day temperature and monsoon-driven rainfall. The strategy has been to grow compatible crops that have canopy and root structures in a manner that their canopies intercept sunlight at varying heights and their roots tap moisture and nutrients from different depths of soil without interfering with the growth of coffee. The diversification of coffee holdings with different compatible crops originated in India much before any systematic initiatives by any agency due to the prevailing conditions and necessities of the coffee growers. Most of the diversification efforts were made by coffee growers themselves in the early years. The diversification has led a region specific intercrops like pepper and areca nut are the main intercrops in Chikmagalur district, while pepper dominated as intercrop Arabica holdings of Coorg region. In contrast, the Arabica holdings in Tamil Nadu had a higher degree of diversification with organe, pepper, bananas, cardamom, lemons, and vegetable crops. The disadvantage of shade cultivation is that it also inhibits overall productivity when compared to coffee grown under open conditions in countries such as Brazil and Vietnam. Coffee is grown mainly in the agrarian countries of the tropical and sub-tropical regions of the world in developing countries while it is mainly consumed by the developed countries.

Coffee Prices

The structural adjustment programme sponsored by the World Bank has suggested abandoning the objective of food self-sufficiency and rely on international trade to obtain food grains, more so if we do not have a comparative advantage. The comparative advantage is a rather nebulous concept (more so its indicator, that is the border prices) there is ample evidence to show that international prices are more volatile. It is being argued that, in today's world, it is possible to bridge the gap between domestic demand and supply by way of food imports.[13] However, a large and poor country, such as India cannot afford to take the issue of sizeable quantities of food imports lightly. The policy of food self-sufficiency, which has remained the cornerstone of our agricultural policy, paid us rich dividends.

The prices of coffee in India are very unstable and are characterized by cycles with short periods of high prices and extended periods of depressed prices, due to variations in supply. The Indian coffee plantation is in no position to influence global prices which are on the basis of the London Terminal Market for Robusta Coffee and New York Terminal Market for Arabica Coffee, although a few plantations cultivate some fine connoisseurs' coffee.[14] The coffee cultivation integrated with the global market, which decides the fate of the growers.[15] When quantitative restrictions were lifted, exports from Brazil and Columbia began to reach India, which is superior in quality and caters to the demand of the connoisseurs in the market. Cheap coffee from Vietnam and Indonesia also reaches India and competes with the Indian varieties.

Consequently, the price of coffee rose in the next few years. In 1994-95 due to unseasonal thunderstorms which completely destroyed the coffee plantation in Brazil the demand for coffee in the international market led to a significant rise in the prices of Indian coffee temporarily. Many growers have attempted to intensify coffee cultivation to increase production and productivity of their plantations. The wrong assumptions led the coffee farmers in Chikmagalur to invest in land, vehicles and real estate which led many farmers into debt crisis. This also coincided with the dismantling of the Indian Coffee Board which was made to believe that the Coffee Board was the reason for the crisis. When the pooling system was strong the growers could sell their output only to the Coffee Board. But when free marketing was allowed it led to the unhealthy practice of distress sale of coffee. The total numbers of registered coffee exporters are about 395. Further the Board issues, under Section 20 of the Coffee Act, 1942, permits for exports of Indian coffee. Additionally, the Certificates of Origin are also issued as per the provisions of the International Coffee Agreement. The method of fixing the minimum release price followed by the Coffee Board was against the interests of growers. According to this method, the first payment was the minimum relief price, fixed on the basis of data on cost of production of growers in the cooperative sector. The withdrawal of the Coffee Board from the marketing of coffee has led to the emergence of intermediaries in trade. The coffee industry has undergone its own process of consolidation, resulting in the emergence of super-large international firms like Proctor and Gamble, Nestle and Chabby control 50 per cent of that market that is produced by 2.5 crore growers and five lakh workers across the world. In Karnataka few companies like Ramesh Exports Limited of Mr. Ramesh P. Rajah, Madhu Jayanthi International of Mr. Ashwin Shah, Mr Allana and Sons Limited of Mr. Arun Biddappa, Mr. V.G. Siddhartha trading company named Amalgamated Bean Company handle most of the cargo that goes outside the country.[16]

The downward trend in prices began in 2000 and intensified over 2001 and 2002. The price of Arabica, which averaged ₹ 90 a kg in 1999 dropped to ₹ 63 a kg in the last quarter of 2001. Over the same period, Robusta fell from ₹ 68 a kg to ₹ 33 a kg. Indias exports 80 per cent of its coffee produce, and there has been a sharp fall in both export quantities and values in the last two years. While the volume of exports has fallen from 2,53,524 tonnes in 2000 to 2,23,782 tonnes in 2001, the value has fallen from ₹ 1,685.24 crores to ₹ 1,136.93 crores in the same period.

The crisis has led to switching away from coffee cultivation to cultivation such as pepper and arecanut due to its un-remunerative nature. The shift in the cultivation has made the farmers resort to a balanced approach of planting a variety of crops because the loss in income due to fall in the price of one crop would be compensated by the income from other crops. The large estate owners of more than 100 acres of land and big farmers who own more than 10 acres of land do not face the risk of investing in a single crop because the gross income they receive from cultivation of coffee is high due to the high volume of their production.

Karnataka Growers Federation and Coffee Debt Relief Package

It has 21 associations affiliated to it from Chikmagalur, Kodagu, Hassan, Chamrajnagar and Dakshina Kannada with the motto: 'Sustainability, Growth and Justice'. It has been representing the cause of growers of coffee and species.

The following are the main objectives of the Association as per the KPA rules:

- To promote and protect in all parts of the world, the interests of the plantation industry carried on in Karnataka.
- To promote or guide legislative and other measures

affecting such industries and to make representations to local, state or other authorities on matters connected with these objects or any of them.

- To collect, classify, circulate and publish statistics and other information relating to such industries.
- To communicate with Planting Associations, Chambers of Commerce, Employers' Federations, Trade Unions and other mercantile and public bodies throughout the world, and concert and promote measures connected with these objects or any of them.
- To advise, represent or assist members on labour, planting, taxation and commercial matters.

Though the Government of India announced an agriculture debt waiver package in 2008, the debts of the growers continued to be a big burden for the growth of the industry. The KGF decided to appraise the Commerce Ministry about the new package which led to differences of opinion with the chairman of the Coffee Board. The tension was regarding the growers over 10 hectares who were kept out of the purview of the package. The package was reaching its final stages when incidentally the elections were declared. The new United Progressive Alliance (UPA) government took office in 2009 and Mr. Moily became the minister for law, and this helped and started the discussion with the new commerce minister Mr. Anand Sharma.[17] The intense lobbying with the government led to the announcement of "Coffee Debt Relief Packages" in 2010. This significantly reduced the burden of the growers below 10 hectares as 75 per cent of the loan was waived off. The glory and triumph of getting the "Coffee Debt Relief Package" sanctioned was due to the long relentless struggle which was carried out with team work, lobbying and peaceful agitation.

The Ministry of Commerce concerned with the problems of the coffee growers implemented a special package in 2012 called Special Coffee Term Loan (SCTL) for the coffee growers.

The different packages announced by the Government

of India and the State Government from 2000 to 2010 are as follows:

(i) 2001-02: Restructuring of the loans to SCTL

(ii) 2002-03: Reduction in the rate of interest on SCTL from 18 percent to 13.5 per cent.

(iii) 2003-04: Rate of Interest on working capital reduced to 9 per cent for loans upto ₹ 50 lakhs.

(iv) 2005: SCTL package of ₹ 281 crores.

(v) 2006: Exemption from permit for cutting silver oak trees.

(vi) 2008: Agriculture Debt Waiver package of ₹ 110 crores.

(vii) 2010: Coffee debt relief package of ₹ 450 crores.

(viii) 2002-2013: Waiver of agricultural income tax of ₹ 600 crores

The package resulted in restructuring/reschedulement of the term loans as well as crop loans taken by coffee growers from commercial banks, providing 5 per cent interest relief to small growers and 3 per cent interest relief to larger growers. These measures were introduced for export of coffee and innovative marketing strategies in the international as well as domestic markets to arrest the decline in exports and also to increase domestic consumption, etc. The government has decided to set up a price stabilization fund with a corpus of ₹ 500 crores to provide relief to the growers of coffee, tea, natural rubber and tobacco.[18]

The growers did not realize the trap they were getting into as in many cases the interest had doubled the principal. The collapse of the coffee prices far below the cost of production and the pressure from the banks forced many growers to abandon their plantations, sell them and some even resorted to the extreme step of suicide. The state government gave the first relief by waving the agriculture income tax for growers below 10 hectares which was further extended to 20 hectares and later to all individuals growers. Though this was a minor relief to the growers they slowly started to believe that organization would bring in some more relief. The National Democratic Alliance government in 2014 announced the rate of interest on

Special Coffee Term from 16.5 per cent to 13.5 per cent and 9 per cent on the working capital loan.

The major criticism against "Special Coffee Term Loan" (SCTL) was that it remained unpaid. The first relief came by a waiver of interest on SCTL from 2002 to 2005 wherein growers had to pay one-third and the remaining two-thirds ware shared by the bank and the Government of India. The government announced the Vidarbaha Package in 2006[19] which included waiver of all interest on all over due loans in 25 districts of the country where suicides were high due to debts. The three districts of Chikmagalur, Hassan and Kodagu were included and this package considerably reduced the interest burden of the growers who had not opted for the SCTL package.[20]

Response of Karnataka Planters Association

The bigger organizations such as Karnataka Planters Association (KPA) affiliated to United Planters Association of India (UPASI) have opposed militant mass protest by coffee growers. The KPA had regular meetings with the union Commerce Minister, the Finance Minister and the Prime Minister. The delegations of growers association along with the Members of Parliament and ministers from Karnataka met the union Finance Minister and the union commerce minister to express their anxiety with respect to the coffee price situation and other related aspects.[21]

The more balanced approach of these associations has been respected by the respective state governments and centre. The KPA held a press conference in November 2002 where the chairman, A.S. Muthanna stated that between 1998 and 2002 the coffee industry had lost up to ₹ 2,000 crores. He warned that the coffee industry was "on the verge of collapse".[22] In the total amount of coffee produced in our country, Karnataka farmers contribute 74 per cent while Kerala farmers contribute 24 per cent. The foreign exchange earnings through the export of tea, pepper, cardamom, areca nuts, ginger, vanilla and other spices from the region amount to thousands of crores of rupees. In view of this crucial contribution, the government should protect and promote the cash crop growers of this region as its responsibility. This sort of severe crash of prices has drained the farmers of their earnings and the steep hike in the input costs due to withdrawal of subsidies, hike in the price of fertilizers, electricity, water, diesel, seeds and plants has made agriculture too expensive.[23]

Coffee Labourers

The coffee plantations are the main source of income and livelihood for a large number of daily migrant workers, including women and indigenous tribal communities settled in the surrounding forest areas. As per the data released by the Coffee Board of India, the average daily number of workers employed on coffee estates has increased from 423,451 in 2003-04 to 479,453 in 2009-10. The response of the trade unions and peasant organizations to the crisis has been sedate as different organizations came together to form a Joint Action Committee and submitted a memorandum to the Government of India. It organized a strike by workers on December 11, 2000 demanding various tax concessions to "Save the plantation industry and its workmen".[24] Earlier there were around 44 unions, now this number is reduced to 12 unions.

The coffee economy is highly labour-oriented with 495 mandays for Arabica, for Robusta 330 mandays. There are 15 lakh workers who are employed directly and indirectly; most of the labourers are categorized as permanent, temporary and migratory. The migratory labourers come from the neighbouring districts especially during the months when there is no agriculture activity in those districts. For example, Harapanahalli in Davangere district is the largest supplier of labourers to coffee growing areas. On an average for a one acre, around 175-200 labourers are required; most of the workers are women. The stipulated daily wage amount is ₹ 247, but they are paid more due to the shortage of labour. The labourers are provided with all the statutory benefits under the Plantation Labour Act, like basic minimum wages, free housing, electricity and schooling. The shortage of labourers is due to various reasons; For example, the younger generation does not want to work in estates and have moved towards cities for work in hotels. In the recent years the shortage of labour has been filled by migratory labourers from Odisha, Bengal and Assam.[25] Apart from the income received as daily wages, workers employed on coffee estates also benefit from fuel-wood and other non-timber forest products available providing alternative livelihoods opportunities. The small growers are represented by the Karnataka Growers Federation (KGF) which is the apex plantation decision-making body in the state comprising of members with coffee, tea, pepper, cardamom and rubber plantations.

Future of Coffee Plantation

The major worry for the plantation is the problems of encroachment where the draft proposal of India to bring plantations under the preview of ceiling has left the entire industry in jeopardy. The Karnataka Land Grabbing (Prohibition) Act, 2007 was passed unanimously by both houses of the Karnataka legislature. The salient features under the Karnataka Act are:

1. It applies to all land belonging to government, local authority, a statutory or non-statutory body and includes a Company, Trust, Society or association of individuals.
2. A land grabber includes whoever unlawfully takes possession of the land or assists in taking possession and also an abettor to such acts, such as public servants.
3. Land-grabbing is punishable by the Special Court with a minimum of one year's imprisonment and a maximum of three years and with fine up to ₹ 25,000.
4. The Special Court will initially consist of a chairman of the rank of serving or retired High Court Judge and two judicial members of the rank of district judges and two other revenue members not below the rank of deputy commissioner of a district.
5. Additional benches can be constituted with a judicial member as chairman and a revenue member.
6. All land grabbing cases in the state will be tried only by the Special Court and the decision of the Special Court

will be final.

7. The Special Court will have powers of the civil court and the Court of Session.
8. Where it is proved prima facie that the land is owned by the government, the burden of proof that the land is not grabbed lies with the accused.
9. In areas where the Special Court is not constituted, a magistrate of the first class can be empowered by the government to try offences under this Act.
10. This Act overrides all other laws. All cases of land-grabbing nature before any other court or authority stand transferred to the Special Court under this Act.[26]

The Bill submitted to the Union Ministry for obtaining the President's Assent in July 2007 had few clarifications sought from the Minority Affairs to include the *Wakf* Board lands and submit the Bill after getting it passed in the Karnataka Legislature. The Bill is still pending with the Revenue Department and indicates the scant importance attached by the government to control encroachment of public lands.

Conclusion

The state government in order to formulate uniform land reform legislation appointed a committee popularly known as the Jatti Committee to make a detailed review of tenancy and agricultural land legislation in different parts of the state and presented its report in September 1957. The recommendations became the basis of the Mysore Land Reforms Act 1961 (later called Karnataka Land Reforms Act, 1961. The 1961 Act included various concessions to different streams of society. There was a conscious delay of eight years in implementing the Act. The delay facilitated *mala fide* transfers of land under different names and the gross misuse of the concession given to widows, minors, etc to hold ownership over the leased out land and granting rights to landlords for resumption of land for personal cultivation—a phrase loosely defined in the Act. The exemptions from ceilings were granted to cooperatives, various educational, religious and charitable institutions were exempted, in particular institutions engaged in industry and business, where the rent was collected. In order to increase the cultivation of coffee the Government of Karnataka had sanctioned land for coffee plantation during the years 1964-1969 on *darkast* (by request) and suddenly stopped. Lands which were brought under coffee cultivation remained as cultivated but were not regularized and the grower's application remained pending. The government has collected *takrar takth* a minimal fine collected for encroaching a piece of land for twenty to twenty-five years and allowed the cultivation. The 1974 Land Reforms Act, continued the trend with regard to the exemptions from ceiling which were granted to cooperatives, sugar mills and joint farming societies. Their cultivation is required for the industry, as coffee plantation requires on-farm or near-farm processing facilities. The breaking of the plantation into small farms owned and operated by economically smaller groups may result in decreased production and in turn will hit foreign exchange.[78] For example, the Karnataka Government issued *saguvali* chits in lands considered as revenue lands which appeared in the government records but later was transferred to forests as in the case of Muskli village in Chikmagalur. This has resulted in farmers losing their lands due to the mistake of the revenue and forest departments between survey sketches done by the Revenue, Forest and Survey of India.

The new export-oriented agricultural policies that are part of agricultural globalization have led to a shift from the production of food crops to commodities for exports, such as cotton, horticulture, sunflower, orchards and eucalyptus. This was particularly noticeable in the southern states of Andhra Pradesh, Karnataka, Tamil Nadu and Kerala. The financial stress has caused epidemic suicides in Warangal district of Andhra Pradesh. The trade liberalization has to budget and cutback in extension and withdrawal of low interest credit from cooperatives and public sector banks. There has been no worthwhile public investment in agriculture and allied sectors, apart from what is minimally required for World Bank financed or other ongoing projects. In the district of Warangal the shift in the cropping pattern from food grains to cash crops like cotton may fetch higher prices, but they also demand a higher level of expenditure. The use of pesticides has increased because the hybrids are very vulnerable to pest attack. Expenditure on pesticides in the district went up to 2.5 million dollar for the entire decade of the 1980s to 50 million dollars in 1997. The financial stress is blamed for an epidemic of suicides in Warnagal district. The agrarian crisis is spurred by agrarian distress of one kind or the other and has been a recurrent theme in the state agrarian sector since 1998.[28] Rural indebtedness appears to be the consequence of inequalities and pressures resulting from specific state-directed strategies in the agricultural sector. This has created the conditions that drive the more vulnerable into hopelessness and suicide.[29]

Suicides have generally haunted the dry rain-fed plains areas of Karnataka, but the coffee distress has not led to peasant suicide.[30] However in contrast the Wayanad district of Kerala with a population of eight lakhs has drawn the media attention where 130 farmers and agricultural workers committed suicides in 2004 due to the price crash of coffee prices. Varkala Radhakrishnan, Member of Parliament from Vayanar told Parliament that the coffee crisis would lead multinational companies to "dictate terms" and the "entire produce will have to be sold according to the whims and fancies". He further said that it would have "an adverse interest in the case of the poor coffee growers of South India, especially Karnataka and Kerala".[31] The state government gave the first relief by waving the agriculture income tax for growers below 10 hectares which was further extended to 20 hectares and later to all individual growers.

Thus Indian coffee farming is characterized by inter-regional variations across different coffee regions. The small growers constitute the majority of the coffee planters in Chikmagalur district who require a region-specific policy for the survival of coffee plantations. The wide variations in annual crops, as well as district variations during different seasons, point to the marked element of unpredictability about coffee as a permanent plant crop. The current practices of intercropping are practised as a supplementary source of income and due to the complementary relationship between the non-coffee plants and trees in coffee estates. Encroachment of forests for coffee cultivation has been done by small, marginal and big farmers for coffee cultivation. The issue of forest encroachment also leads to the question of forest laws and especially the Forest Conservation Act 1980, which was enacted to check the diversion of forest land to development projects. The Forest Conservation Act arose mainly because land records are poorly maintained and the act was also based on the premise that state governments have mala fide intentions and are incapable of protecting their forests. The interface involves the state at three levels—central, state and local where the diversion of forest land is decided by the central government, but routed through the state government with a clearance from the chief secretary and the chief conservator of forests.

References

1. Dr. Leslie Coleman has been considered as the father of organized coffee research in India.
2. The tea production was more labour-intensive than coffee, and unlike coffee it required a year-round labour force.

3. Coffee Guide (2014): *A Manual of Coffee Cultivation*, published by Coffee Research Station, Chikmagalur District, Karnataka, pp. 195-200.
4. Ibid., pp. 208-211.
5. Kate, Macdonald (2007): 'Globalizing Justice within Coffee Supply Chains? Fair Trade, Star Bucks and the Transformation of Supply Chain Governance', *Third World Quarterly*, Vol. 28, No. 4, p. 795.
6. Coffee (2001): 'Hard Times', *Economic and Political Weekly*, 1 September, pp. 3332-33.
7. C. Upendranath (2010): Coffee Conundrum: Wither the future of Small Growers in India?, Discussion Paper No. 3, Centre for Development Studies, Thiruvananthapuram, pp. 27-28.
8. Utsa, Patnaik (1996): 'Export-Oriented Agriculture and Food Security in Developing Countries', *Economic and Political Weekly*, Vol XXXI, No. 35, 36, Special Number, September, pp. 2429-49.
9. Stefano Ponte (2001): 'Behind the Coffee Crisis', *Economic and Political Weekly*, November 24, pp. 4410-4417.
10. Gerard, Greenfield (2001): 'Vietnam and the World Coffee

Crisis: Local coffee Riots in a Global Context', December, www.oxfam.org.uk.

11. C.V. Joy (2004): 'Small Coffee Growers of Sulthan Bathery, Wayanad', Centre for Development Studies, Kerala, p. 34.
12. Pulneys, Shevroys and Annamalais in Tamil Nadu and Nelliampathis in Kerala are the other sources of Arabica coffee. M.S. Narayana (2014): 'Size Distribution of Estates, Inequality and Poverty: Evidence for India's Household Coffee Farmers', *Journal of Asian Policy,* Vol. 7, No. 1, Routledge, pp. 18-40.
13. Madhura, Swaminathan (2002): *Weakening Welfare: The Public Distribution of Food in India,* Left Word, New Delhi, p. 8.
14. The world of specialty coffee has developed with a level of sophistication with fine coffee which is synonymous with refined taste. The three best examples are the Monsooned Malabar, Mysore Nuggets, Extra Bold and Robusta Kaapi Royale.
15. Parvathi, Menon (2002): 'The cup of Woes', Vol. 19. *Frontline,* Issue 06, 16th March, pp. 49-51.
16. Raji (2004): 'Bitter Coffee, Crisis of the Indian and Global Coffee Industry', *Vimukthi Prakashana,* Bangalore.
17. Interview with B.S. Jayaram President of Karnataka Growers Federation on June 17, 2015.
18. Karnataka Growers Association (2006): Letter written to Shri Kamal Nath regarding relief package for coffee growers, dated 27th May, Saklespur, Karnataka.
19. Vidharbha region in Maharashtra (the north eastern region of the state) is predominantly a cotton belt and most of the farmers committing suicides in the area are cotton growers. The major farmers committing suicide are small and middle-scale farmers, with less than 4 hectares of land. The major political leaders like Sharad Pawar, have consistently supported the cause of sugarcane, but the cotton farmers haven't received any support from the government. See Ritambhara Hebbar (2010): 'Framing the Development Debate: The Case of Farmers' Suicides in India' In *Democracy Development and Decentralization in India: Continuing Debates* (ed), Chandan Sengupta and Stuart Cordbridge, New Delhi, Routledge, pp. 84-111.
20. Karnataka Growers Federation (2013): Annual Report from the President's Desk.
21. Memorandum of Crisis in Coffee and Relief Sought, submitted to Honorable Minister, Mr. Vidya Sagar Rao, the then Minister of State for Commerce and Industry, on behalf of Coffee growers of Karnataka, Kerala and Tamil Nadu, July 2, 2003.

22. "Coffee Industry on Verge of Collapse", *Deccan Herald,* November 11, 2002.
23. Interview with Mr. Prasanna, Gram Panchayat Member, Shirivase Village, Chikmagalur Taluk on June 21, 2015.
24. Plantation Workers May Strike on December 11, *Financial Express.*
25. Interview with George Austin, Communist Party of India, Taluk Secretary of Coffee Labour Union on June 20, 2015.
26. Task Force for Recovery of Public Land and its Protection (2011): Greed and Convenience, Government of Karnataka, Bangalore, pp. 69-70.
27. M.A.S. Rajan (1979): *The Land Reforms Law in Karnataka,* Bangalore Government Press, pp. 45-46.
28. Parvathi Menon (2003): 'Death and Distress', *Frontline,* Vol. 20, Issue 24, November-December.
29. R. Vasavi (1999): 'Agrarian Distress in Bidar', http:/ / www.iisc.ernet.in / nias / bidar.htm.
30. The social investigation teams of CPI (ML) (People's War) undertook a rural survey in some of the coffee growing villages of Chikmagalur district in late 2001.
31. Krishna, Prasad (2004): 'Farmers Form Platform for Resistance', *People's Democracy,* Weekly Organ of the Communist Party of India (Marxist) Vol. XXVI, No. 36, September.

3

Centralization of Forests Through the Forest Conservation Act (1980) and Supreme Court Intervention

Introduction

The environment struggles have opened up the contradiction between the interests of the forest dwellers and conservation of forest wealth and maintenance of ecological balance propounded by the British.[1] Ramachandra Guha's classic work *Unquiet Woods* has suggested that the idea of scientific forestry practised and implemented as a conservation strategy was implicated in several colonial agendas for rule and domination. The forest has been defined in the Government Forest Act 1865 (Act of VII of 1865) as "land covered with trees, brushwood or jungle, and declared to be Government Forest under the Act". The act was applicable to the forests in control of the government and did not cover private forests. It made no provision regarding the rights of the users. The Act of 1865 was replaced with the more comprehensive Indian Forest Act of 1878 which divided forests into four categories:

(a) Those forests, the preservation of which is essential on climatic or physical grounds.
(b) Forests which afford a supply of valuable timber for commercial purposes.
(c) Minor forests; and
(d) Pasture lands. The last two categories of forests were relatively less productive of timber and were meant for meeting local needs of biomass.[2] The Forest Act of

> 1878 empowered the local government to levy duty on timber produced in British India or brought from any place beyond the frontier of British India, thus encouraging revenue from forests. The successive forest laws in 1865, 1878 and 1892 established government ownership of nearly the entire forest cover of India for the sake of timber extraction.

The Indian Forest Act of 1927 which set aside forests for different purposes and gave them an administrative designation indicating their purpose, but did not define forests. The act enabled the formation of a Village Forest Panchayat of the villagers to manage forest use and solve the problem of open access and free riding. The Government of India Act, 1935 created a dual system of government by setting up provincial legislation and assigning with the issue of forests. After independence, the Constitution of India retained the provisions of the Government of India Act 1935 and retained forests as a state subject in the seventh schedule.

After Independence, the role of the forest department changed to that of a custodian of forests for people. The Forest Department continued the organizational structure or legal framework arrangements of the colonial structure which led to the exclusion of people from the forest management. The National Forest Policy of 1952 reinforced the exclusive rights of the state to manage forests to meet 'national needs'. These areas meant to ensure the supply of forest produce to industry, defence and communications and the realization of maximum revenue as consistent with the needs.[3] The wood-based industries such as pulp, paper and plywood were well established, and their demand for raw material became an important consideration in the management of the forests. In the early stages of development, wood-based industries depended on species naturally in the forests led to the collaboration of influential groups such as industrialists, timber, traders, agriculturists and government. The clearance of forests to the wood-based industries at very low prices, released land for the expansion of agriculture. The National Commission on Agriculture (1976) advocated the commercialization of agriculture at all costs and disregarded the benefits derived from the forests. The Ministry of Forests was originally a part of the Ministry of Agriculture where the commercial bias was evident in this statement that, "free supply of forest produce to the rural population and their rights and privileges have brought destruction to the forests and so it is necessary to reverse the process. The rural people have not contributed much towards the maintenance or regeneration of the forests. Having over-exploited the resources they cannot in all fairness expect that somebody else will take the trouble of providing them with forest produce free of charge."[4] However this process could not continue for long as the availability of naturally growing raw material declined, requirements of wood-based industries could be met either by tapping new areas or by growing the required species in plantations. The report published by the National Commission on Agriculture in 1976 stressed the gap between the demand and supply of wood, and the frequent confrontations between local forest users and the state over scarce resources. For example, the commission had recommended 75 million hectares in the country; 48 million hectares were to be identified as production forests directed towards meeting the requirements of wood-based industries. In the 1980s an important shift in the forest policy from pure commercial species to mixed species can be seen in the social forestry which were to be developed for the welfare of peasants. Social forestry did not lead to any transfer of rights over forests, but became part of the beneficiary-oriented programmes such as the Hill Area Development Programme (HADP), the Drought Prone Area Programme (DPAP), and the Desert Development Programme (IDRP) supported by International Aid agencies. The state government of Karnataka took up Social Forestry Projects in 1983-84 with the financial assistance from the World Bank and Overseas Development Administration, to help the rural community for meeting the day-to-day needs of firewood, fodder and small timber for the people.[5] The World Bank identified three elements for a new strategy where the private sector should be actively involved in forestry. The state should restrict its intervention to social forestry and conservation, and NGOs and voluntary agencies should be promoted for people's participation.

The National Commission of Agriculture advocates more centralization and enactment of a revised All India Forest Act. The Forest Bill shifted 'forests' from the 'State List' to the 'Concurrent List' and prohibited non-forest use of forest land without central government approval. This powerful legislation has, to a large extent, curtailed the indiscriminate logging and release of forestland for non-forestry purposes by state governments.[6] The Bill has encroached upon the power of the states for while previously forestry was in the State List and the states could decide their own policies, now the Centre will, through the Bill, be directing the Forest Policy for all states. In the process, the state will be reduced to mere administrative and executive machinery.[7]

The Forest Conservation Act, 1980

The Forest Conservation Act of 1980 was enacted in order to check rapid deforestation due to forestlands being released by state governments for agriculture, industry and other development projects (allowed under the Indian Forest Act) the federal government enacted the Forest Conservation Act in 1980 with an amendment in 1988. The Act made the prior approval of the central government for de-reservation of reserved forests, logging and for use of forestland for non-forest purposes. The Forest Conservation Act 1980 was an attempt by the centre to introduce some long-term thinking into otherwise short-sighted conversion of forests to other uses. This powerful legislation has, to a large extent, curtailed the indiscriminate logging and release of forestland for non-forestry purposes by state governments. The conflict between the centre and states in their alternate conception of use of forests led the central government to pass an ordinance, 1980 which later became an act the same year. The act requires the states to seek prior permission for diversion of land, which is more than 10 hectares for development projects. The inability and incompetence of state governments to obey the Supreme Court have little motivation to change local policies to function under the guidelines that do not reflect their local political situation. The close link of forests, wildlife and environment are interconnected, but the regulatory system treats them as largely independent from each other.[8] The environmental policies and laws followed by the state to protect land, air, water and forests of the country are violated by the commercial and industrial companies which are patronized by the political and bureaucratic system. The Ministry of Environment and Forests (MoEF) is primarily concerned with the planning, promotion and coordination of the implementation of India's environmental and forestry policies and programmes. Its primary concern is related to the conservation of the country's natural resources including lakes, rivers, biodiversity, forests and wildlife, ensuring the welfare of its animals and prevention of pollution. These objectives are well supported by a set of legislative and regulatory measures, aimed at the preservation, conservation and protection of the environment. The Ministry of Environment and Forests has been viewed as a soft regulatory hurdle which needed to be crossed before any diversion of forest land. The final decisions of the MoEF were subject to final approval of the Supreme Court which led to a relatively better appraisal of projects. The genesis of the Godavarman case was the reluctance of the central as well as the state governments to take tough environmental decisions relating to environment in general and forests in particular. Thus, the engagement of the Supreme Court began on a continuing basis with the issue of forest conservation.[9]

Supreme Court Intervention

The Public Interest Litigation based judicial activism has transformed from a passive arbiter of ordinary disputes and giving relief to the disadvantaged groups.[10] Under the leadership of Justice V.R. Krishna Iyer and P.N. Bhagwati the Supreme Court gained in stature and legitimacy covering a wide spectrum such as road safety, pollution and illegal structures. In 1981 a PIL was filed to protect the rights of pavement dwellers in Bombay and the Court gave a historic judgment that held that the Right to Life included the Right to Livelihood, and hence, the pavement dwellers were arbitrarily evicted, as their livelihood was dependent on where they lived. However, in 1985, one of the first environmental cases was filed as a PIL to stop limestone quarrying in Dehradun. This drastically changed the nature of jurisprudence, because the Court held that the Right to Clean Environment took priority over the Right to Livelihood. Thus, the interests of the mineworkers were sacrificed in order to protect the Mussoorie hills from degradation. Such a judgment completed the transition in PIL from the rights of weaker sections of society to the right to enjoy clean environment. The decision emphasized that people should be able to live in a healthy environment, but said nothing about the right to work in such an environment. Thus, it created an artificial divide between employment and environment. The court emerged as redresser of grievances and in the eyes of the public as an agent of social change. In India courts have been used to direct the government to enforce laws. The environmentalists in Europe took the route of electoral politics to bring about changes in the social and economic order that would be conducive to healthy living from the polluting industries.

The Supreme Court's intervention on forest conservation over the last two decades is unparalleled in terms of its scope and extent. The Supreme Court's role in environmental governance raises the question as to why there is a need for such intervention because the failure of the legislature and executive have not been effective in curbing pollution and environmental degradation.

The Court's role with respect to forests has undergone a change with enlarging the scope of existing conservation laws particularly the Forest Conservation Act 1980 leading to negative social, ecological and administrative effects.[11] With reference to case No. 202 of 1995 a civil writ petition titled T.N.Godavarman vs Union of India was filed in the Supreme Court, also known as the 'Forest case' which entertained a petition related to the large scale illegal felling of timber and denuding of the forests in Gudalur Taluk of Nilgiri in Tamil Nadu.[12] The large-scale illegal felling of timber and denuding of the forests continued even after the notice had been issued by the state governments of Tamil Nadu. The main focus of the petition was illegal felling and with the similar Case No. 171 of 1996 which dealt with the deforestation in Jammu and Kashmir. The meaning of 'forest' is to be as per dictionary definition irrespective of ownership and court orders are to apply all lands entered in any government record as 'forest'.[13] This was selectively used by the state and the central government stopped the states from doing this by making guidelines to this effect. The Forest Conservation Act made the permission of the centre mandatory for two more activities like clear felling of forests and creating any right on forest land through safe, transfer, lease, mortgage or any other mechanism for any person including any institution or company. The forest land includes all lands recorded as forests in government documents and thus revenue forests, panchayat forests and even private forests included in its holds. This powerful legislation has, to a large extent, curtailed the indiscriminate logging and release of forestland for non-forestry purposes by state governments. Initially the definition of 'forest land' was assumed to be only that land which has been legally notified as forest as per the Indian Forest Act or Reserved or Protected Forest.[14] Over time its mandate has been extended even to lands with preliminary notifications where rights are yet to be settled, in addition to "any area recorded as forest in the government records".

The cases are being heard under the 'continuing manadamus' whereby the courts rather than passing final judgments, keep passing orders and directions with a view to monitor the functioning of the executive. On the other side of the legislation the Supreme Court orders have curtailed the indiscriminate logging and release of forest land for non-forestry purposes by state governments. While the federal government imposed such restrictions, it did not simultaneously evolve a mechanism to compensate state governments for loss of timber logging revenues.[15]

The order of the Supreme Court was at the behest of a senior advocate (the Amicus) that local state issue of forests assumed national importance on forest conservation. The enlargement of the decision with regard to other states context where the Supreme Court tagged together and also directed the authorities as well as the High Courts that the "authorities are not required to act on the directions given by the High Court... matters in respect of the same subject matter and that the High Court or any other court would not entertain any matter the subject matter of which is covered by the scope of these matters". The Supreme Court became the sole arbitrator regarding forest-related matters and all such issues in the country were solely heard by it.

The Court also went on to issue notices to the Chief Secretaries of all state governments and made them parties in view of the nature of the petitions and points involved therein. The Court issued fresh notices on September 23, 1996 to all state governments as they had not complied with the last order. The Supreme Court orders were and probably would remain the single most important order that completely changed the forestry debate in India. The Court orders led to a complete banning on felling of trees in all 'forest' areas. There was a misconception about the true scope of the Forest Conservation Act 1980.[16]

"The Forest Conservation Act, 1980 was enacted with a view to check further deforestation which ultimately resulted in ecological imbalances and therefore the provisions for the conservation of forests and for connected matters under the FCA, must apply to all forests irrespective of the nature of ownership or classification".

The confusion regarding the definition of 'forest land' was assumed to be only that land which has been legally notified as forest as per the Indian Forest Act or Reserved or Protected Forest. Over time its mandate has been extended even to lands with preliminary notifications where rights are yet to be settled, in addition to "any area recorded as forest in the government records". The Forest Conservation Act is the primary legislation for conservation of forests. The meaning of 'forest' used in the Forest Conservation Act must be understood according not only for its dictionary sense, but also any area recorded as forest in government records, irrespective of the ownership or classification thereof which is significant because the issue of conservation was brought into the definition of forest. Section 2 of the Forest Conservation Act clearly stated that certain activity in the forest area which is commercial in nature is prohibited without the prior approval of the central government all over the country. The directions of the central government meant that felling of trees was to remain suspended except in accordance with the working plans of the state government, as approved by the central government.

The forest conservation law in India is now impacted not only by the outcome of the Godavarman case but also the ongoing litigation concerning national parks and sanctuaries through the Centre for Environment Law, WWF vs. the Union of India. It was passed in 2000 prohibiting the de-reservation of any forest, national park and sanctuary without the approval of the Supreme Court.[18] The Court has also passed orders prohibiting a range of activities in national parks and sanctuaries without its approval. The reconstitution of the Forest Advisory Committee and National Board for Wildlife has led to a relatively greater scrutiny of proposals with a marginal increase in the rate of rejection of projects especially in ecologically sensitive areas in the era of neoliberal reforms.

There is a tremendous pressure on forests in the neoliberal reforms period according to the estimates by the Ministry of Environment and Forests where about 9.55 lakh hectares have been diverted between 1980 and 2004. Between 1980 and 2003, 8.73 lakh hectares of forest land were diverted for various development activities in different states, about 3.73 lakh hectares, that (is 42.70 per cent is from Madhya Pradesh, Maharashtra (9.16 per cent), Uttar Pradesh (8.70 per cent), Gujarat (6.4 per cent), Arunachal Pradesh (5.07 per cent), Kerala (4.67 per cent) and Karnataka (4.18 per cent). The important preconditions for approving proposals relates to compensatory afforestation—offsetting forestland diversion by growing trees on non-forestland spread over an equivalent area, or an degraded forestland that is twice the size of the tract in question. The Forest Conservation Act was enacted to control deforestation and forest diversion for non-forestry projects such as dams or mining.[19]

The diversion of forest land has been described as a Forest Clearance Act because of clearance done at faster rate for economic growth. The importance of forest lands in people's lives is the fact that 800 interlocutory applications (IAs) have been filed in the case, ranging from the North East to the Andamans to Madhya Pradesh. The increasing number of cases made it difficult to examine each and every issue in detail and pass appropriate judgments has led to the creation of Central Empowered Committee (CEC). The Supreme Court constituted the Central Empowered as an advisory for the Honourable Court orders by its order dated May 9, 2002 and its reliance was placed on Section 3(3) of the Environment (Protection) Act, 1986 to set up High Powered Committees, Empowered Committees, Forest Protection Authority and later on the Central Empowered Committee.

Section 3(3) of the Environment (Protection) Act, 1986 reads as follows:

"The central government may, if it considers it necessary or expedient so to do for the purposes of this Act, by order, published in the official gazette, constitute an authority or authorities by such name or names as may be specified in the order for the purpose of exercising and performing such of the powers and functions (including issue directions under Section (5) of the central government under this Act and for taking measures with respect to such of the matters referred to in subsection (2) as may be mentioned in the order and subject to the supervision and control of the central government and the provisions of such order, such authority or authorities may exercise the powers or perform the functions or take the measures so mentioned in the order as if such authority or authorities had been empowered by this Act to exercise those powers or perform those functions or take such measures". The increasing number of pending cases before the Supreme Court made it difficult for the court to examine each issue in detail and pass appropriate orders. The Forest Conservation Act did not provide any opportunity for setting up Tribunals or Authorities to adjudicate on such issues. The CEC set up by the Ministry of Environment and forests on direction of the Supreme Court provided an avenue for grievance redressal for saw mill owners, encroachers, contractors, and other affected people started approaching the court, to render justice, faster if not effectively.[20]

Central Empowered Committee

The main functions of the CEC are to place the non-compliance cases before it, like encroachment removals, implementations of working plans, compensatory afforestation, plantations and other conservation issues. The CEC consists of five members and their main task is to monitor and ensure the compliance of the Supreme Court's orders. The CEC may decide its own procedures for dealing with the pending affidavits filed by the states in response to the orders made by the committee and their recommendations placed before the Honourable Supreme Court for order. The process prescribed under this notification could bring together local communities, project-affected people, government agencies, project proponents, planners, consultants, and NGOs in decision-making processes. The convergence of these actors for environmentally sustainable and locally appropriated decision-making has occurred partially in a few cases. The CEC assumed the role of the executive in administering its own interpretation of the law in addition to its specific orders. The Supreme Court passed on responsibility for grievances and for all the problems that arose from its orders to the CEC, and once again failed to respect the responsibilities of the Ministry of Environment and Forests.

The Supreme Court directed the chief secretaries of Odisha, West Bengal (in the Sunderbans), Karnataka (Western Ghats), Tamil Nadu (the Nilgiris), Maharahstra, Madhya Pradesh and Chhattisgarh (Aravalli and Satpura region) and Assam to file a reply to this IA in relation to the steps required to prevent encroachment of forest land and to indicate the steps taken to clear earlier encroachments.[21] The ban on felling of trees in the forests was the only measure possible as the timber lobby nexus especially in North East, was losing 31,700 hectares of forest every year, according to the Ministry of Environment Affairs. But it caused hardship to saw mill owners, those employed in timber-based activities and small private forest owners. The issue of encroachment initially rose in 1999 when three

NGOs approached the Calcutta High Court at Port Blair in the Andaman and Nicobar Islands who demanded the following:

(i) Removal of all encroachments from the tribal reserve.
(ii) A ban on all mining or any other non-forest activities in the Little Andamans.
(iii) Restrictions on construction of any road within the tribal reserve within a radius of half a kilometre.
(iv) Complete ban on felling trees in the Little Andamans.

Based on the recommendations of the CEC report, "one of the major reasons for decimation of the forests is the growing extent of encroachments".[22] The Supreme Court observed that regularization takes place subject to imposition of conditions such as compensatory afforestation, the regularization becomes effective without conditions ever being fulfilled. In view of this fact, the Court was of the opinion that the central government should consider, that the conditions imposed in relation to regularizations are fulfilled first before any regularization is granted. The Revenue Department in order to spread cultivation has been a facilitator as revenue is linked to taxation and the extent of land under cultivation.

Encroachment of Forest Land

The provisions of FCA agreed to regulate the pre-1980 encroachments and permit their regularization and stop regularization of post-1980 encroachments. In the case of pre-1980 encroachments, the state government had evolved certain eligibility criteria with the local needs and conditions and had taken decisions on regularization of such encroachments but could not implement them due to the Forest Conservation Act 1980. Following the pressure of the encroachers in 1991, the Karnataka Government petitioned the Government of India to regularize about 17,007.23 hectares (in 21,569 cases) of forest land encroached upon prior to April 1978. The centre had the areas surveyed and in an order dated May 17, 1996, agreed to the regularization of 14,848.83 hectares (involving 19,348 cases).

The following categories of persons shall only be regularized but subject to certain conditions. It was only to be done to an extent of 3 acres or 1.2 hectares in individual cases (including forest encroachment), and in the case of persons belonging to the Scheduled Castes and Scheduled Tribes, landless marginal agricultural labourers and those holding an insufficient extent of land-up to three acres of agricultural land. The person concerned should be a domiciled for at least 10 years in a village adjacent to which the forest land encroached by him lies. In the case of landless marginal agricultural labourers the encroacher or his family should not hold or own any agricultural land anywhere in Karnataka and the total annual family income should not exceed Rs. 8,000. The order of the Government of India had decreed that encroachments should not be regularized in the midst of forests, on steep slopes or in the middle of national parks or sanctuaries. Eligible encroachers from these areas are relocated on the fringes of forests, on areas recovered from encroachers.[23]

The directive of the MoEF meant that 1978 should be the cut-off year for legalizing encroachment. Those who encroached later should be evicted subject to certain conditions. It ignores the other circular of 1990 stating "Review of disputed claims over forest land arising out of forest settlement[24] and disputes regarding *pattas*/leases/grants involving forest land, which has a considerable bearing on deciding what, constitutes an 'encroachment'. In 1990, the 29th report of the Scheduled Castes and Scheduled Tribes Commission under B.D. Sharma had drawn out a clear, unambiguous framework to settle the encroachment issue, keeping in mind both conservation interests and livelihood security for Adivasi and forest dwellers. In a set of six guidelines, it suggested that all encroachments made prior to the Forest Conservation Act be settled and those made after that be carefully examined, distinguishing the claims of the tribal people from those of encroachers.[25] Besides making it mandatory for the states to come up with schemes to provide alternative means of livelihood to those affected, the recommendations also sought to involve village communities in settling disputes and ensuring lasting solutions. The report covered disputes regarding *pattas*, leases and grants involving forest land and suggested that centrally sponsored schemes involve members of the Scheduled Tribes and the rural poor in afforestation projects for degraded forests. However, the report has been consistently ignored by policy makers on the question of encroachment.

The Supreme Court's intervention of even eligible regularization of pre-1980 encroachments and de-reservation of forest land or protected areas (irrespective of whether these have been finally notified after due settlement of rights) has led to discontent among the forest dwellers. Along with this the Supreme Court has also banned the 'removal of dead, diseased, dying or wind fallen trees, drift wood and grasses, from all national parks and wildlife sanctuaries. This was interpreted by the MoEF as direction to evict encroachers, although there is no express order of the Supreme Court to evict. The Ministry of Environment and Forests (MoEF) used the above references in the court proceedings to issue a directive to all states/union territories on May 3, 2002, to summarily evict "all illegal encroachment of forestlands" before September 30, 2002. The coercive means were employed, from setting fire to houses and destroying crops created havoc among the Adivasis in India for the last 200 years.

The faulty settlement process leaves the definition of forests whether it applies only to reserve forests or other dense forests are classified as revenue land has evaded the FCA and fails to distinguish between 'unsettled claims' and 'encroachments'. It was in this context which led to campaigning against evictions, led to a high level meeting on January 19, 2005, the Prime Minister Mr. Manmohan Singh decided that a new Act should be drafted and tabled in the budget session of Parliament. The Government of India introduced the Scheduled Tribes (Recognition of Forest Rights) Act, 2006 to strengthen the tribal empowerment process.[26] The contentious issue with the forest rights has been the assertion led by conservationists claiming that the act will end up destroying all of India's forests which will result in the decline of tigers. On the other side the human rights, social activists has seen the act which will transform the Adivasis' existence and save India Forests, destroyed by the industry. In some North Eastern states, the conflicts between older Adivasi residents or non-resident settlers, In the Western Ghats the communities are largely non-tribal and the economy is relatively prosperous and where substantial forest rights were granted to forest dependent households at the individual rather than community level but in a discriminatory manner (landed versus landless). The Forest Department has identified B.L. Shankar and his relatives had encroached on an area of 27.67 acres in Survey No. 4 of Kenjigegudda Coffee Estate Village (KGCEV) in the Thatkola reserve forest. According to the Survey of India report, 147 instances of encroachment (accounting for 611.23 acres) had taken place in the reserve forest. Of these 147, 100 persons had encroached upon 3 acres or less (accounting for a total of 118.613 acres), 19 persons had encroached on between 3 and 5 acres (totalling 79.96 acres), and 10 had encroached on between 5 and 10 acres (59.5 acres). Interestingly, the majority of the encroachment (adding up to 353.16 acres) was committed by just 18 people, each of whom had encroached on an area in excess of 10 acres. Despite the Supreme Court order to evict encroachers in the Thatkola reserve forest the state government is yet to act on the orders and the process of surrender remains on paper and the encroachers enjoy the fruits of the land even now.[27] There is a constant demand from political parties to permit regularization, because besides plantations, in many of these encroached areas there are schools, colleges, roads, government offices and even houses built under various government schemes for weaker sections of society.[28] The state politicians have used the FCA as a convenient target and have generated an anti-environmentalist rhetoric at state-level politics. The tussle is at multiple levels, like local communities who want to use forests for their livelihood purposes, state apparatus in the form of non-timber forest products or wanting to give it for mining or other short-term activities.[29]

In Kudremukh common property resources such as forests are encroached upon for coffee cultivation. The local government officials often act in connivance with local elites. The pressure from the political parties to regularize under public pressure, has also led to environmental damage. The encroached lands are under non-poor rather than the poor, even if some poor may gain land, the remaining poor would be deprived of access to common lands. The absolute ownership by the state management is also subjected to severe limitations, as it brings the state into direct conflict with the local people dependent on them for a livelihood.[30] The state has to ensure equitable and sustainable use particularly when the people's collective action breaks down and has to play a catalytic role to ensure fair play. The Chikmagalur Superintendent of Police Madhukar Shetty and District Commissioner Harish Gupte tried to resolve the crisis by distributing the excess land from Bobsale estate near Khalsa, which had 500 acres from encroachment and tried to regularize land for rehabilitation of the contract workers of KIOCL Company. The collective pressure of coffee estates led to the transfer of SP and DC transferred to different places in the state. These failures by the social movement falter by portraying a homogeneous community where such divisions affect the marginalized groups that the movement intends to benefit.

The issue of forest encroachment was rampant due to the high value of lands led the Karnataka Government to constitute a Joint Legislature Committee in July 2005 under the Chairmanship of A.T. Ramaswamy to enquire into the matter and suggest solutions for future encroachments. The Forest Department has booked 7,846 Forest Offence Cases (FOCs) under the Karnataka Forest Act involving about 30,000 acres. The Assistant Conservator of Forests has issued orders only in the 1,193 cases and has not issued orders in the remaining 6,653 cases and in no case has the encroachment been removed. The response of the Karnataka Forest Department in halting forest loss has been slow, due to the local political and social considerations. Several political leaders are demanding a dilution of the Forest Conservation Act 1980 by protecting the cause of an underprivileged forest encroacher and literally using him as a "human shield". We are requesting the Centre to permit regularization as besides plantations in many of these encroached areas there are schools, colleges, roads, government offices and even houses built under various government schemes for the weaker sections of the society.

Karnataka Forest Department

The vast majority of the forest covers are under the direct control and management of the state forest department which has no administrative control over large tracts of forest areas including reserved forests. There are significant areas of forests that were not part of the reserved forests or village forests in the Western Ghats districts of Karnataka which has shown a lack of coordination between the forest department along with other departments. Karnataka covers a total land area of 191,791 square kilometres, accounting for 5.83 per cent of the total geographical area of the country, with a forest cover of 22.61 per cent of the total geographical area of the state. The state accounts for a total of 43,356.45 square kilometres of forest cover of which reserve forests and protected forests share 2,955.10 square kilometres and 3,585.22 square kilometres respectively. The remaining forest area, 10,117.92 square kilometres come under unclassified forest, 49.05 square kilometres under village forest while 54.07 kilometres comes under private forests in the state. The Department of Forests, Ecology and Environment is responsible for the conservation and development of forest ecosystems, and ecological resources. Therefore, the Forest Department should play an important role in terms of prompting not only its core conservation activities but also the general welfare of the people depending on the forest resources. The responsibilities of the Forest Department include sustainable management of forests, conservation of wildlife, restoration of degraded forests, afforestation across barren lands, promotion of social forestry, protection of forests from fires and illegal poaching, soil and moisture conservation in the forest area, meeting the demands of timber, industrial woods, firewood, bamboo and other non-timber forest products (NTFPs). For administrative purposes the state has been divided into 13 circles and these 13 circles are further divided into 40 territorial divisions, 30 social forestry divisions, 11 wildlife divisions, and 1 wildlife subdivision, 9 forest mobile squads, 5 research units and 1 training circle.

The Karnataka Forest Department has four categories of forests: Reserve Forests, Village Forests, Protected Forests and Private Forests. The first two categories are 84 per cent of the total 'forest' area while the other categories constitute only 1.2 per cent. The inheritance of different sets of regimes inherited by the state has led to difficult understanding of forest tenure regimes in the Western Ghats of Karnataka. The forest land refers to the legal control of the forest department. However, many lands that are not officially declared forest or natural growth of trees are under the revenue department.[31]

The ambiguity with relation to certain forests called 'C and D lands' held by the Revenue Department were transferred to the Forest Department for afforestation activities under the social forestry programme with regard to Gomals/Gauchars of Shimoga and Chikmagalur and Paisaris in Kodagu[32] are revenue/village lands used and managed by the local communities by the village as common grazing grounds belong to all. However these lands are contested due to the repeated cancellation and leased out to the state owned corporations such as Mysore Paper Mills and Karnataka Cashew Development Corporation. The constitution of these forests were arbitrary and was done by the colonial state on the basis of people's need which was set aside that can be used by local communities to meet their subsistence requirements of fuel wood, leaf manure, small timber and fodder.

The Forest Department plays the role of regulator or monitor concentrating on enforcing essentially the rules against tree felling, wereas the Revenue Department takes care of the legal forests and non-forests. These lands are being encroached by coffee growers and political leaders who have made land grants or regularized to various categories of households in the post-FCA.[33] These forest tenures are discriminatory because they are assigned to traditional arecanut landholders in Uttara Kannada, whereas paddy and arecanut are concentrated in Shimoga and Chikmagalur. The district forests are lands such as Betta lands, Bane lands, Jamma Malai, Forest Peramboke,

Paisari, kans, Kumki, Amruth Mahal Kaval, Assessed Waste, Kharab, Inam and Wet Lands, lakes, kumki lands or the lands classified as forests in revenue records.[34] These are the privileged lands assigned for various purposes at the time of survey settlement or assigned for certain privileged with certain conditions. These districts forests are notified by the Revenue Department and basically managed by the Revenue Department. The records are with the Deputy Commissioner and the management prescription is supposed to be prepared by the Deputy Commissioner of the district in issuing the ownership of these lands.

Details of Total Areas Recorded as 'Forests' Identified by Expert Committee

S.No.	*Particulars*	*Area in Ha*
1.	Reserved Forests	28,18,905.63
2.	Protected Forests	4,11,533.54
3.	Village Forests	9,504.17
4.	Private Forests	31,228.90
5.	C and D Class of Land	2,03,982.61
6.	Wooded Areas	7,03,309.67
7.	Uruduve	2,634.76
8.	Bane Lands	1,07,481.65
9.	Coffee Saguvali Malai	3,218.38
10.	Devara Kadu	7,747.76
11.	Paisaris	55,111.77
12.	Kumki	6,853.42
13.	Amruth Mahal Kaval	22,328.92
14.	Mangroves	927.00
15.	River Catchments and Erosion Prone Areas	3,031.06
16.	Assessed Waste Land	1,97,154.36
17.	Inam Land	4,552.40
	Total	45,89,506.00

The directions of the Honourable Supreme Court of India in their interim order dated February 12, 1996 in the Writ Petition Civil No. 202/1996 had ordered the state government to constitute an expert committee:

(i) Identify areas which are forests irrespective of whether they are notified, recognized or classified under any law irrespective of their ownership of the land of such forests.
(ii) Identify areas which were earlier forests but stand degraded, denuded or cleared and
(iii) Identify areas covered by plantation trees belonging to the government and those belonging to private persons.

The Karnataka Forest Department has said that identification of forests is a continuous process which had in the earlier report excluded bane lands, coffee Suguvali Malai, Paisari and Kumki while submitting to the apex court. The Committee Members deliberated on these issues and suggested that the Coffee Saguvali Malai was a private land, but other lands like Bane, Paisari and Kumki lands should be considered as district forests, which have the features of the forest. The MoEF in 2007 decided to define forests in the Indian context to develop ecologically sound and socially desirable definitions of forests. The definition of forests has attracted a lot of criticism in defining what constituted a "Forest" is being undertaken in an transparent, undemocratic and unscientific manner. The definition comprehensively attacks the possibilities of extending any form of protection to grasslands, for instance which are amongst the most productive ecosystems. If grasslands have survived, it is mainly because communities have protected them (as in the case with Amrit Mahal Kavals in Karnataka, which have been degraded by government neglect or actively destroyed by government diversion resulting in ecological and humanitarian chaos. Similarly, this kind of articulation results in dubious interpretations and may be used by state governments to promote diversion of ecologically sensitive areas to 'developmental' purposes without proper evaluation. The discrepancy in the dictionary meaning of the forests by the Godavarman case has been argued for moving away from the legal forest to a physical forest. The Forest Department has been strangely shy of protecting forest lands apart from making periodical references to the Godavarman Tirumalpad verdict by the Supreme Court. Under the FCA, the state government has to secure the permission of the union government for diverting forestland to non-forest areas. The definition problem of forest with binary divisions of forest/ non-forest has led to deconstruction of a forest that performs varied functions like the benefits of shade cultivation with coffee plantation. This should lead to a more nuanced and locally specific in place of the uniform approach of forest rights which takes into account the ecological, cultural, legal and administrative diversity across the country.

Conclusion

The chief ministers of different states have been very critical of the Forest Conservation Act 1980. The inability and incompetence of state governments to obey the Supreme Court recommendation reveals a gross failure of cooperation. The Forest Conservation Act has changed the ownership and management of forests only on the approval of the central government. The Supreme Court's creation of national and local forest management policies has interfered with the work of MoEF, which are responsible for managing India's forests and wildlife which are closely tied to the Supreme Court decisions. The other concerns are the insufficient funding which has made it difficult for the MoEF to manage India's forests effectively, especially given the country's size and the attempt to protect forests in name only at the expense of India's rural populations. This shifted the political articulation from the states to the centre as whether a patch of forest should be preserved or used for development activities came to be guided by national interest as opposed to regional interests. The Supreme Court has used the national interest argument to justify the centralization of powers in its own hands. The initial orders may have been justified; however, the implications of this sweeping and continuing intervention by the judiciary are far more doubled-edged than the celebratory accounts of the Godavarman case would suggest. The Supreme Court should move beyond judicial adventurism and focus on improving the quality of forest-related jurisprudence. The initial Godavarman cases were justified, but the situation with respect to forests was different, with the entry of the private sector, has changed the nature of decisions emanating from the Court. Finally the Supreme Court should motive state responsibilities for managing forests among the various parts of the government by enforcing the Article 48A of the Directive Principles of State Policy of the Indian Constitution. The state should be encouraged to prepare a comprehensive legislation because the land administration is under the purview of the state government. The repeated u-turns and confusions in the policy framing and execution are at the behest of vested interests in industry and the rural dominant caste with political, economic and social status of the rural elite will make it difficult to formulate a policy framework and to apply it. The environmental policies and laws followed by the state to protect land, air, water and forests of the country are violated by the commercial and industrial companies which are patronized by the political and bureaucratic system. The enforcement agencies failed to enforce laws has led to social movements and difference of opinions between formal government institutions and various other organizations such as interest and pressure groups, industries and environment headed by the members of civil society and local communities.

The Supreme Court intervention in forest issues has changed the situation where the decisions of the Ministry of Environment and Forests were subject to final approval from the Supreme Court and led to a relatively more detailed appraisal of projects. The court decisions are also guided by the orders in the Centre for Environment Law, WWF vs Union of India passed in 2000 prohibiting the de-reservation of any forest, national park and sanctuary without approval of the Supreme Court.[35] The Court has also passed orders prohibiting a range of activities in national parks and sanctuaries without its approval. The reconstitution of the Forest Advisory Committee and National Board for Wildlife has led to a relatively greater scrutiny of proposals with a marginal increase in the rate of rejection of projects especially in ecologically sensitive areas. The genesis of the Godavarman case was the reluctance of the central as well as the state governments to take tough decisions relating to the environment in general and forests in particular. The reconstitution of the Forest Advisory Committee and National Board for Wildlife has led to a relatively greater scrutiny of proposals with a marginal increase in the rate of rejection of projects, especially in ecologically sensitive areas.

The pressure of development in the depletion and diversion of forest land for non-forest use initially was for agriculture which found impetus towards enhancing food production and modernization. The diversion of land/forest land for these development projects towards hydel projects, mining has increased in the recent years that have been approved through various policy initiatives like forest policy, industrial policy, mining policy and Special Economic Zones to serve the neo-liberal agenda of the state. The diversions for mining industries are justified with the logic of national need and sustainable development in the economically backward and well forested areas has been given sanction for these industries for regional development and creation of employment besides adding revenue to the exchequer. The impact of mining often led to resource degeneration as well as socio-economic problems like unemployment and influx of skilled labour outside. The other issues with mining are handling of immense quantities of waste, environment impact assessment, designing environment management plans, effective mine closure and restoration of ecological balance. Unfortunately, development projects continue to adversely impact the environment and all mining including underground mining requires prior approval of the Forest Conservation Act has been seen as a major hindrance in the continuance of projects.

References

1. Madhav Gadigil and Ramachandra Guha (1983): Forestry in British and Post-British India: A Historical Analysis, *Economic and Political Weekly*, 18 (43), October 22, pp. 1882-1896. Also See Ramachandra Guha (1988): *Unquiet Woods*, Oxford University

Press, New Delhi.

2. The difference between pre-colonial and colonial policies were although 'there was no functional harmony in pre-colonial times, there were surplus land and did not attempt to outlaw or suppress any specific form of land use by hunters, shifting cultivators and peasants all coexisted. See Mahesh Rangarajan (1996): *Fencing the Forest: Conservation and Ecological Change in India's Central Provinces, 1860-1914,* Oxford University Press, New Delhi, p. 16.
3. Pari Baumann (1998): 'The Persistence of Populism in Forest Policy', *Journal of Peasant Studies,* Vol. 25, No. 4, July, pp. 98-101.
4. Richard P. Tucker (2012): *A Forest History of India,* Sage Publications, New Delhi, pp. 212-13.
5. S. Parameshwarappa (1999): 'Developmental Forestry in Karnataka and Conservation of Biodiversity', *Karnataka Forest Department,* Bangalore.
6. Akhileshwar Pathak (1994): 'State, Environment and Law', *Economic and Political Weekly,* December 10, pp. 3138-41.
7. Walter Fernandes and Sharad Kulkarni (1983): *Towards a New Forest Policy: People's Rights and Environmental Needs,* Indian Social Institute, New Delhi, p. 146.
8. Geetanjoy Sahu (2014): *Environmental Jurisprudence and the Supreme Court: Litigation, Interpretation, Implementation,* Orient Blackswan, New Delhi, pp. 12-33.
9. Ritwick Dutta (2003): 'Courts and Environmental Justice: Critical Issues', *Social Change,* Vol. 33, No. 2&3, June-September, pp. 24-35.
10. Shoba Agarwal and Dunu Roy (2000): Our Land, Our Minerals, Our Rights, *Report of the First Convention, Mines, Minerals and People* (Mm&P), April 28 to May 1, Hyderabad, India
11. The debate of accountability between the legislature and the executive as they are accountable to the people by way of elections, but the role of judiciary as a distinct role criticized for encroaching upon the domains of other organs. Justice Krishna Iyer said long back in 1982, "Independence of the Judiciary is a myth. It overlooks numerous tie-ups with the executive and business houses". See A.K. Roy (1997): 'Can Courts Run the Country?', *Economic and Political Weekly,* October 11, pp. 2579-81.
12. Armin Rosencranz, Edward Boenig and Brinda Dutta (2007): 'The Godavarman Case: The Indian Supreme Court's Breach

of Constitutional Boundaries in Managing India's Forests', *ELR News and Analysis*, 37, Washington, pp. 10032-42.

13. The Forest Bill, 1980 tries to formulate certain definitions very widely. Thus forest includes any land containing trees and shrubs, pasture lands and any land whatsoever which the state government may, by notification, declare to be forest for the purpose of this Act.
14. Sharachchandra, Lele (2007): 'A Defining Moment for Forests?' *Economic and Political Weekly*, Vol. 42, No. 25, June 23, pp. 2379-2383.
15. Ritwick Dutta and Bhupender Yadav (2011): *Supreme Court on Forest Conservation*, Universal Law Publishing Company, New Delhi, p. 47.
16. Ibid., pp. 47-52.
17. Sharachchandra Lele (2007): 'A Defining Moment for Forests?' *Economic and Political Weekly*, Vol. 42, No. 25, June 23, pp. 2379-2383.
18. Sarin, Madhu (2014): 'Undoing Historical Injustice: Reclaiming Citizenship Rights and Democratic Forest Governance Through the Forest Rights Act' in *Democratizing Forest Governance in India* (Ed) by Shaarachchandra Lele and Ajit Menon, Oxford University Press, pp. 100-146.
19. Assem Shrivastava and Ashish Kothari (2002): *Churning the Earth: The Making of Global India*, Penguin Viking, p. 124.
20. 'The Forest Encroachment Issue', Note Prepared by Kalpavriksh, Pune.
21. Archana Prasad (2004): *Environmentalism and the Left*, Leftword Books, Delhi, pp. 34-40.
22. Sharachchandra Lele (2011): Rethinking Forest Governance: Towards a Perspective Beyond JFM, the Godavarman and FRA, *The Hindu Survey of the Environment*, pp. 95-103.
23. Ravi Sharma (2003): 'Eating up Forest Land', *Frontline*, Vol. 20, No. 6, pp. 51-2.
24. Forest settlement refers to the settlement of rights process followed by the government when it acquired forest land and notified them under various categories. The process involves conducting an inquiry into the rights (habitations, agriculture, use of forest resources, etc) exercised by people or over the forest being notified and documenting them. For certain categories of forests the process also involved extinguishing these rights

after giving compensation. See Syed Ajmal Pasha (1994): 'Uncultivated Lands: Institutional Aspects of Their Use and Management in Karnataka', Institute for Social and Economic Change (ISEC), Bangalore.

25. Archana Prasad (2003): 'Forest Encroachments: Guidelines and Implications of Recent Orders', *People's Democracy* (Weekly Organ of the Communist Party of India (Marxist), Vol. XXVII, No. 1, January 05.
26. Madhu Sarin (2002): Who is Encroaching on Whose Land? *Seminar*, No. 519, November, pp. 1-10.
27. Ritwick Dutta and Bhupender Yadav (2011): *Supreme Court on Forest Conservation*, Universal Law Publishing Company, New Delhi, pp. 205-208.
26. Karnataka Growers Association (2006): Letter Written to Shri Kamal Nath Regarding Relief Package for Coffee Growers, May 27, Saklespur, Karnataka.
27. Muzaffar, Assadi (2004): 'Forest Encroachments, Left Adventurism and Hindutva', *Economic and Political Weekly*, February 26, Vol. 39. No. 09, pp. 882-885.
28. M.V. Nadkarni and Syed Ajmal Pasha (1989): *Political Economy of Forest Use and Management*, New Delhi, Sage Publications Private Limited, pp. 79-91.
29. Srinidhi, A.S. and S. Lele (2001): *Forest Tenure Regimes in the Karnataka Western Ghats: A Compendium*, Institute for Social and Economic Change, Bangalore.
30. Betta lands or *Soppina betta* are an individual owning an acre of areca plantation was given privilege over to mulching material in their arecanut gardens. *Kans* are protected forests which are given for the privilege for coffee, pepper, gum and honey and also green manure as per the Section 134(3) and 138(3) of the Karnataka Forest Manual. *Paisari* lands are revenue wastelands under the control of the revenue department, allotted to the landless for housing and crop cultivation under '*Darkhast*' (literally meaning 'request') grant of land to the landless on request. *Kharab* land is a wasteland; non-arable land that is in possession of the government. *Bhane* land is part of the protected forest land granted for service of holding of wet land which is allotted to be held free of revenue by cultivators for grazing and to supply leaf manure and fire wild and small timber required for agricultural and domestic purposes of the cultivator. *Kumki/ Hadi* (Hadya) lands are also government forestlands under

the private control and use of the local farmers. *Amrut Mahal kavals* are government lands used and controlled by the Animal Husbandry Department (AHD). *Devara Kadu*/Sacred Forests are forests set apart for some object of worship and are still managed and used by the local committees, through temple committees. The revenue department in order to spread cultivation has been a facilitator because as revenue is linked to taxation and the extent of land under cultivation. Syed Ajmal Pasha(1994): 'Uncultivated Lands: Institutional Aspects of Their Use and Management in Karnataka', Institute for Social and Economic Change (ISEC), Bangalore.

31. In other states the community rights in Kumaon or Chottanagpur were the status of orange areas in Madhya Pradesh and Chhattisgarh, has been a contentious issue because it has been 'undemarcated protected forests' in forest records, and also as revenue land in revenue records. These lands are termed as *chote jhaar ke jangal or Bade jhaarr ka jungle* (that is, Organe Area/undemarcated PF which include *nistari* forests set aside by the British to meet villagers' fuel and fodder needs), *Jhudpi jungle* and unclassified forests in Maharashtra and protected forests in Odisha. These also include cases in which land was assigned by the Revenue Department supposedly from revenue lands, but eventually these were found to be notified forest land even though assignees were not dispossessed of their holdings. Sharachchandra Lele (2002): 'A Defining Moment for Forests', *Economic and Political Weekly*, June 23, p. 2381.
32. Karnataka Forest Department (2002): Report Constituted Expert Committee-I, Aryana Bhavan, Bangalore.
33. Sarin, Madhu (2014): 'Undoing Historical Injustice: Reclaiming Citizenship Rights and Democratic Forest Governance Through the Forest Rights Act' in *Democratizing Forest Governance in India* (ed) by Shaarachchandra Lele and Ajit Menon, Oxford University Press, pp. 100-146.

4

Mining, Pollution and Workers' Rights of the Kudremukh Iron Ore Company Limited

Introduction

The development of the large-scale steel industry in India from 1890-1907 was largely due to the changing conflicts of interest involving steel and capital in Britain, India and in the world arena.[1] The emergence of mass production of steel in the world market and the development of railways and communication led to the formation of cartels dividing up world markets. This also influenced the colonial governments towards industrialization which led to the Kolar Gold Fields in 1890 which attracted the proletarian workforce and was responsible for an overall reduction in migration from the state. The Kolar Gold Fields (KGF) has been functioning for the past 120 years.[2]

The Karnataka state domination is often associated with industry but it is arguably more widespread agrarian economy, especially the old Mysore area that had an established network of tanks and canals[3] had drastically transformed the economic and social relations in the countryside.[4] The first major steps at industrialization started in 1911 when the Mysore Economic Conference[5] under the initiative of Sir M. Visvesvaraya (the Dewan of Mysore) who started the notion of 'Industrialize or Perish' was a pioneer in the establishment of the basic consumer goods industries.[6] The commencement of the Sivasamundram Dam, which was constructed in 1902, marked the beginning of a new era in industrialization. The other important feature of his regime was to carry out a survey of natural resources, the report which was published in 1913. In 1922 the Department of

Industries and Commerce was reorganized in order to give a greater emphasis to the development of industries in the state.

The Mysore State was considered as the dominant actor, but the aim nevertheless was capitalism, which led to certain contradictions in the case of Mysore, controlled by an imperial centre, which was in opposition to peripheral industrialization. The new mixed economy approach was followed in the 1930s by private entrepreneurs and was supported and encouraged by the government which came to be known as the Mysore model of development. The government was a shareholder in 12 companies and the role of the state still became stronger which was due to weak private capital. The striking feature of the economy before independence was the dominance of industrialization with the small-scale iron and steel plant at Bhadravathi in Shimoga district in 1923.[7]

The decade 1931-41 recorded the highest degree of industrial activity in the state like Mysore Iron and Steel Works, Aircraft Factory, the Mysore Chemical and Fertilizers, Mysore Sugar Company and Mysore Paper Mills were directly owned or aided by the government. Further with the onset of the Second World War, some new production activities were initiated in the state which includes manufacture of starch for textile purposes, vegetable dye stuff, radio sets, cement, etc.

The emphasis on state-owned industries were concentrated only in erstwhile old Mysore and Bangalore, which forms a major part of present Karnataka was a major factor which led to uneven development of Karnataka.[8] The shift in power had an impact on the pattern of economic development and the need to correct the imbalance between the southern and northern regions.

Karnataka had a strong tradition of state-led industrialization and Bangalore owes much of its growth to the establishment of several public sector industries in the 1950s, which in turned spawned a thriving small-scale sector of ancillary units. This also gave rise to many technical training institutes, which provided the technical work force, absorbed by a burgeoning industrial base. The economic development depends largely on the 'quality, quantity, structure and the geographical distribution of the subsoil resource endowment in a country.[9] The rapid industrialization was a key goal of India's economic policies in the early phase of its post-independence era to achieve a higher standard of living for the population with economic growth must be pursued with equitable growth.

The era of Nehru's "Planned Economy" were large Public Sector Units (PSUs), was seen as the more effective instrument than the markets or private sector. The Public Sector Enterprises (PSE) in India, which may be owned either by the central and state governments, covers a wide range of heavy machinery and infrastructure related goods. The Public Sector enterprises were established partly because of the underdeveloped markets at that time, and the assumed inability of the private sector to raise investment for large industries. The crisis after the mid-960s to the late 1970s had both political and economic dimensions and their respective spheres were not completely separated from each other. The collapse of investment in the organized manufacturing sector with low savings, limited investment, sluggish industry, a steep rise in the money supply and a sharp decline in agricultural production were the prominent features of economic administration. The problems were also complicated by international 'price revolution' and a phase of 'stagflation' in the world economy. The situation gave rise to multiple political pressures, youth movements and working class protests which culminated against the failures of the government in terms of checking corruption, controlling price rise, creating employment, and providing relief to the poor. The measures that increased regulation through three enactments which were enacted to curb foreign capital were the Monopolies and Restricitive Trade Pratices (MRTP) Act 1969, the Indian Patents Act 1970 and the Foregin Exchange and Regulation Act (FERA) 1973. The public sector expanded through the nationalization of banks and the general insurance sector and of infrastructure sectors—coal, iron and steel, copper and oil. The nationalization in many industriddddes, the concept of joint sector was promoted for major projects in the core and heavy industry sectors involving private capital. The changes in the licensing and regulatory regimes was an effort made to induce private investment in industry were liberalized in the 1970s as those not involving foreign exchange expenditure and smaller investments were de-licensed. However, access to foreign exchange and technology and even entry of private capital became more restricted and were concentrated towards promoting particular industries that had an import substitution or foreign exchange saving character. These factors were very influential for the particular reference to mining in Kudremukh by collaborating with foreign capital.[10]

Kudremukh Iron Ore Company Limited

In Karnataka, the well-known high-grade iron ore deposits are in the Kudremukh-Bababudan belts of Chikmagalur district which have magnetite types of ores, whereas Sandur-Chikkanyakanahalli in Bellary district has hematite type of ores.[11]

Source: Kudremukh Iron Ore Company Limited

The National Mineral Development Corporation (NDMC) carried out detailed exploration in 1965, and after three years of investigation at a cost of ₹ 50 lakhs, proved that deposits were extensive. It secured a lease area of 5,218 hectares of land in the Bhadra reserve forest on lease from the Government of Karnataka for a period of 30 years starting July 25, 1969. The lease area also included 310 hectares of land in Nellibeedu; and also included an additional area of 1,174 hectares at a later stage in Gangadikal. However, on October 6, 1972, the

NDMC surrendered 613 hectares of land to the Government of Karnataka on the condition that additional lands would be leased out in due course for prospecting mining in Nellibeedu and Gangadikal. The consideration of the steep expenditure involved in setting up mining operations and the consequent burden on ensuring profitability led to the plan continuing at a slow pace during the 1970s.

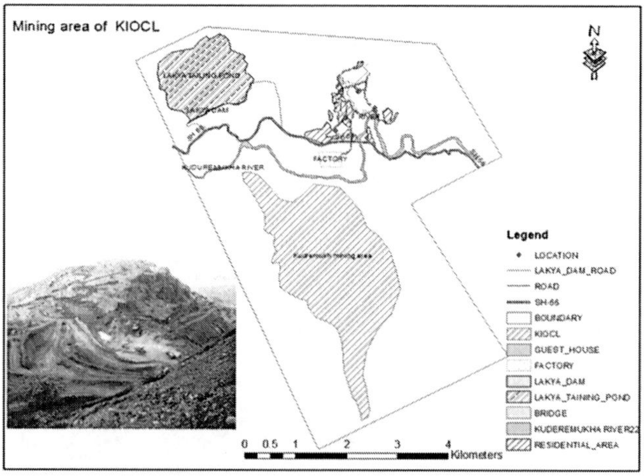

Source: Kudremukh Iron Ore Company Limited

The financial agreement between the Government of Iran and India, led to the production of iron pellets where the former extending credit of 630 million US dollars and the latter promised production and delivery of 150 MT iron ore concentrate to the National Iranian Steel Company. The plant facilities and mining was commissioned in 1980 and the first shipment of concentrate started from October 1981. The euphoria was jolted by the collapse of the Shah's regime in 1979 which resulted in the abrupt end of the Iranian aid. When the production of iron ore began in the 1980s, it had no buyers; hence the production capacity was brought down to 5 million tonnes per year. However, Rumania came forward to buy iron ore concentrate and agreed to set up a pelletization plant at Mangalore with an annual capacity of 3 million tonnes of pellets. After 1986, the company was able to enter the markets of Japan and China and KIOCL made its highest profit of ₹ 140 crores in 1991. The protest against Kudremukh gained momentum only from 1994 when the company started pushing for the extension of its lease, which was due to expire in 1999 to continue mining for another 20 years.

Pollution

The general notion of environmental degradation is a process by which our environment, air, water and land are contaminated, over-exploited and destroyed. The differing principles used for assessing environmental damage and the differing emphasis laid by societies on environmental resources and their use, make the definition of environmental degradation difficult and complex. The important substances which pollute water have been identified as traditional organic waste, waste generated from industrial activity, chemical agents for fertilizers and pesticides for crop protection and silt catchments. The major legislative action in the area of environmental protection came into force with the enactment of Water (Prevention and Control of Pollution) Act of 1974 and Air (Prevention and Control of Pollution) Act of 1981 were the initial measures adopted to control pollution.

The Ministry of Environment and Forests, which is the apex body in the field of environment, acts through the Central and State Pollution Control Boards for implementing pollution control laws. Under this act and these boards prescribe standards for the discharge of effluents or the quality of the receding waters. The disposal of polluting matters in streams, wells and sewers or on land in excess of the standards established by the state boards. It stipulates that consent must be obtained from the state board before taking steps to establish any industry, operation or process, discharge of sewage or trade effluents into a stream, well or sewer or onto land. The important regulatory mechanisms used in pollution control or prevention mechanism are (a) No Objection Certificate (b) Consent and (c) Standards. The pollution control boards have the necessary powers to enforce pollution standards and compel industries to adopt either clean technologies or clean-up whichever seems to be appropriate. The government has categorized industries into 'Red', 'Orange' and 'Green' depending on the severity of pollution generated by industries. The other changes include the National Conservation Strategy and Policy Statement on Environment and Development in 1992 which has laid guidelines for integrating environmental considerations into India's process of development. The guidelines including environment impact assessment of all development projects right from the planning stage was made mandatory. The environment safeguards and protection measures were to be incorporated in policies and in the implementation of development projects, create environment consciousness through education and mass awareness.

In Kudremukh the 'Gangamoola' is the birthplace of three major rivers—Tunga, Bhadra and Nethravathi. The river Tunga, which originates in the midst of the forest, flows northwards and then turning to the east joins river Bhadra at Kudali in Shimoga district far from the mining site. The river Nethravathi first flows westwards, then turns to southwest, to join the Arabian Sea in an estuary at Mangalore. Only Bhadra the river flows downwards towards Balehonnur via Jamble, Nellibeedu and Kalasa near KIOCL. The river forms an important lifeline for the people of Karnataka and Andhra Pradesh, providing sustenance and livelihood to the millions of people living downstream.[12] With over 7,000mm of annual rainfall that Kudremukh receives, open cast mining is an extremely dangerous operation here, and results in adverse impacts on a thickly forested and river area. The washing down of large amounts of silt during the monsoons from the mines has resulted in high rates of siltation of feeder streams and to the Bhadra river. The opposition against the KIOCL centred on river Bhadra that originates a short distance from the Lakya dam, into which the KIOCL released its industrial pollutants leading to the silting of rive Bhadra.

During 1991-94 the height of the Lakya dam[13] was increased by 35 metres, which was done without obtaining permission from the Karnataka State Forest Department and in 1994 due to record rainfall of up to 1000mm the Lakya dam breeched and the KIOCL township and the villages downstream up to the

Bhadra reservoir were evacuated in response to this alarm.[14] In 1994, the Government of Karnataka accorded sanction for issuing a prospecting license[15] over an area of 310 hectares of forestland at Nellibeedu within the Kudremukh National Park for a period of three years subject to certain conditions. The KIOCL violated the prospecting license stipulates by constructing roads over 19 kms length and 6 metres width inside the national park on very steep slopes. The individual members from different organizations like Mr. Shekar Singh, Former Planning Commission Advisor along with Ms. Malati Sen of the World Wild Fund for Nature and Mr. Chandi Prasad Bhat of the Chipko Andolan wrote to the then Union Minister of Environment Mr. Kamal Nath urging him to revoke the prospecting license granted to KIOCL.[16]

With the expiry of the mining lease on July 24, 1999 the management of the KIOCL appointed the National Environment Engineering Research Institute (NEERI), Nagapur to prepare a Comprehensive Environment Impact Assessment report for the extension of lease for another 20 years. The NEERI report which was in favour of the company has also led to the various studies with regard to pollution levels by various institutes and non -government organizations. Another report submitted to the company on the flora and fauna impact study done by the Centre for Ecological Studies, Indian Institute of Science concluded that the overall impacts of the mining and associated activities on the ecology has a direct effect on the loss of habitat and fragmentation of an important tract of tropical rainforest in the Western Ghats. The Ashoka Trust for Research in Ecology and the Environment carried out a scientific study on the impact of mining. The topography and rainfall characteristics, in combination with the opencast mining, road building and other land-surface disturbances caused by KIOCL operations, are likely to lead to high sediment discharges in the Bhadra river system in the short and long term. The study focused on the poor attention given to water quality and the omission of wet-season sampling of streams. Environmentalists say that KIOCL's measures to check pollution have had very little impact.[17] The main thrust of the Company's mining is eco-friendly as would be evident from the various activities undertaken by it and vast sums of money spent on the preservation of nature and environment in addition to prevent pollution.[18] The Karnataka Vimochana Ranga (KVR) affiliated to CPI (ML) based its campaigns against mining operation is an export-oriented and the pollution caused to river Bhadra may also affect the Tunga river. The KVR also focused on Gangadikallugudda to 'Save Tunga Origin' in 1994, which gained momentum in places such as Sringeri, Koppa, Thirthahalli and Shimoga. KVR activists undertook a cycle *Jatha* (procession) from Sringeri to Harihar to enlighten the people on the consequences of the mining operation. The campaign later merged to form the Tunga-Bhadra Ulisi Okkuta (Save Tunga-Bhadra Forum). The movement did not exclusively deal with environment issues, but follow an integrated approach by linking poverty, social justice, inequality, rural development and health issues.

The fight against the KIOCL was joined by several prominent writers such as K.P. Purnachandra Tejasvi, U.R. Anantha Murthy[19] and social worker H. Sudershan played a key role in persuading the Government of Karnataka to stop the mining.[20] The delegation led by U.R. Ananthmurthy[21] submitted a Memorandum to the then Chief Minister Mr. S.M. Krishna and pleaded not to renew the mining lease and ordered the Kudremukh Company to "pack Up" as the company had done enough.[22] The other institutions like religious Mutts intervened for closing the company which not only control funds but also influence public opinion and intervene for the purpose of patronage distribution.[23] In April 2001 a slide show was organized by D.V. Girish of the Nature Conservation Guild, Chikmagalur and Niren Jain of Kudremukh Wildlife Foundation and WILDCAT-Chikmagalur regarding the ill-effects of mining in Kudremukh to several cabinet Ministers Mr. D.B. Chandre Gowda, Minister of Law and Parliamentary Affairs, Mr. Sager Ahmed, Minister of Transport and other politicians. The concerned individuals also approached the High Court of Karnataka where the case was disposed due to the Supreme Court direction in the IA No. 207-2210/97 that "in view of the fact that in matters pending in this court and throughout the country, it is appropriate that no aspect of this matter be considered separately by another court in any form". The High Court gives the liberty to the concerned individuals to approach the Supreme Court for judgment.

Kudremukh Iron Company Limited Case in the Supreme Court

In 2001, K.M. Chinnappa, a retired forest officer and trustee of the NGO Wildlife First, in association with the Delhi-based NGO, LAW-, filed an Interloculatory Application in I.A 670 with the Supreme Court in the Godavarman Thirumalpad vs Union of India Case in which K.M.Chinnapa appealed for the mines to be closed and the lease areas to be included in the National Park.[24] The main reliefs sought were:

(a) To direct the MoEF to withdraw the illegal 'temporary working permission' for mining activities.
(b) Direct KIOCL to stop polluting the Bhadra river due to open cast mining.
(c) Take action against KIOCL for illegal encroachment in the forest and for the destruction of forests in the Kudremukh National Park.
(d) To stop KIOCL from laying a new slurry pipe line in the forest of the National Park.

The company is boosting states revenue by payment of royalty, sales tax and entry tax to the tune of ₹ 2.5 crores annually.[25] The MoEF promptly went ahead, issued a year's Temporary Working Permission (TWP) to KIOCL in 1999, and extended by another year, because of the Karnataka government's submissions that the area concerned would not form a part of the area notified as a national park. The TWP was conditional, with one of the conditions being the state government's final notification on the constitution of the KNP by September 30, 2000.

The Court observed: "Before we part with the case, we note with concern that the state and the central government were not very consistent in their approach about the period for which the activities could be permitted. Reasons have been highlighted to justify the somersault. Whatever is the justification, it was only imperative that due application of mind should have been made before taking a particular stand and not to change colour like a chameleon, and that too not infrequently."[26]

The increasing number of pending cases before the Supreme Court made it difficult for the Court to examine each and every issue in detail and pass appropriate orders. The Forest Conservation Act, 1980 did not have any provisions for setting up tribunals or authorities to adjudicate on such issues. When the affected people started approaching the Court, the need was felt to urgently set up a system in place to render justice faster if not more effectively. This led to the setting up of high powered committees, empowered committees, forest protection authorities and later on the Central Empowered Committee. The KIOCL case was referred to the CEC for hearing the parties and taking note of the materials placed before it. The recommendations made by the CEC were based on a documentary film called *Mindless Mining* made by filmmaker Shekar Dattatri.[27] The film was submitted as audio-visual evidence in the Supreme Court to stop mining inside the national park. The film claimed that farmers using the Bhadra Reservoir Command Area (located downstream of mining) would be losing irrigation potential due to the heavy siltation in the reservoir from the mining site at Kudremukh. The documentary was used by CEC to stop mining operations by KIOCL and "Restoration and Winding Up" has to start so that the company can restore all mined lands, plants and protect the region from further degradation. The exploitation of the Kudremukh iron ore follows no principles in law; the valuable rainforest has a greater value to human life than iron ore.[28]

The recommendation of the CEC to the Supreme Court led to the final judgment for closing the KIOCL by 2005. The Supreme Court has emphasized the need to set up special courts cases involving environmental pollution, ecological destruction and conflicts over natural resources with one professional judge and two experts drawn from the Ecological Sciences Research Group keeping in view the nature of the case and the expertise required for its adjudication.

"The courts' inability to handle complex science-rich cases has recently been called into question, with the widespread allegation that the judicial system is increasingly unable to manage and adjudicate on science and technology issues. Critics have objected that judges cannot make appropriate decisions because they lack technical training, that the jurors do not comprehend the complexity of the evidence they are supposed to analyse and that the expert witnesses on whom the system relies are mercenaries whose biased testimony frequently produce erroneous and inconsistent determinations. If these claims go unanswered, or are not dealt with confidence in the judiciary will be undermined as the public becomes convinced that the courts as now constituted are incapable of correctly resolving some of the pressing legal problems of our day."[29] However, in recent years there has been a lot of criticism against PIL, which has a public interest because of the political motive and as a strategic part of their job description. The resources and willingness to litigate public causes limited by their own internal agenda-setting interests in addition to the other apparent and external factors of the government behind such decisions.[30]

The Supreme Court has become the most powerful institution of the state because it enjoys enormous power and the arbiter of disputes between citizens and the state, and between states and the union, and directs the government in closing down industries.[31] The central feature of the labour law system is the strong presence of the state due to import substitution, planned development period of post-independence India (1950-76). The 1974, All India Railway Strike and its severe repression by the government, followed by the Emergency in 1975 when industrial actions were massively curbed.

Trade Union Movement

The question which arises at this point is that trade unions have to adapt to the new challenges as well as alternatives to the present policies.[32] The trade unions were mainly formed for protecting the interests of workers or employees against those who would harm them could be the employers, state or any agency identified as such. The trade union politics are dictated by the major political parties in the Kudremukh Iron Core Company launching their own struggles by different unions to protect the interest of the workers. The affiliation of the trade union with the party politics is an important feature of the trade union party politics. The most important feature of the labour movement after the 1970s saw the regional parties like the Shiv Sena starting their own labour wing called Bharatiya Kamgar Sena. It was widely believed that the Shiva Sena had the backing of the industrial houses to curb the influence of socialists and communists in the labour unions. The gradual withdrawal of the state and the sharp reduction of trade union power has led to the informalization and structural dualism in the labour market reflected in the Bombay textile strike of 1982 led by Dr. Datta Samant. The conflict in the Bombay textile strike also reflects on the trade union leaders coming out of the political parties or not directly affiliated to the federation to continue their struggle as independent unions. Datta Samant who was elected on a Congress ticket from Kurla left the Congress and Indian National Trade Union Congress (INTUC) in 1978 and became an independent union leader, thus setting a new trend in the trade union movement. He started a number of unions covering Association of Engineering Workers' Mumbai General Kamgar Union, and Maharashtra Mill Workers' Union.

The other independent union leaders who came into prominence were Shankar Guha Neogi who organized the contract workers in the iron-ore mines of Dalli Rajhara near Bhilal in Madhya Pradesh. The other prominent name is A.K. Roy who organized the coal-mine workers in the Dhandad-Jharia of Jharkhand. The main purpose of independent unions was that the trade union federations were more concerned with the problems of the permanent workers in the organized sector. Unfortunately the independent trade union leaders like Datta Samant and Shankar Guha Neogi with their popularity have been killed owing their activities in the trade union movement.

The other reason for the crisis has been ascribed to

the vigorous and rapid process of disinvestments and the withdrawal of the state government means the closure of the public sector units. In different parts of India like Orissa, Chhattisgarh and Jharkhand these conflicts are raising issues on better compensation packages, but often communities are raising serious objections to the notion of development itself that is being promoted by the state. The serious criticism against the public sector companies in the area of public relations, at a time when the torrent of false propaganda let loose against the company, did not defend itself by placing facts before the people, which was a serious lapse on the part of the KIOCL Company. The workers union due to restraints in public sector units gave the details to the Democratic Youth Federation of India (DYFI), proposed that mining should be extended for a period of 20 years (up to 2019) by KIOCL without any hindrances. The extension of lease should be subject to the following conditions and priority given to the closing operation of the mine during the last 3 years of the extended lease period.

The trade unions have opposed the closing down of the company and organized nationwide strikes, *bandhs* and rallies in different parts of the country, but these had no effect in changing the policies. It is therefore evident that the traditional forms of protest have lost their strength concerning labour.[33] The division of the labour is further divided between the employed and the unemployed, between regulars and temporaries, between employees and contract labour, and so on. The vertical division within the enterprise making one set of workers control another set of workers, has led to inter-worker conflict

Protest of Trade Unions Against the Closure of Kudremukh Iron Company Limited

The issue of workers' rights has been greatly highlighted with the introduction of 'liberalization, privatization and globalization implying that the period prior to 1991 was a golden era of labour unions. There was a fundamental continuity of labour unions before the reforms. The Trade Unions Act allowed for the registration of unions, but did not require employers to recognize them or engage in negotiations with them, not did it protect union members from victimization. The other major defect with regard to workers' rights was about the assumption that most workers would not be covered by labour legislation. Thus various acts like Factories Act, Employees State Insurance Act, Employees Provident Fund Act, and Payment Gratuity Act did not cover establishments with less than ten workers. These loopholes provided the space for the large businesses for evading labour legislation, splitting their establishment into several fictitious businesses and subcontracting production to smaller establishments. Such strategies resulted in the large informal workers who were not legally registered as workers, and their employment is not recorded. The workers' rights have always been weak and the major obstacle for forging a strategy of resistance was the existence of multiple fault lines within the labour force along lines of gender, caste, religion, ethnicity employment status, and so on.[34]

The Central Trade Unions that are recognized by the Company are Kudremukh Employees Union affiliated to (Indian National Trade Union Congress). It is affiliated to the Congress Party and was formed in 1947. Its ideology was close to the Gandhian view of cooperation rather than confrontation. Kudremukh Shramashakti Sangathane affiliated to (HMS) broke away from the All India Trade Union Congress (AITUC) to form a new political party called the Praja Socialists Party. The basic premise was to draw the non-communist and non-Congress trade unions into its fold with Royalists and Indian Federation of labour merged to form the Hind Mazdoor Sabha (HMS). The third union Kudremukh Mazdoor Sangh affiliated to (BMS) is affiliated to the Bharatiya Jan Sangh and have argued against the closing of the company. They have articulated their protest on party lines by taking different routes to protect the workers.

Kudremukh Shram Shakthi Sanghatan

In India the civil society campaigns are supported through the intervention of Public Interest Litigation (PIL) in the Supreme Court. The social movements' engagement with the law depend on the extent to which they can frame their demands and engage in struggles that avoid direct confrontation with state sovereignty and its ideological foundation of developmental nationalism. The Supreme Court has used its right to enforce and interpret the Constitution. In the initial phase the conservative and status quoits character came in between for more radical reforms in relation to socio-economic and the defence of individual rights. For example, the Supreme Court interpreted the right to property to negate land reforms, nationalization of banks, etc. But these changes were rectified and in recent years the Supreme Court has become more sensitive to social issues, from the rights of women, workers, ecology, social justice and social discrimination.

The emergence of green attitudes coincides with the Supreme Court's interpretation of constitutional promises in favour of the poor, the illiterate, and the disadvantaged people, liberated *locus standi* from the narrow clutches of justice and developed a new jurisprudence of social action, known as public interest litigation. These cases pertain to the issue of environmental pollution caused by industrial units due to the failures of the state in protecting the right to a healthy environment and the rights to health are an integral part of the right to life under Article 21 of the Indian Constitution.[36] The Public Interest Litigation (PIL) was intended to ensure legal rights to people who because of poverty, helplessness, disability or socially or economically disadvantaged position, was unable to reach the court themselves. The growth of environmental disputes is one of the main elements in the growth of Public Interest Litigation, where the Supreme Court plays an activist role. Judicial activism in the initial phase was the direct result of the creative imagination of Krishna Iyer and P.N. Bhagwati. In its second phase this activism was empowered by environment concerns, and here again the initiative taken by Justice Kuldeep Singh stood out.[37]

The Public Interest Litigation (PIL) based judicial activism has transformed from a passive arbiter of ordinary disputes and giving relief to the disadvantaged groups under the leadership of M.C. Mehta the Supreme Court gained in stature and legitimacy covering a wide range of cases such as industrial pollution, violations of Forest Conservation Act due to mining activities and a different trend in cases involving infrastructural projects. The collaboration of NGOs and lawyers are well structured and experts who are capable of producing the facts and materials to convince the court of the importance of a particular environmental problem. It has changed the nature of decisions emanating from the court like Tarun Barat Singh, Alwar vs Union of India. These cases involved widespread illegal mining in a notified national park and a tiger reserve, where the Court ordered that the mines be closed. The cases taken up by the civil society campaigns are supported through the intervention of Public Interest Litigation (PIL) in the Supreme Court. The Supreme Court has used its right to enforce and interpret the Constitution, where it is called upon to ensure observance of enacted laws made by the state to protect the environment and ecology of an area. The Kudremukh Shram Shakthi Sanghatan[38] filed Application No. 1374/2005 for reconsideration of the judgment stating that it was against the principles of natural justice and prayed that the same be heard with 1010/2003 filed by KIOCL[39] as the subject matter of both applications were substantially similar. The concept of natural justice has undergone a great deal of change in recent years. In the past it was thought that no one shall be a judge in his own cause and no decision shall be given against a party without affording him a reasonable hearing has changed with quasi-judicial inquiries must be held in good faith, without bias and not arbitrarily or unreasonably. The public interest litigation has been criticized as 'publicity interest litigation' by Justice B.N. Kripal in the BALCO Employees Union vs Union of India and also asserted that PIL is not a pill or panacea for all wrongs. The debate of accountability between the legislature and the executive as they are accountable to the people by way of elections, but the role of judiciary as a distinct role criticized for encroaching upon the domains of other organs. Justice Krishna Iyer said long ago in 1982, "Independence of the judiciary is a myth. It overlooks numerous tie-ups with the executive and business houses".[40]

Kudremukh Mazdoor Sangh

The KMS has argued that closure of mining activity at Kudremukh will create a severe hardship to employees and indirectly a setback to our economic development.[41] The Kudremukh Mazdoor Sangh protested on behalf of the 2500 direct employees of KIOCL, who along with their families will count around 10,000 people who are indirectly dependent on KIOCL by the closure of mining activities.

Most of the employees have reached a halfway mark in their service and they may find it very difficult to get employment elsewhere.[42] The employees of Kudremukh belong to the age group of 40-45 years, which means they are neither young nor old; hence, their condition is precarious. There is no recruitment in the company as per government directives and under the scheme of Voluntary Retirement Scheme (VRS), which was in force up to June 30, 2000; around 74 employees belonging to various categories including officers have retired. Around 800 members have opted for VRS and the maximum amount received by an individual is around 6,50,000 lakhs for executives and around 1,100,000 lakhs for non-executives.[43] Most of the children of the employees are studying in various classes at Kudremukh and they have to get new admission on their respective class and respective places.[44] It also criticized VRS as a part of privatization which appears attractive to workers who are facing insecurity in their jobs.[45] KMS organized a huge protest in Managlore in collaboration with Sri Jayakrishna Parisara Premi to draw the attention of the state, and also protested in Bangalore in collaboration with the Rakshana Vedike under the leadership of Narayana Gowda.[46]

Kudremukh Employees Union

The Kudremukh Employees Union affiliated to the Indian National Trade Union Congress (INTUC) led a team to New Delhi to meet Congress Ministers and submitted a memorandum to them. The KEU took a procession in New Delhi to highlight the issue; and one of the banners had a message: *We have come to Delhi seeking justice against the closure of KIOCL by NGOs*. The KEU met senior Congress leaders like Margret Alva, Oscar

Fernandes, Janardhana Poojary, Dayanidini Maran, Ramvilas Paswan and finally Sonia Gandhi and expressed the fear that the closing of the mining would lead to the Naxalite menace. The company has not taken care of the workers, and this led to a socially unstable situation.[47]

The unions blocked the Mangalore-Mumbai highway with *Rasta roko* (road blockade) and raised slogans against 'environmentalist' as a mark of protest against the closure of mining operations. The workers union also burnt the effigies of Jnanpith awardee Dr. U.R. Ananthamurthy, environmentalists Ullas Karanth, Praveen Bhargav and Niren Jain. A memorandum submitted to the government through MLA J. Krishna Palemar expressed sympathy with the workers and blamed the inefficiency of the state and central governments for the closure of KIOCL. Palemar stated that "Had the KIOCL been a private firm, it would not have been closed" and demanded a high-level enquiry against environmentalists who had received foreign funds to force the closure of KIOCL. The trade union response in which unions organize rank-and-file members, putting power behind their demands was missing and daily wage workers ware left from the purview of the workers unions and there was no rehabilitation process offered to them.

Daily Wage Workers in Kudremukh

The term 'unorganized' and 'informal' sectors have been used to refer to related but slightly different aspects of the economy. While the former pointing towards smaller units where workers remain unprotected by unions the latter stands particularly for production or distribution that is not formally registered. In both cases workers or self-employed labouring masses remain out of the legal and social security cover. The management with its bureaucratic centralization had been manipulating regular unions and the issue of daily workers has been left unorganized.[48] The management used to control the daily wage workers[49] through the contractors for different works in the company[50] like welding, fitting, cleaning, greasing, civil works, cable handling, masonry work, sweeping, serving in canteens and maintenance of gardens. The contractors had a good understanding with the management and the daily wage workers were paid around ₹ 71 per day. On paper, they showed more but in reality the manipulations were so much that if anybody tried to organize the workers or encouraged them to raise their voices; their entry passes were not renewed.[51]

Strength of the Daily Wage Workers as on February 23, 2007

S.No	*Village*	*Total Number of Families*	*Total Population*	*Daily Wage Workers*
1.	Vinobhanagar	329	1,144	345
2.	Jamble	62	196	61
3.	Nallibeedu	104	413	122
	Total	495	1753	528

Source: Kudremukh Daily Wage Workers

Political leaders have visited Kudremukh and have given assurances and nothing has come to the relief of destitute families of daily wage workers.[52] The daily wage workers have urged the state government to intervene, protect their interests, and ensure a decent living for them. The issue was also linked with the local people in the nearby villages of Jamble, Neelibedu, and Samse[53] who were dependent on the company for their livelihood either as permanent employees of the company or as contract labourers who had their own grievances against the company regarding employment opportunities for their families or relatives. The company closed due to the total collapse of administration, rather than mining, which is very systematic with no pollution.[54] The major conflict in the era of neoliberal reforms requires trade unions to fight for freedom of association and collective bargaining rights for every worker and for all labour legislation to cover all workers regardless of their place of work or the number of workers in it. Such a strategy would require a conscious strategy of building solidarity and combating divisions within the labour force. The common strategy of eliminating trade unionism was to deny sections of workers of the right to engage in it. The management was assisted by the ambiguities in the Industrial Dispute Act, which protects the collective bargaining rights of only those who are designated as 'workmen'.

The trade unions urged the state government to allot block numbers 13, 14, 15, and 17; of Ramanadurga in Bellary district[55] for mining as an alternative but private parties had already taken away a lion's share of the Ramanadurga mining block. In July 2005, the district administration recorded the movement of over 5,000 trucks on a single day through Bellary city to Mangalore Port. The district administration has now set up a task force to conduct random checks of transport permits. The illegal mining in iron-ore rich Bellary has deprived the state administration of an enormous revenue around ₹ 3000 crore in two years, according to the government's estimates.[56] The revelation by the Karnataka Lokayukta Report had drawn extensively from U.V. Singh, a senior official who highlighted the irregularities of the mining operators and owners including (state Chief Minister, Minister for Health, and the Minister for Tourism G. Janardhana Reddy.[57] The central government in order to check illegal mining of iron and manganese ores set up a commission in 2010 headed by M.B.Shah to suggest remedial measures. The report has criticized the view that illegal mining of the ores was on the Chinese demand during the Beijing Olympics and booming export market. The report was rejected by the Union Ministry of Mines who blamed the poor governance at the state level that has left illegal mining unchecked.[58]

Conclusion

In India public sector enterprises were established partly because of the underdeveloped markets at that time and big industries like Kudremukh were seen as the pride of industrialization. The entire debate on reforms whether we should privatize an enterprise or not seems to be centred on whether it is a profit or a loss making enterprise. The central and state governments have gone out of their way to bail out

KIOCL, and in the process ignored the law of the land. The Karnataka Government's predicament stems from the fact that it cannot be instrumental in the closure of a profit making company, with nearly annual earnings of $150 million foreign exchange. The company is boosting states revenue by payment of royalty, sales tax and entry tax to the tune of ₹ 2.5 crores annually[59] (See Appendix I.d and I.e). The three unions setting aside their union affiliation argued that NGOs like Wildlife First are not doing this simply out of love for 'lion-tailed Macaques' or 'Niligiri Marteus' or out of sympathy for the 'peasants' dependent on the Bhadra reservoir. The river Bhadra is also polluted due to the various industries in Bhadravathi town or the Birla owned poly fibre factory in Kumarapatnam near Harihar is poisoning the entire Tungabhadra river. NGOs are silent about the atrocities being perpetrated by the private sector industries on nature and environment.[60] The serious criticism against public sector companies in the area of public relations, came at a time when a torrent of false propaganda was let loose against the company. It did not defend itself by placing facts before the people, which was a serious lapse on the part of the KIOCL Company. The campaign was also led by big coffee planters against the company because of shortage of labourers in coffee estates. The villagers who are working in the company if closed would become destitute and be compelled to work in the nearby coffee estates.

The Supreme Court in a series of orders in the Godavarman case, dealt with the mining cases taking place in forest areas. The Supreme Court has emphasized that it is not against mining per se but against mining which is in violation of the Forest Conservation Act 1980, and also mining in National Parks and Sanctuaries.[61] The Supreme Court in the final judgment ordered the closing of the Kudremukh Iron Ore Company Limited highlighting the importance of the environment and protection of biodiversity. The Supreme Court order in the Kudremkuh case is important because the Court had emphasized the need to implement the provisions of the Convention on Biological Diversity:

"Duty is cast upon the government under Article 21 of the

Constitution of India to protect the environment and the two salutary principles which govern the law of the environment are: (i) the principles of sustainable development and (ii) the precautionary principle. It needs to be highlighted that our country has acceded to the Convention on Biological Diversity and therefore, it has to implement the same."

Kudremukh region is rich in biodiversity and is recognized as one of the 12 mega-biodiversity centres of the world and has two of the 18 identified hot spots (Western Ghats and Eastern Himalayas) of the world. The importance and uses of biodiversity in India include its ethical values, ecosystem services and values of biodiversity. Livelihoods, health and food security in India have been facing several threats. The causes of biodiversity loss are manifold with rapid expansion of agriculture and industry; large-scale development projects like mining, dams and highways are major threats to biodiversity through destruction and degradation of habitat.

The awareness of hot spots is a recent development but none of these considerations appeared to have weighted in when Kudremukh Iron Ore Company Limited started its mining operations. The Supreme Court in the final judgment ordered all mining operations to cease as per the recommendations made by CEC that the company should be closed by 2005.[62] The Supreme Court orders are not against mining per se but against mining which is in violation of the Forest Conservation Act, 1980 and also mining in National Parks and Sanctuaries. The Supreme Court final order for closing the company draws attention to the importance of Sustainable Development and the need for balance between Ecology and Development has to be maintained for future generations.

References

1. Vinay Bahl (1994): 'The Emergence of Large-Scale Steel Industry in India Under British Colonial Rule, 1880-1907', *The Indian Economic and Social History Review,* Vol. 31, No. 4, p. 459.
2. The Kolar Gold Fields (KGF) has been functioning for the past 120 years. With a one time workforce of 36,000 workers it has now been reduced to just 4,000 workers. It was taken over during British rule by an Englishman John Taylor in the 1880s and

nationalized by the Government of India after independence. It has so far produced 850 tons of gold. For this 4,600 workers died in accidents alone, 6,000 workers were disabled, 11,000 workers suffered from silicosis (lung disease caused by inhalation of crystalline silica dust). Also See Report of the First Convention: Mines, Minerals and People: *Our Land, Our Minerals, Our Rights,* from April 28 to May 1, 2000, Hyderabad, Andhra Pradesh.

3. Esha Shah focuses on understanding how power relations operate and orchestrate the domain of technological designs and by that means resource distribution in order to reproduce. Esha Shah (2003): *Social Designs: Tank Irrigation Technology and Agrarian Transformation in Karnataka, South India,* Orient Longman, New Delhi, p. 18.
4. Narendar Pani (1988): 'Political Economy of Karnataka 1950-1955: An Overview', *Journal of Social and Economic Development,* Vol. I, No. I, January-June, p. 69.
5. The Mysore Economic Conference was held in 1911 as an economic-political counterpart to the representative assembly was to have the following composition: President (The Dewan of Mysore), Vice-President (the members of the council) Members (selected heads of departments), Deputy Commissioners, prominent agriculturists, merchants. etc). See Sunil, Khilnani (1997): *The Idea of India,* Penguin Books, p. 38.
6. Y.G. Krishnamurti (1941): *Sir M. Visvesvaraya: A Study,* Popular Book Depot, Bombay.
7. The Mysore Iron Works did not take off due to the lack of coal in southern India whereas wood available in the large forest area of Shimoga could be converted into charcoal. Owing to the lack of infrastructural facilities in the area and financial point of view the project was to be completed in 1919 but was extended to 1923 during which the prices of iron had gone down to less than half of what they were when the scheme was sanctioned. See Bjorn, Hettne (1978): *The Political Economy of Indirect Rule Mysore 1881-1947,* Curzon Press, London, pp. 269-274.
8. Narendar Pani (1988): 'Political Economy of Karnataka 1950-1955: An Overview', *Journal of Social and Economic Development,* Vol. I, No. I, January-June, p. 64.
9. N. Naganna (1999): 'A Structural Analysis of India's Mining Sector in the Context of Development Planning', *Indian Journal of Economics,* Vol. LXIX, Part III, No. 274, pp. 279-30.
10. Surajit Mazumdar (2012): 'Industrialization, Dirigisme

and Capitalists: Indian Big Business from Independence to Liberalization', Nehru Memorial Museum and Library, Occasional Paper, New Delhi, pp. 12-13.

11. T.N. Venugopal (2006): 'Mineral Resources of Karnataka and Challenges for its Extraction', Department of Mines and Geology, *Geological Studies*, No. 387, Bangalore, pp. 1-3.
12. Interview with Subhash Kharbare, Employee of KIOCL on March 10, 2006, Bangalore.
13. The project generates a very large quantity of slime for which a dam has been built at Lakya to store the fine tailings left after separating the concentrates.
14. Praveen, Bhargav and Niren Jain (2004): 'Battle for Kudremukh': *The Hindu*, January 4.
15. Prospecting license (PL) granted for undertaking operations for purpose of exploring, locating or providing mineral deposits. The other kinds of mineral concessions recognized in Indian Law are Reconnaissance Permit (RP) which is granted for preliminary prospecting of a mineral through regional, aerial, geographical or geochemical surveys and geological mapping. See Vagholikar, Neeraj, Kaustubh A.Moghe and Ritwick Dutta (2003): *Undermining India: Impacts of Mining on Ecologically Sensitive Areas*, Kalpavriksh, Pune, p. 7.
16. Under the liberalized policy, mining activity with respect to as many as 13 minerals earlier reserved for the public sector, are open to the private sector for exploitation. These were iron ore, manganese ore, sulphur, chrome, gold, diamond, copper, lead, zinc, molybdenum, tungsten, nickel and platinum. Around 15 minerals removed from Part C of the First Schedule of the MMRD Act, leaving only 11 minerals, for which the permission of the central government for the grant or renewal of mining lease (ML) and prospecting license (PL).
17. Mahalakshmi Parathasarthy (2001): 'Escalating Ecocide in the Kudremukh National Park', Fact-Finding Report, *Nagarika Seva Trust*, Gurvayanakere, Dakishna Kannada.
18. The KIOCL Company in their eagerness to raise forests as speedily as possible, the Forest Department planted 80 lakhs of acacia (*Acadia Auriiculoformics*), eucalyptus and casurina everywhere in plenty in the 1970s and 80s. It would have been understandable if these exotic species were planted only on barren lands and bald hills where nothing else grows, but there was no justification in planting them even in Malnad and the

west coast where the indigenous species of these trees could be grown easily.

19. U.R. Ananthmurthy is the most influential representative of the '*navya*' (modernist) movement in Kannada literature. He joined hands with "Tungamula Ulisi", a movement to protect the source of the river Tunga with K.G. Sridhar who led the movement in Thirathhalli of Shimoga district.
20. Praveen Bhargav and Niren Jain (2004): "Battle for Kudremukh": *The Hindu*, January 4.
21. The delegation included the leader of the opposition of the legislative council, Mr. K.H. Srinivasa, Mr. B.L. Shankar, Mr. K.B. Mallikarjun, Mr. A. Jnanendra and Mr. Visvesvara Hedge. The former state government official, Mr. Yellappa Reddy, and the noted environmentalist, Mr. Ullas Karanth were also part of the delegation. *The Hindu*, July 19, 2001.
22. Harsh Sethi (2001): 'Movements and Mediators', *Economic and Political Weekly*, January 27, Vol. XXXVI, No. 4, pp. 269-270.
23. See Atul Kohli (1987): 'Karnataka: Populism, Patronage and Piecemeal Reform' in *The State and Poverty in India*, 145-85, Cambridge, Cambridge University Press, p. 152.
24. Praveen Bhargav and Niren Jain (2004): "Battle for Kudremukh": *The Hindu*, January 4.
25. The Mangalore port receives ₹ 3 crores annually by way of port charges and another ₹ 2.5 crores as land rent charges as the ore and pellets are exported to China, Iran, Australia, Turkey and Japan and the company signed fresh contracts in 2000-01. The company has exported 210 million tons of ore concentrate and its mining zone has a stockpile of weathered ore of about 140 million tons and beneath it another 350 million tons of primary ore, enabling operations for another 20 years.
26. K.N. Murthy and D.V.R. Seshadri (2011): 'Kudremukh Iron Ore Company Limited (KIOCL): The Death Knell and Beyond', *Vikalpa*, Vol. 36, No. 2, April-June, pp. 133-137.
27. See Shaker Dattari (2007): 'Wildlife Films, Do They Have a Future in India', *Sanctuary Asia*, Vol. XXVII, No. 1, Mumbai, pp. 18-29.
28. Memorandum submitted by Kudremukh Shram Shakti Sanghatan to Valmik Thapar to honourable Chairman and Members of the Central Empowered Committee during his visit

to Kudremukh on September 30, 2002.

29. Ritwick Dutta (2003): 'Courts and Environmental Justice: Critical Issues', *Social Change*, Vol. 33, No. 2&3, June-September, pp. 24-25.
30. Ridwanul Hoque (2006): 'Taking Justice Seriously: Judicial Public Interest and Constitutional Activism in Bangladesh', *Contemporary South Asia,* 15 (4), December, p. 409.
31. The judicial orders of the Supreme Court resulted in the closure of polluting and non-conforming industries in Delhi, the capital city, throwing out of work an estimated 2 million people in a population of 12 million people through public interest litigation by bourgeois environmentalism. See Amita Baviskar, (2003): 'Between Violence and Desire: Space, Power and Identity in the Making of Metropolitan Delhi', No. 175, *International Social Science Journal*, pp. 89-98.
32. Sharit K. Bhowmik (2002): 'Coping with Economic Liberalization: Alternative Trade Union Strategies', Vol. 45, No. 4, *The Indian Journal of Labour Economics*, pp. 1339-1346.
33. The first manifestation of discontent among the workers in Mysore manifested only in 1920 and even this late awakening did not take any organized form. The great depression in the 1930s labour saw the labour force becoming more and more organized, but the ruthlessness of the government was also on the increase. Although the Trade Union Act was passed in 1926 the Mysore Government saw no reason to extend it and as a result, the trade unions had to register themselves as charitable institutions up to 1942. The union movement in KIOCL however never met with great difficulties because the state was the principal industrial entrepreneur, the employer's interests therefore largely became identical with the state interest, and as a result, union activities were looked upon as anti-state activities. See Chandrashekar, S (1985): *Dimensions of Socio-Political Change in Mysore 1918-40,* Ashish Publishing House, New Delhi, pp. 116-17. Also See Rakhahari, Chatterji (1980): *Unions, Politics and The State: A Study of Labour Politics*, South Asian Publishers, New Delhi, pp. 43-52.
34. Rohini Hensman (2012): 'Workers, Union and the Left: Responding to the Global Crisis', Nehru Memorial Museum and Library, Occasional Paper, New Delhi, p. 9.
35. Indian National Trade Union Congress (INTUC), All India Trade Union Congress (AITUC), Centre of Indian Trade Unions (CITU), Hind Mazdoor Sabha (HMS), Bharatiya Mazdoor Sangh (BMS),

United Trade Union Congress (UTUC) National Organization of Labour (NLO), National Federation of Indian Trade Unions (NFITU), United Trade Union Centre (LS).

36. S.P. Sathe (2002): *Judicial Activism in India: Transgressing Borders and Enforcing Limits*, New Delhi, Oxford University Press, p. 224.
37. The M.C. Mehta vs. Union of India also known as the *Kanpur Tanneries or Ganga Pollution Case* is among the most significant water pollution case. The opening part of the judgment discusses the various legal provisions and the legal duties of municipal bodies and pollution control boards. The Court then goes on to appreciate the evidence of the level of pollution. It is important to note here one of the effective strategies adopted by M.C. Mehta which seems to be the deciding factors for his success. All the cases involve detailed scientific investigations and the reports are produced before the Court as evidence. M.C. Mehta's work is painstaking, his research and scientific study meticulous. The results of investigations are displayed in self-explanatory tabular form to highlight the magnitude of environmental damage. So well employed is his use of facts and figures, which the Court is struck by the severity of the problem and feels compelled to interfere. Another noteworthy strategy adopted in these cases is offering the Court feasible alternatives, which balance preservation of the environment with development of industries. In the case following the alarming details given by M.C. Mehta about the extent of pollution in the river Ganga due to the inflow of sewage from Kanpur only, the Court came down heavily on the Nagar Mahapalika (Municipality). The Court emphasized that it is the Nagar Mahapalika of Kanpur that has to bear the major responsibility for the pollution of the river near Kanpur city
38. Circular of Kudremukh Shram Shakti Sanghatan dated December 26, 2005.
39. On November 19, 2003 the Kudremukh Iron Ore Company filed application No. 1010/2003 praying the court to appoint an independent committee to examine the matter on the ground that an interested person was a member of the CEC and also with a prayer to allow the KIOCL to continue the mining for 20 years producing evidence in abundance in support of it.
40. A.K. Roy (1997): 'Can Courts Run the Country?', *Economic and Political Weekly*, October 11, pp. 2579-81.
41. The BMS has severely criticized the political leaders for not

taking an interest in decision-making for the continuation of mining. BMS has gone from door to door of the ministers of Karnataka and central government. Interview with Kulkarni, member of BMS, on September 26, 2007, Kudremukh.

42. Memorandum Submitted by Kudremukh Mazdoor Sangh to Valmik Thapar on September 30, 2002.
43. Interview with Anwar Pasha Kudremukh Employees Union Affiliated to Indian National Trade Union Congress (INTUC), January 29, 2007, Mangalore.
44. Valmik Thapar (2002): Horrors of Kudremukh: A Photographic Report on Mining in Kudremukh National Park from September 30 to October 1.
45. Ramesh P. Babu (2007): 'Optional or Imposed / An Ex-Post Evaluation of Voluntary Retirement Scheme in BALCO', *Economic and Political Weekly*, Vol. XLII, No. 21, May 26, pp. 1934-41.
46. The assertion of "Kannadiga" by the Karnataka Rakshana Vedike laying emphasis on the fact that the development of people is directly linked to the development of language. The recent "Cauvery agitation" is seen as a potent force which believed in violent methods of protest.
47. Nandini Gooptu (2007): 'Economic Liberalization, Work and Democracy', *Economic and Political Weekly*, Vol. XLII, No. 21, May 26, p. 1926.
48. Navin Chandra (2002): 'Organizing Labour: 'The Question of Form and Content', *The Indian Journal of Labour Economics*, Vol. 45, No. 4, pp. 1329-37.
49. The AITUC affiliated to the Communist Party of India started to mobilize the contract workers during the period 1982-83 but the company has not recognized it. The split in the Communist Party into Communist Party of India and CPI (M) split the AITUC in 1970. The CPI (M) formed their own union called Centre of Indian Trade Unions (CITU) .
50. Letter written to Shri Manmohan Singh by Kudremukh Daily Wage Workers Union, on February 9, 2006.
51. The pay scale of the regular workers followed the rules of the central government, whereas the contract workers the rules of the state government rules and the differentiation between them in salary, living conditions also made a huge difference by the claims made by the company were in total contrast with the

situation of the contract workers.

52. Interview with Periyaswamy, Secretary of the Kudremukh Daily Wage Workers Union, on September 25, 2007, Kudremukh.
53. The rehabilitation of 63 families who gave up their lands to the company have been rehabilitated in Jamble, Nellibeedu and Samse villages and given alternative land of 2 ½ acres of alternative land and one person in each such family has been given a suitable job in the company. The company has constructed a 5-bedded and well-equipped hospital for its employees and primary health facilities at Nellibeedu and Vinoba Nagar. More than 3,000 children from Malleswara and nearby villages receive quality education in the Kendriya Vidyalaya, Junior College and primary schools run with the assistance of the company.
54. Interview with Ramesh, a taxi driver in Jamble, on September 27, 2007, Kudremukh.
55. In the year 1964, the Karnataka Government through a Gazette Notification reserved the Ramanadurg area for mining by the state and/or by the public sector units. The Mineral Concession Rules 1960 provided that the state government with the consent of the central government may permit private companies to mine in such a reserved area. In pursuance of this relaxation, the Karnataka government in the past has allowed some of the private parties to mine in some Ramanadurg areas. The boom began when the centre opened the country's iron ore reserve to private enterprise in 1999.
56. The coalition government between BJP-JD(S) in 2008 came to power owing to the mines lobby and the money power of the Reddy brothers consisting of the trio of G. Janardhan Reddy, G. Karunakara Reddy and G. Somashekara Reddy, along with their trusted aid B. Sriramulu failed to protect thousands of labourers who were depending on KIOCL by not allowing mining in the region but gave permission for illegal mining in Bellary.
57. The Bailadila mines in Rajandgaon which supplies iron ore to the Bhilal Steel Plant where the mine workers were organized by Shankar Guha Neogi under the banner of Chhattisgarh Mukti Morcha (CMM) until he was brutally murdered in 1991 by state agents in collusion with the mining mafia.
58. Sugaandh Juneja (2012): 'Ministry Indifferent to Illegal Mining',

Down to Earth, January 31.

59. The Mangalore port receives ₹ 3 crores annually by way of port charges and another ₹ 2.5 crores as land rent charges as the ore and pellets are exported to China, Iran, Australia, Turkey and Japan and the company signed fresh contracts in 2000-01. The company has exported 210 million tons of ore concentrate and its mining zone has a stockpile of weathered ore of about 140 million tons and beneath it another 350 million tons of primary ore, enabling operations for another 20 years.
60. Kudremukh Mining: Reality and Myth (2001): 'A Report by the Fact-Finding Team of Democratic Youth Federation of India (DYFI) Udupi District Committee', Published by Pragathipara Janasamudaya Prakashana, Mangalore, p. 4, (in Kannada).
61. Ritwick Dutta (2003): 'Courts and Environmental Justice: Critical Issues', *Social Change*, Vol. 33, No. 2&3, June-September, pp. 24-5.

5

Biodiversity Conservation and Rehabilitation from Kudremukh National Park

Introduction

The political ecology in the 1970s has been dominated by the two discourses which appeared after the Club of Rome Report in 1972 under the banner of 'Environment' and 'Development'. The 'development' camp was committed to the cause of accelerating economic growth through industrialization for increasing human welfare, while the 'environmentalist' camp was concerned with the preservation of endangered species, as well as with the maintenance of an overall ecological balance.[1] In order to protect biodiversity, national parks and wildlife sanctuaries have been established to promote *in situ* and *ex situ* conservation programmes in India. The national parks are concerned with selected keystone species of both ecological and aesthetic value, including those which have become endangered due to significant degradation in their habitats. Currently, there are 89 national parks and 496 wildlife sanctuaries covering 1.83 million square kilometres in the major bio-geographic zones of India. In addition to widen the scope of conservation strategies, UNESCO proposed the creation of Biosphere Reserves in the early 1970s. These reserves were set up with the basic objective of conserving and developing a knowledge base about a particular biodiversity of a region, including the local communities which should be actively involved in conservation programmes. These cover about 21,067 square kilometres of Biosphere Reserves[2] since 1979, adding to these another seven are proposed, forming the major biogeographic zones of India.

The actual management of these reserves continues to be based on the convention-protected areas approach, with the Forest Department in Charge. The survey of the Indian Institute of Science in a survey of seven BRs noted that reconciliation of people-park conflict has to incorporate the local communities in the planning process. The international conference gave impetus to the growth of International Environmental Law and International Organizations like the International Union for Conservation of Nature (IUCN), International Biological Programme (IBP) and Man and the Biosphere Programme (MAB) argued for export-led policy inputs and 'good' science for various global environmental issues backed by massive technical and scientific capacities supported by bureaucracies for the future of development and economic growth. The growing pace of development anxieties and their global implications failed to bridge the gap between the 'First' and the 'Third' World over conflicting views and approaches to issues of environment and development. The Third World countries argued that the 'First World Environmentalism' ignored or downplayed the impacts brought on by the colonial exploitation and widespread poverty in former colonies. In recent years, however authoritarian solutions to the environmental crisis have been abandoned, but there is always an authoritarian edge somewhere in ecological politics which rests upon scientific-technical rationality that is science-led solutions within an administrative state armed with the strong regulatory bureaucratic process of political-economic decision-making.[3] In 1987 the World Commission For Environment and Development (Brundtland Commission) succeeded in building a conceptual bridge between the two discourses and offering the definition of 'Sustainable Development' that meets the needs of the present without compromising the ability of future generations to meet their own needs.

Sustainable Development

The Brundtland Report ended by suggesting that the United

Nations should organize 'an international conference to review progress and programmes that will be needed over time to set benchmarks and to maintain human progress within the guidelines of human needs and natural laws.[4] This resulted in a Global Convention in Rio de Janeiro to take part in the 'Earth Summit', which represented the boundless hope that humanity could come together to solve its mounting global ecological crisis with grave concerns and public awareness regarding the ozone layer, global warming, and the rising rate of species extinctions resulting from planetary destructions of ecosystems.[5] The main agenda of the summit was to launch sustainable development for the twenty-first century.

Sustainable development is essentially a policy and strategy for continued economic and social development which is not detrimental to the environment and natural resources on the quality of which continued activity and development depend. The notion of sustainable development takes different meanings in different contexts; it usually implies a growth in productive activities which does not result in the irreversible depletion of natural resources.

These agreements aim to gain the commitment of official state bodies to conserving tracts of land for wildlife and ecosystem conservation, reducing air pollution, and supporting allegedly sustainable forms of development. Besides international funding, such strategies receive favourable international media support and form part of an ideology of wise global resource management among many Western conservationists. The claim that wilderness prevention is equivalent to biodiversity is also an empirical claim that went unchallenged and was hailed as comprehensive rather than a sectoral approach to conservation of biological resources. There are different interpretations of sustainability like what is to be sustained? How long does it have to be sustained? At what level does sustainability operate? Can sustainability be measured? Is it an ecological concept or social one?[6] The problem with the vagueness and generality of this definition has increased, but sustainable development remains very much an operational phrase within the development literature.

The international agreements on sustainable development aim to evolve an integrated approach to solve environment-related conflicts at regional and global levels. In India the courts, in particular, the higher ones often cite these provisions while passing a verdict on certain environmental issues. The United Nations Conference on Environment and Development outlined 27 principles while agenda 21, consisted of 40 chapters. The conventions led to changes in the Indian context such as the National Biodiversity Act. The international agreements law making process is highly skewed during preparation of drafts as well as in the lobbying for their acceptance. The post-Rio Conference has witnessed a retreat by governments and commercial interests of private sectors from the areas that governed the conservation use and trade in environmental resources. But on the other side the different campaigns, organizations, tribunals and movements have focused on the adverse effects of environmental crises.[7]

Biodiversity Conservation

The major global problems discussed at Rio were deforestation, climate change and the loss of biodiversity. The Convention on Biological Diversity signed by the Indian government is the first treaty to deal with the entire range of life forms found on earth, including wild plants and animals, crops and livestock and micro-organisms. The significance of biodiversity conservation is viewed in three ways. Firstly, biodiversity provides enormous economic benefits in the form of food, medicine and industrial raw materials and has the potential for generating more. Secondly, it supplies an array of essential services to humanity such as clean air, modification of climatic extremes, degradation of wastes, recycling of nutrients, creating of soils, controlling of diseases, and regulation of hydrological cycles. Finally, the ethical and aesthetic values, that is plants and animals are independent of monetary valuations and are a source of irreplaceable wonder, spirituality and inspiration to humanity.[8] The economic argument of protection of biodiversity stems from different concepts of value attached as market values, ecosystem values, existence values, and intergenerational values.[9]

The "biodiversity conservation" movement argues that resources must be set aside and "protected" from the people.[10] Biological conservation must be based on science but scientific investigation is not the only output required for effective conservation and even when there is substantial information, prudent conservation policies are not assured. It can never be proven in a relatively short period of time that human-related activities have been the cause of species extinctions. The sustainable use approach of biological resources succeeds in raising local interest and involvement in conservation of widespread and non-charismatic forms of biological bio-diversity of human use. But a lack of any definition has resulted in multiple meanings suiting convenience.[11] Sustainable development with its universal appeal is also its weakness allowing it to be co-opted and redefined in ways that actually limit its goals and hence the societal change needed to achieve them. The concept has been popularized by international agencies and governments, NGOs and the corporate sector. The Earth Summit also resulted in international conventions on biodiversity, wetlands, and forestry and the negotiations underway on climate change.[12] The World Bank identified three factors for a new strategy. First, where the private sector should be actively involved in forestry, second where the state should restrict its intervention to social forestry and conservation, and third, where NGOs and voluntary agencies should be involved in promoting people's participation. The principle of reducing human dependence on natural resources, and winning their thrust and protection, through eco-development in buffer zones of protected areas incorporated in the National Wildlife Action Plan has since become the cornerstone of conservation action today.[13] The logic of eco development is to provide alternative means of livelihood to people through a variety of development initiatives, thereby reducing their dependence on resources outside protected areas.

The Biodiversity Diversity Act 2002 was enacted to achieve conservation and sustainable use of the country's biological sources. The contribution of local and indigenous communities to the conservation and sustainable utilization of biological resources through traditional knowledge, practices and innovation provides for equitable sharing of benefits with such people arising from the utilization of their knowledge, practices and innovations. Biodiversity is a multi-disciplinary subject involving diverse activities and actions which involves the central government, state governments, institutions of local self-governmental organizations, industry, etc. The Botanical Survey of India and the Zoological Survey of India carry out the surveys of floral and faunal resources in the country. The Forest Survey of India uses remote sensing technology to assess the forests and tree cover with a view to developing an accurate database for planning and monitoring. The reports are published at the district, state and national levels, besides considering animal species for planning suitable conservation measures.

Conservation Concerns

The environment question across the world has been steadily growing since the 1970s which now appears to be undergoing a dramatic reconsideration. Rachel Carson's *Silent Spring* showed the inter-connectedness between seemingly minute levels of pesticides which could become concentrated in food chains and thus pose a serious environmental problem. But apart from banning a few toxins, the chemical industry triumphed, seeing an expansion of the production of chemicals.[14] An extreme ecological stand was taken by the *Limits to Growth Study* produced by the Club of Rome. It predicted that unless technology changed its current course, the world was in danger and running out of its resources.

At the Stockholm Conference in 1972 Indira Gandhi posed the question "is not poverty and need the greatest polluter?" She went on to argue that "the inherent conflict is not between conservation and development" but "between environment and the environment and reckless exploitation of man and earth in the name of democracy". The reference made here is to the people who live in and around forests who could hardly be urged to save wildlife unless their conditions of living were improved.[15] She also stressed on ban tree-cutting in ecologically sensitive areas which was targeted against the contractors and commercialization. The close relationship she developed with a variety of wildlife enthusiasts like Kailash Sankahala and Salim Ali, for example gathered a huge support base among the middle class who took up the cause of wildlife in India and in the Western world were scientists were in the forefront of conservation. The conservation gained impetus as a class of ex-hunters turned conservationists from the erstwhile princely states joined the campaign along with representatives of international agencies, such as the World Wild Fund (WWF) and International Union for Conservation of Nature and Natural Resources (IUCN). This group of environmentalists successfully brought pressure on the government to create a network of national parks and sanctuaries all over India to protect endangered wildlife, overlooking the claims of local residents. This group of conservationist believed that without state intervention, deforestation and wildlife depletion would be accelerated, given the pressures on forests from local communities and also from industrial, commercial and development projects.

The Stockholm Conference resulted in the emergence of the Wildlife Act of 1972 which has led to the changing nature of forests as wildlife sanctuaries, national parks, conservation reserve, community reserve and tiger reserve.[16] The WPA does allow declaring "any area considered necessary" as a protected area without any rigorous process of justification. The WPA and its subsequent amendments require all legal and customary rights in national parks to be extinguished while severely restricting them in wildlife sanctuaries.[17] This act also prohibited hunting[18] of wild animals and birds scheduled in the Act and the areas led to declaring as national parks and wildlife sanctuaries, which are the dedicated habitat for wildlife and no activities, in these areas. The Project Tiger was established in 1973 with the objective to "ensure maintenance of a viable population of tigers in India for scientific, economic, aesthetic, cultural and ecological values to protect and increase tiger numbers in selected forest areas. The scheme has been implemented in the 17 states of India and Karnataka has been at the forefront of conservation of tigers in several protected areas of the state: Bandipur Tiger Reserve, Rajiv Gandhi (Nagarahole) Tiger Reserve, Bhadra Tiger Reserve and Anshi-Dandeli Tiger Reserve. The scheme has been providing assistance by the Government of India providing 50 per cent support for recurring items and 100 per cent support of non-recurring items. The emergence of the Wildlife Act of 1972 and Forest Conservation Act 1980 has led to the changing nature of forests as wildlife sanctuaries and national parks.

The effort has led to restoring a viable population of important animals such as tigers, elephants, lions, rhinoceros and of late Project Elephant launched in 1991-92 aims at ensuring long-term survival of identified viable populations and restoring their lost and degraded habitats and also aims to mitigate man-elephant conflicts. The other programmes like eco-development integrates the ecological and economic parameters for sustained conservation of ecosystems In order to complement *in situ* conservation, attention has been paid to *ex situ* conservation by establishing botanical gardens and animal parks. There are about 33 botanical gardens for conservation of plant diversity and several zoos and parks for *ex situ* preservation of wildlife. The conflict around protected areas has led to the physical displacement of people which has resulted in negative, social and economic impacts all over India. In this background we will analyse the conflict with reference to Kudremukh National Park in the Western Ghats of Karnataka.

Kudremukh National Park

1. The park derives its name from the highest hill peak "Kudremukha Peak" (1892 mts).
2. Area spreads over 600.57 sq km.
3. It falls in the middle of Central-Western Ghats (Part of Sahyadri Hill Ranges)
4. Home for Lion-Tailed Macaque (LTM,) Malabar civet cat, tiger, elephant.
5. Located in three districts: Udupi, Dakshina Kannada and Chikmagalur

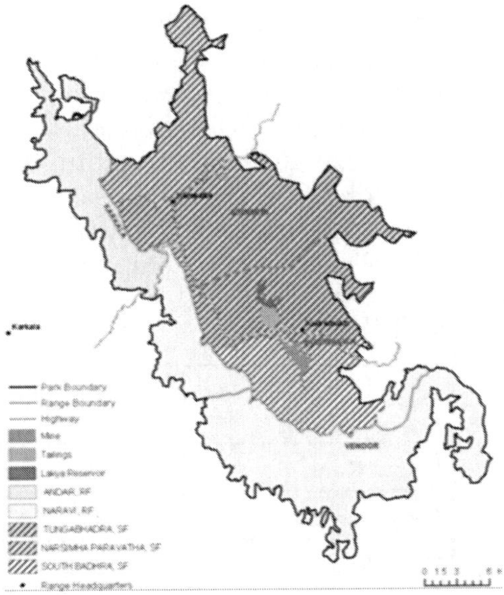

The Western Ghats was coming under severe pressure from private capital and inappropriate utilization for resources led to the Save Western Ghats March in 1987-88 along the 2500 kms involving around 150 voluntary organizations from the states of Kerala, Tamil Nadu, Karnataka, Goa and Maharashtra. This was an important event as the Kudremukh is one of the largest blocks of tropical wet evergreen forests in the Western Ghats. The Western Ghats, the natural resource pool of the country, play a crucial role in shaping the topography, climate pattern and the environment system of the nation besides living laboratories of biodiversity. The Western Ghats region occupies (53,950 square kilometres) in the second largest portion (27.67 per cent) of the Western Ghats and lies within the boundaries of Karnataka and Maharashtra (36.48 per cent). The total area of the Western Ghats in Karnataka measures about 44,300 square kilometres and has five national parks and 15 wildlife sanctuaries and a part of Nilgiri Biosphere. India qualifies as one of the top 13 biodiversity richest countries of the world, due to its high rate of endemism and biodiversity richness Western Ghats have also earned their status as one of the 18 biodiversity hotspots of the world.[19] The Western Ghats are a chain of forested hills that run from the north to the south of the west coast along the Arabian Sea. The Western Ghats rise to great heights in Anaimudi (2,695 metres) in Kerala, Kudremukh (2,071 metres) in Karnataka and Doddabetta in Tamil Nadu. In Kudremukh forests are incredibly beautiful because of the grasslands and shola forests, rolling hills, peaks, gushing rivers and streams. The shola forests signify the typical wet evergreen forest diminutive in physical stature but rich species.

National Parks in Karnataka

Place	*Location*	*Area Notified (sq kms.)*	*Year*
Anashi	Uttara Kannada	250.00	1987
Bandipur	Chamarajanagar	874.20	1974
Bannerghatta	Bangalore	104.27	1974
Kudremukh	Chikmagalur, Udupi and Mangalore	563.00	1987 and 2001
Nagarhole (Rajiv Gandhi)	Mysore and Kodagu	643.39	1983

Source: Kudremukh Wildlife Division

Protected Area in Karnataka

The Kudremukh National Park is administered and protected under the Karnataka Forest Act 1963, Karnataka Forest Rules 1969 and Wildlife Act 1972. The Deputy Conservator of Forests, Kudremukh Wildlife Division with headquarters at Karkala, administers the national park.[20] Kudremukh was initially notified as a national park when K. Ullas Karanth with support from the Government of Karnataka identified the lion-tailed macquae as an endangered species specific to the region.[21] The lion-tailed macques were used as a 'flagship' species to conserve the entire biotic conservation of wildlife population in the region. In 1987, the first notification brought the mining KIOCL area under the purview of the Wildlife (Protection) Act, 1972 which disallows any non-forestry operations, including mining, within a protected area.[22] The major policies with

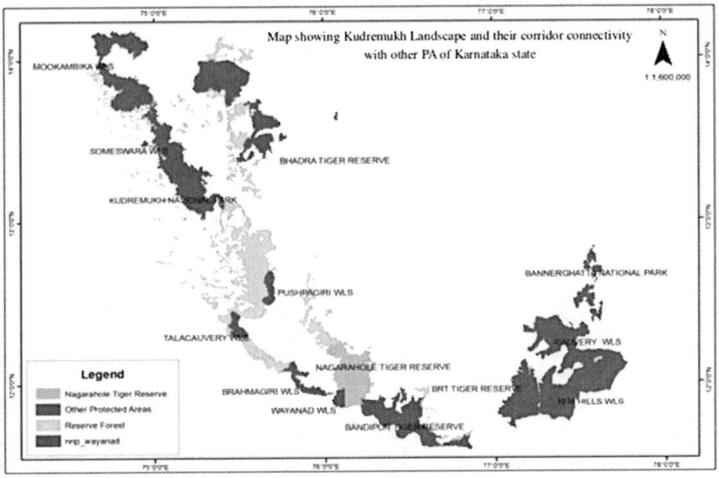

Source: Kudremukh Wildlife Division

regard to national parks can be traced to the British period where large chunks of forest were kept aside from the local people and were termed as Reserved or Protected Forests under the Indian Forest Act. The major policies on reserved forests were declared during the period 1914-16 with reference to KNP which included two reserved forests and three state forests, which were brought together to constitute the national park.[23]

Reserve Forests of Kudremukh National Park

S. No.	*Name of the District*	*Name of the Reserved Forest*	*Notification No. & Date*	*Extent (in acres)*	*Remarks*
1.	Udupi	Andar Reserved Forest	G.O.No.26 Rev., dated March 14, 1891	19,445.22	U/S 16 of Madras Forest Act
2.	Udupi & Dakshina Kannada	Naravi Reserved Forest	G.O.No.96 Rev., dated February 28, 1900	58,954.85	

3.	Chikm-agalur	South Bhadra State Forest	R.1777-80-FT-87-13-14, dated August 29, 1914	20,914.78	U/S 17 of Mysore Forest Regul-ation
4.	Chikm-agalur	Tunga Bhadra State Forest	G.O. No. R.296-9-FR.96-15-6, dated July 07, 1916	49,838.60	
5.	Chikm-agalur	Narasimha-parvatha State Forest	R-8426-29-FR-94-15, dated March 01, 1916	16,745.00	
		Total		1,65,898.45	

Source: No. C3/CR/30/KNP/99-2000 Office of the Deputy Conservator of Forests, Kudremukh Wildlife Division, Karkala.

Reserved Forests Constituting National Park

S. No.	Name of District	Name of the Reserve Forest	Extent (in acres)
1.	Udupi	Andar	19,445.22
2.	Udupi & Dakshina Kannada	Naravi	58,594.85
3.	Chikmagalur	South Bhadra	20,914.78
4.	Chikmagalur	Tunga Bhadra	49,838.60
5.	Chikmagalur	Narasimha-aprvatha	16,745.00
	Total 1,65,538.45 or 600.57 sq km		

The Kudremukh National Park is administered and protected under the Karnataka Forest Act 1963, Karnataka Forest Rules 1969 and Wildlife Act 1972. The Deputy Conservator of Forests, Kudremukh Wildlife Division with headquarters at Karkala, administers the national park. The top down approaches to forest management which depended on maximizing timber production and revenue from these and other forests have been subject to increasing criticisms. The Deputy Conservator of Forests, Kudremukh Wildlife Division with headquarters at

Karkala, administers the national park. There are four ranges located at Belthangadi, Karkala, Kerekatte and Kudremukh. There are two sub-divisions one at Kudremukh and one at Kundapur. All these offices are newly created and the executive staff is drawn from the respective territorial divisions, which contribute to the area of the national park. The state forest, which forms a part of the national park, is quite big in size. In total, there are 86 compartments-20 each in Karkala and Belthangadi, 21 in Kudremukh Wildlife Range and 35 in Kerekatte Wildlife Range.

The Kudremukh National Park is spread over an area of 563 square kilometres and falls in three districts namely, Dakshina Kannada district (158 square kilometres), Udupi district (89 square kilometres) and Chikmagalur district (316 square kilometres).[24] It falls approximately in the middle of mid-Western Ghats (the stretch between Goa and Nilgiris).[25] The World Conservation Union (IUCN) sets international benchmark standards for protected area management. In the IUCN classification, there are eight categories of protected areas, ranging from strict Natural Reserve (Category I) to multiple uses Management Area (Category VIII). By its very nature, it holds a number of endemic floral and faunal species. The highly endangered species such as the Flying Lizard (*Draco dussumieri*), Flying Snake (*Chrysopelea ornata*), King Cobra (*Ophiophagus hannah*), Shield Tail Snakes (*Uropeltidae spp.*), Travancore Tortoise (*Indotestudo forsteni*), Forest Cane Turtle (*Geoemyda silvatic*) and several endemic frogs. Forty-three species of fishes are found in the rivers and streams of Kudremukh National Park.

The Western Ghats are rich in biodiversity and are recognized as one of the 18 mega-biodiversity centres of the world.[26] The biodiversity conservation emphasis on beyond the conservation area has also questioned the over emphasis on tigers to the exclusion of other species, habitats and ecosystem processes. The other concern is related to the conservation ideology; targets and method are not clearly defined and understood in so many different ways, because there is no single overarching agreement on what constitutes effective conservation.[27] There is no unanimity with regard to conservation as biologists have emphasized the wildlife and argued for the distance between people and wildlife. Social activists argue that people are part of the problem and they should be involved in conservation through community conservation programmes. Some of the conservationists have also argued for relocation of people for better conservation.

The local communities in wildlife–rich areas are seen as enemies of the conservationist cause and are physically displaced or denied access to these areas. The approach is therefore not only anti-human; but is also shortsighted from the wildlife conservation point of view. The wilderness designation, to the exclusion of humans is an expression of the cultural and economic imperialism of the rich countries. The people of poor countries cannot afford the luxury of a "museumized nature", nor does such an imposition usefully serve the long-term interests of either humans or non-humans. The idea of wilderness[28] is to erase the very history it seeks to deny and represents a false hope of an escape from the responsibility in which our past and return to the dream of a natural landscape that supposedly existed before. The conservation ideologies based on a higher cause overlooks the problematic consequences of its policies because it is a good cause undertaken for posterity on behalf of nature, wherein people do not expect any ill effects. Wilderness has served as an important vehicle for articulating deep moral values regarding our obligations and responsibilities to the non-human world.[29] In the larger process the wider human dimensions of wildlife conservation sideline the rights of the local people in and around the national park.

Settlement Process

The final notification of the Kudremukh National Park was issued in 2001 when the assistant commissioners under the Wildlife Protection Act initiated the 'settlement processes'. The process of settlement involves conducting an inquiry into the rights (habitations, agriculture, use of forest resources, etc.) exercised by people in the given area and extinguishing these rights after compensation offered. Since the last 10-15 years, the government has promised the tribals that their areas will be regularized in their favour but that promise has not been fulfilled so far. The tribals have questioned the Forest Department regarding the formation of National parks as in 1997 the Mangalore District Forest Officer sent a notice, which was supposed to be given to the people who had *pattas* (legal land holders). However only a few people got the notice apart from KIOCL and the survey numbers, notified as KNP.[30]

The local inhabitants interpreted this as a process of land acquisition for the national park intending complete evacuation of dwellers from the park area. The issue also got interconnected with the agitation against KIOCL mining, and gradually picked up momentum. The national park was reduced to 563.29 square kilometres from the original 600.32 square kilometres, which does not include any of the revenue villages, *patta* lands, revenue lands, *gomal* lands and such other areas, which do not form any part of the above mentioned state forests and reserve forests. Notices were issued to each resident within the limits of the national park calling for a list of their assets and claims. The Government of Karnataka handed over the park according to the map as there was no proper survey conducted to locate the habitation of tribals and hence their areas were left out of the park.[31] The legal lands holding at the time of notification of Reserved Forest were treated as enclosures.[32] These enclosures were located within the overall area of national park, which were not notified for the purpose of the national park. This affected the tribals,[33] namely Gowdlu, Malekudiya and Marathi Naiks traditionally living in the purview of Kudremukh National Park. Together they consist of 90 hamlets belonging to 40 revenue villages, with 1299 families, who did not possess *patta*[34] (land rights certificate) and hence were labelled as encroachers.[35] The rights of the local communities were neither recognized nor recorded and hence with the creation of Kudremukh National Park the tribal communities fear displacement from their homeland.[36]

KNP in Karnataka covers about 61,000 hectares spread over three districts—Dakishna Kannada (Belthangadi), Udupi (Karkala) and Chikmagalur (Mudigere, Koppa and Sringeri). The legal land holding at the time of notification of the Reserve Forest was treated as enclosures. There was discrimination and arbitrariness in relation to the land and some of them were excluded in the process. The alienation of communities is an important factor and the focus on tiger conservation in national parks and sanctuaries have been on paper but in reality there are many pressures, which the state and Forest Department are not able to manage. The communities around or inside the park are constantly fighting a battle with the state enforcement. The idea of 'pristine myth' of untouched nature has shown how the establishment of these conservation areas such as community conservation areas, watershed-based projects and the management of buffer zones of biosphere reserves in the daily lives of the people who live in and around the park have often been contested due to disputes over the location, coverage and management of these territories. This has often resulted in the forced relocation of the economically poor and socially disadvantaged and the conservationists have been criticized for their elitist approach to conservation.

Alienation of Tribal Population

In Karnataka the tribal population constitutes 6.95 per cent of the total population of the state. Currently there are 50 Scheduled Tribes in Karnataka notified according to the Constitution (Scheduled Tribes) Order (Amendment) Act 2003. The most notable tribal population comprises some of the best known tribes like the Soligas, Yeravas, Todas, and Sisshis. The tribes such as the Gowdlus, Malekudiyas and Marathi Naiks traditionally live in the interior forest area of Kudremukh and are not primitive people. The tribal economy has been traditionally centred on land and resources of the forest and even today land constitutes an important source of livelihood for the majority of the tribal population. The Malekudiyas speak Tulu which is a dialect spoken by all communities in the region of Dakishna Kannada. The Marathi Naiks and Gowdlu speak Kannada in the Chikmagalur district. Kudremukh National Park consists of 90 hamlets belonging to 40 revenue villages, with 1,299 families staying within the purview of the national park.

Village-wise Details of People Residing inside Kudremukh National Park

Abstract of the Kudremukh National Park					
S. No.	*Name of the District*	*Total No. of Villages*	*No. of House-holds*	*No. of People*	*No. of Cattle*
1	Chikmagalur	16	243	1,150	847
2	Udupi	6	294	1,611	1,576
3	Dakishna Kannada	10	762	3,407	4,508
			1,299	6,168	6,931

Source: Kudremukh Wildlife Division, Karkala, Dakshina Kannada.

Abstract of the Kudremukh National Park				
S. No.	*Name of the Village*	*No. of Households*	*No. of People*	*No. of Cattle*
1.	Samse	328	1,579	2,031
2.	Malavanthige	3	6	-
3.	Kere	91	374	603
4.	Muduba	53	286	275
5.	Gulganjimane	33	172	229
6.	Balekadi	43	233	431
7.	Budabishoppa	5	14	39
8.	Thalavanthikodige	1	5	7
9.	Tharolikodige	15	61	59
10.	Kitlamanekodige	9	-	-
11.	Hadi	33	74	194
12.	Malnad	35	31	106

13.	Shirlu	40	211	251
14.	Balegere	49	259	133
15.	Hadikerur	19	88	142
16.	Matholi Estate	5	14	8
	Total	762	3,407	4,508

Source: Kudremukh Wildlife Division, Karkala, Dakshina Kannada

Udupi District				
S. No	*Name of the Village*	*No. of Households*	*No. of People*	*No. of Cattle*
1.	Andar	157	653	537
2.	Kabbinale	44	201	118
3.	Mala	4	25	23
4.	Idu	1	5	-
5.	Nuralbettu	35	255	156
6.	Kervase	2	11	13
	Total	243	1,150	847

Source: Kudremukh Wildlife Division, Karkala Dakshina Kannada

Dakshina Kannada District				
S. No.	*Name of the Village*	*No. of Households*	*No. of People*	*No. of Cattle*
1.	Sulkerimogru	25	137	95
2.	Navar	9	55	20
3.	Shirlala	10	61	54
4.	Kuthloor	45	260	105
5.	Naravi	6	43	26
6.	Navur	27	158	88

7.	Nada	3	18	5
8.	Laila	1	4	3
9.	Savanalu	7	48	63
10.	Malvanthige	161	827	1,117
	Total	294	1,611	1,576

Source: Kudremukh Wildlife Division, Karkala, Dakshina Kannada

The issue of relocation and rehabilitation has acquired centre stage in the context of biodiversity conservation crisis in nature conservation of India. Biologists have identified several proximate causes for the tiger's dramatic decline; loss of habitat, conflicting land-use, over hunting of the tigers prey species by people, and killing of tigers to protect livestock or to meet commercial demand of their body parts. The human settlements inside the forests with agricultural fields has fragmented the habitat for wildlife, especially for large fauna such as tigers, hornbills, and lion-tailed macaques that require habitat vast stretches of undistributed forests for their survival in terms of dietary habits and home ranges. The high rate of human population growth has resulted in small landowners who are unable to make a satisfactory living on small fragments of agricultural land (less than two hectares) into encroaching nearby forest or common lands. As their families grow, this leads to expansion of land through illegal forest clearance whereby encroachment becomes the most serious threats to the integrity of the reserve forest.[37] The other issue in conservation considerations is not dependent on ecological considerations, but on rural politics on the basis of which people have demanded facilities like hospitals, schools, roads, communication and bridges.[38] The increased access of the human population in these forest areas will facilitate more land, and market-driven exploitation of forests and wildlife products. In India the focus of private capital into natural resources management began first through the social forestry projects. The Act was uncertain about the status of land under shifting cultivation in Odisha, Andhra Pradesh, Madhya Pradesh and North Eastern states, where no compensatory mechanisms were settled. Even the state governments worked out no compensatory mechanisms if they were to be settled elsewhere. The environmental safeguards have been frequently violated due to the opposition from industrialists and politicians who argue that when all the regulations are being removed, and the economy is witnessing a fast growth why impose environmental regulations?

Relocation

The magnitude of displacement due to development projects has increased manifold. According to studies, as many as sixty million people have been displaced and affected due to various development projects in the country from 1947 to 2000. The beneficiaries of development and the victims of displacement have not changed over the years. Development induced displacement is inevitable as development would usher in economic growth, equity and prosperity. The number of displaced people in India has been estimated at between 10-40 million people affecting their livelihood, heritage and identity. The involuntary displacement of people owing to acquisition of their land for developmental activities across India is a major issue. The movements towards displacement raised the issue of unequal distributions of costs and benefits, Adivasis and forest people brought in the issue of marginalization and alienation of land from their traditional sources. The social movements have tended to concentrate on issue-based coherence rather than comprehensive political cohesiveness. The formation of the National Alliance of People's Movement (NAPM) in 1992, claims that they are a collection of 'like-minded groups and movements' which retain their 'autonomous identities'. The limitations of these formation is the multi-class alliance as in the case of Narmada Bachao Andalon whereas the alliance of rich farmers, Adivasis or tribals suggest that the social and class alliance may only hold for the issue and the basic class antagonisms remain and prevent attempts at expanding the movement into different realms of struggle.[39]

The wildlife protection through giving incentives to relocate human population to less ecologically sensitive areas is seen as a magic solution which benefits both human and wildlife and a new paradigm of site-specific, incentive driven through participatory voluntary settlement.[40] In 2004 the Karnataka government presented the rehabilitation plan for voluntary resettlement of 201 families, inside the national park, where infrastructure development was not possible and hence they needed to be relocated in the first place. The rehabilitation plan was sent to the Planning Commission in 2006. The Commission gave recommendations along the lines of the Tigers Task Force appointed by the Prime Minister Manmohan Singh to look into the tiger crisis in the country and to prepare a tiger conservation plan. The conservation induced displacement has led to vulnerability over their natural environment. The Tiger Task Force (TTF) estimates that there are 1,500 villages within the 28 tiger reserves and roughly 65,000 families (around 3,25,000 people) have to be resettled to create people free core areas in these reserves. The Tiger Task Force recommends minimizing conservation induced displacement or treating it as a last resort for protecting habitats and species due to the poor record of the government in effective relocation. It emphasized community conservation, but one of its members Valmik Thapar has argued that tigers and humans simply cannot coexist.The final notification of the national park was issued only in June 2001, relocation needs huge resources, and net outcome will be social and cultural displacement of the people. The Forest Department asserts that relocation is not the solution for Kudremukh National Park, as people have been residing for centuries and reserve forests are about a hundred years old. Relocation needs huge resources and net outcome will be social and cultural displacement of the people.

Budget Expenditure of Relocation

Total Cost	Rs. 147.95 crores
	Rs. 122.33 crores for land acquisition
	Rs. 25.62 crores for rehabilitation
Total villages	32

Families	1,299 (6168 persons)
Total Land Enclosure within KNP	1,129 hectares

Phase–I	
Families	201 (671 persons)
Cost	Rs. 18.35 crores
Ex-gratia	Rs. 4.81 crores
Acquisition	Rs. 16.86 crores
Rehabilitation	Rs. 5.45 crores

Source: Karnataka Forest Department.

The conservation induced displacements affects the tribal groups although there have been several cases of non-tribal relocations such as the Corbett Tiger Reserve, and Bhadra Tiger Reserve which were successful models for relocation.[42]

The Government of Karnataka initiated the relocation of villages from Bhadra to improve the conservation potential and to reduce the human-wildlife conflicts. The Bhadra land acquisition, resettlement and rehabilitation project relocated 413 families from 10 villages. The rehabilitation package included a house, transportation allowance of Rs. 5,000 and a range of civic amenities such as roads, drains, sanitation, drinking water, electricity, school, post office, hospital, playground, shopping complex and place of worship. The Forest Department with the help of NGOs was able to coordinate relocate packages, but the major worry with relocation was the lack of adequate provision of technical and financial inputs required for successful creation of agricultural land outside the national park. The lack of administrative transparency by the Forest Department with local participation or expert involvement as well as inadequate financial commitments has led to a crisis of forest management.

The collaboration of the District Conservators of Forests (DCFs) in their individual capacities with scientists, conservationists and local people has been rare in the Indian context. The DCF Anita Arekal raided the Kudremukh Wildlife Division (NGO) office which had been aiding rehabilitation of communities living within the park. The DCF also filed cases against environment activists Ullas Karanth and Niren Jain for trespassing into the national park, interrogating their sources of funding, registration details, and permission sought to conduct surveys. The matter was taken up by the CEC which held that the raid was not justified and asked the state government to take disciplinary action against Anita Arekal's actions as "illegal and without justifications". The gains of collaboration can be learned from Nepal where independent scientists engaged in active dialogue on a range of issues with government officials, NGOs and villagers living on the fringes of the national parks. There is a strong demand for self-rule which is opposed to a uniform administrative structure across India which would enable tribes to evolve politically autonomous units. The scheduled areas are those specified by the President on the recommendation of the Governor of a state or union territory. It is presumed that the schedule areas would be those inhabited mainly by members of the Schedule Tribes. The 5th schedule provides for tribal advisory council with 3/4th representation from ST groups and the 6th schedule provides for district autonomous units for North Eastern states. The list of schedule areas is amended from time to time but states like Tamil Nadu, Kerala, and Karnataka are not included as scheduled areas.[44]

Tribals and Autonomy

The articulation of Dalits has been through the question of representation while the Adivasis' articulation of democracy has been through the question of autonomy. The tribal groups in Jharkhand have demanded autonomy which has taken the form of separate statehood, in the North East; autonomy has taken the form of tribal secession, in Chhattisgarh as it is about economic autonomy. The tribal autonomy is being constructed upon a strong notion of the self and is predicated upon a similar imagined construction of the other, the latter defining the existence of the former. The forest was a private space like Devara Kadu/Sacred Forests are forests set apart for some object of worship and are still managed and used by the local committees, through temple committees in the Western Ghats. The Department of Tribal Welfare was formed significantly to address the needs of Scheduled Tribes in Karnataka. The concept of the Tribal Sub-Plan and its counterpart the Special Component plan emerged in the National Fifth Five Year Plan. The objectives of the Tribal Sub-Plan are poverty alleviation including programmes in agriculture, animal husbandry, sericulture, horticulture, village and small industries as well as all-employment generating schemes such as Swarna Jayanthi Swarozgar Yojana. The active role of B.D. Sharma has been raising issues concerning tribals and formed the Bharat Jan Andolan to influence the government to set up a committee to look into tribal issues. Subsequently a committee under Dilip Singh Bhuria was set up to extend the provisions of Part IX of the Constitution concerning panchayats in the scheduled areas. The recommendations of the committee were incorporated in a constitution amendment which was known as the Panchayat Extension to the Scheduled Areas 1996 (PESA).[45] The constitutional provisions have enacted a number of acts in order to uphold tribal rights from land tenancy acts and revenue codes to the Panchayat (Extension to the Schedule Areas) Act of 1996, which have not been implemented in Karnataka. According to PESA, gram sabhas are empowered to preserve their cultural identity, community resources, modes of dispute resolution, and equally important the right to approve government plans, programmes and projects within their jurisdiction.[46] The PESA has remained largely unimplemented, as land and decentralization are state subjects. The failure of the Karnataka State, have been reluctant to uphold legislation such as PESA and the Forest Rights Act that could discourage such investment for corporates.[47] The most noteworthy feature of PESA is that it empowers gram sabhas at the hamlet (or groups of hamlet level as opposed to the level of the unwieldy gram panchayats. This was done so as to safeguard and preserve the traditions of tribal people, to protect land alienation within scheduled areas to control and give consent to local development plans and to consult in matters of land acquisition and rehabilitation.

The overall picture is of protective legislation, with toothless bodies which have largely failed to protect the tribals. The interface of tribal areas and Maoism has been fighting the state with the ultimate goal of capturing state power, but in actuality Maoism promises quite something else—namely, creating zones of functional autonomy for tribals by keeping the state and its institutions at bay within a state. In states like Odisha, Chhattisgarh and Jharkhand the Naxalite movement also gained ground due to protests against discrimination over non-timber forest produce (NTFP) and land rights. This has led to stringent forest officials who deny tribals access to forest dwellers without any livelihood sources. The tribals acknowledge that, though many do not agree with their working through violence, attacks on security forces and locals, but have brought the tribal issues into the forefront of government discussions which were taken for granted. The centralized bureaucracy driven visions of conservation and development has failed and in its place PESA and FRA offer an open system of decision-making, transparency and accountability as no other system with space to raise and address all concerns.

Forest Governance

The shift in the National Forest Policy recognized the need to decentralize control over 'nature resources' and involve NGOs in the process of protecting forest lands through Joint Forest Management in which local resource users would be involved in collaboration with the Forest Department. Under JFM, communities were encouraged to regenerate degraded forest lands with the promise of a share of the resulting produce (primarily timber). Many communities prefer to harvest non-timber forest produce, and the rigidity of the rules (which require only the benefits of timber to be shared) hampers people's participation. The state governments still control every aspect of JFM insisting that they have the power to dissolve village communities.[48]

The shift in the forest management to forest governance can be seen with the Forest Rights Act, 2006 which recognizes and vests forest rights of Scheduled Tribes and Other Traditional Forest Dwellers / Communities whose rights could be recorded earlier. The focus shifts from single agency to local citizens, the judiciary, civil society groups, and also multiple layers of government. The major emphasis of forest governance is to identify and implement institutional arrangements and processes that will transparently and fairly balance between these conflicting objectives. The framing and implementing Forest Policy has always been a political process, but also has led to a simplistic vision with regard to 'community' between Non Government Organizations (NGO) approaches. It fails to address the question of inter and intra-community equity as well as by social movements fighting for forest rights has contributed to marginalization of a section within the local community.[49] The hindrances in the forest governance stem from the Forest Department which was set up as the owner, manager, police and policymaker. The development lobby is also against the power given to local communities over forests because it would come in the way of diverting forest land for diverting mining, hydropower projects, etc.[50] The Forest Department also asserts that the propaganda regarding relocation schemes, sudden abolition of traditional forest rights, and severe shortage of trained staff, infrastructure and equipment in the wildlife division due to which it was not possible to completely interact with the people in all the enclosures and convince them about the view of the government.

Conclusion

The tribals feel that the large contradiction of land is not by the people who owe an acre or two but by the big coffee estates with thousands of acres where the government is very silent and have a strong influence on them.[51] The tribals are caught in a difficult situation of neither being able to pursue their traditional lifestyle because of the restrictions imposed by wildlife law on the one hand and on the other hand avail compensation and seek a resettlement package. The land question has once again emerged in rural India and especially among the tribal population of India because it ensures a sense of ownership of land and a sense of psychological security for the tribal population. In the recent development there is a demand by the central government to name KNP as a tiger reserve. With the KNP becoming a tiger reserve, the centre will provide funds to the state under the Project Tiger for relocating families in the vicinity. The state government is against the declaration of the KNP as a tiger reserve and heritage tag accorded to the Western Ghats, because it would affect the tribal communities owing to the pressure from vested interests like forest encroachers, mining, timber, smugglers and poachers.[52]

The conservation impact of human populations has led to the case of preservation via relocation of tribals around Kudremukh National Park which has been built on the hypothesis that humans and wildlife cannot coexist. Therefore if natural areas have to be safeguarded, people have to be relocated outside the forest area. The tribals and local inhabitants living in and around forest areas have been demanding regularization of their land which has been overlooked for a long time. Conservation efforts are solely achieved through building trust and respect with all parties concerned. The confidence building is a crucial part of that trust-building process; the people living near our protected forests are not in dialogue with the officials. The impression that the Forest Department is bent on evicting the tribals has led to a complex of fear and distrust among the tribal population who are alienated from their land and livelihood are being influenced by the Maoist ideology.[52]

References

1. Amita Baviskar (1997): 'Ecology and Development in India: A Field and its Future', *Sociological Bulletin*, 46, 2, September, p. 196.
2. The Seven Biosphere Reserves are Nokrek (Megahalaya), Nilgiri (Tamil Nadu, Karnataka, and Kerala), Nandadevi (Uttar Pradesh), Great Nicobar (Andaman and Nicobar Islands), Gulf of Munnar (Tamil Nadu), Manas (Assam) and Sundarbans (West Bengal).

3. David Harvey (1993): 'The Nature of Environment: Dialectics of Social and Environmental Change', *Socialist Register*, p. 21.
4. Gilbert Rist (1997): *The History of Development: From Western Origins to Global Faith*, Zed Books, London, p. 188.
5. John Bellamy Foster (2007): 'The Ecology of Destruction', *Analytical Monthly Review*, February, Vol. 4, No. 11, pp. 1-13.
6. Dunu Roy (2003): 'Emerging Paradigms in Environmental Conservation and Management', *Social Change*, June-September, Vol. 33, No. 2&3, pp. 2-3.
7. Prakash Sinha (2000): 'International Obligations', New Delhi, *Seminar*, 492, pp. 51-56.
8. L.K. Arun, B. Jayashankar, Kurian Mathew Abraham (2001): 'Biodiversity Conservation and Livelihood of Tribesfolk: A Case Study of Periyar Tiger Reserve', Discussion Paper No. 37, Centre for Development Studies, pp. 5-8.
9. Rajeev Dhavan (2000): The Wealth of Nations Revisited, *Seminar*, No. 492, p. 19.
10. T.P. Sreedharan, (2004): 'Biodiversity of Kerala: A Survey of Kalliasseri Panchayat, Kannur District', Discussion Paper No. 62, Kerala Research Programme on Local Level Development, Thiruvanthapuram, p. 11.
11. M.D. Madhusudan, and Shankar Raman, T.R. (2003): "Conservation as if Biological Diversity Matters: Preservation versus Sustainable Use in India", *Conservation and Society*, 1, New Delhi, Sage Publications, pp. 49-57.
12. This was followed by the creation of the United Nations Centre for Sustainable Development goals by the World Bank resulting in the World Summit on Sustainable Development in Johannesburg in 2002. The focus of the summit brought back the issue of poverty alleviation, resulting in the Millennium Development Goals (MDGs) taking centre stage. The Sustainable Development Goals is back in focus as it is set to replace or complement the MDGs that expired in 2015.
13. Ashish Kothari, Solani Suri, and Neena Singh (1995): 'Conservation in India: A New Direction', *Economic and Political Weekly*, October 28, p. 2761.
14. J. Bellamy Foster and Brett Clark (2008): "Rachel Carson's Ecological Critique", *Analytical Monthly Review*, Vol. 5, No. 11, pp. 1-5.

15. Mahesh Rangarajan (1996): 'The Politics of Ecology: The Debate of Wildlife and People in India', *Economic and Political Weekly*, Special Number, September, pp. 2391-2409.
16. The conservation of forests, grasslands, and wetlands, in India which have become national parks and sanctuaries after independence were also the old hunting grounds of Indian princes, which were developed under the British colonial rule. Hunting was also an important pastime and the integral life of the princely states and wild animals like tigers, lions, and leopards were not protected and their hunting was a valued sport. See Divyabhanusinh (1998): 'A Princely Bequest', *Seminar* 466, June, p. 42.
17. Vasant Saberwal, Mahesh Rangarajan and Ashish Kothari (2001): *People, Parks and Wildlife: Towards Coexistence*, Orient Longman.
18. Divyabhanusinh (1998): "A Princely Bequest", *Seminar* 466, June, p. 42.
19. S.G. Neginhal (2011): *Forest Trees of the Western Ghats (includes Eastern Ghats and Deccan Plateau*, Bangalore, p. 12.
20. This division was brought into being in G.O. No. AHFF.83. FNG-92 dated May 2, 1992.
21. With regard to declaring an area as a national park, Section 35 of the Wildlife Protection Act, 1972 provides "whenever it appears to the state government that an area, whether within a sanctuary or not, is by reason of its ecological, faunal, geo-morphological or zoological association or importance, needed to be constituted as a national park for the purpose of protecting, propagating or developing wildlife therein or its environment, it may be notification, declare its intention to constitute such area as a national park".
22. Valmik Thapar (2003): *Battling for Survival: India's Wilderness Over Two Centuries* (ed), Oxford University Press, p. 244.
23. G.O. No. AHFF.42.fwG.87, dated September 2, 1987.
24. In 1997, Dakishna Kannada district was divided into Mangalore and Udupi districts and Mysore district was divided into Mysore and Chamarajanagar districts.
25. The Western Ghats comprise a total area of 160,000 sq kms containing two biosphere reserves, eight national parks and 39 wildlife sanctuaries in six states: Gujarat, Maharashtra, Goa, Karnataka, Tamil Nadu and Kerala. This region is broadly grouped as northern (covering Surat in Gujarat to Goa, Central

(Goa to Niligiri mountains in Tamil Nadu and Southern Western Ghats (south of Palghat).The Kudremukh National Park comes under the Global Tiger Conservation Priority-I, under the format developed jointly by the Wildlife Conservation Society (WCS) and World Wide Fund-USA.

26. Anja Nygren (2000): 'Environmental Narratives on Protection and Production: Nature-based Conflicts in Rio San Juan, Nicaragua', *Development and Change*, Vol. 31, p. 809.
27. M.D. Madhusudan and Rohan Arthur (2007): Succeeding Poorly or Failing Better? *Seminar*, No. 577, pp. 74-78.
28. The influence of 'deep ecology' appeals to the notion of 'human essence' or human potentiality from which humanity has become fundamentally alienated from nature. The defence to restore the lost connection by modern technology, commodity production, the utilitarian approach to nature, appeals to the root of an intuitive, contemplative phenomenological search for 'self-realization'.
29. Ashish Kothari (1997): *Understanding Biodiversity: Life, Sustainability and Equity*, Orient Longman, p. 36.
30. Interview with group of villagers in Adikesu, Sringeri Taluk, Chikmagalur on November 15, 2006.
31. D.C. Srikantappa (2001): 'Letter Written to Shri Atal Behari Vajpayee, Former Prime Minister of India', April 25.
32. The major policies on reserved forests were declared during the period 1914-16 with reference to KNP which included two Reserved Forests and three State Forests, which were brought together to constitute the national park. The Indian Forest Act of 1927 set aside forests for different purposes and gave them an administrative designation indicating their purpose. Many forest areas that were declared "reserve forest" under IFA have received additional protection and have been named as a sanctuary or national park under the Wildlife Protection Act of 1972 in recognition of their values as critical habitat for wildlife.
33. According to the 2001 census, there are 34.6 lakh tribes in the state, constituting 6.6 per cent of the total tribal population. The tribal population is concentrated in the 5 districts of the state: Bellary, Bidar, Chitradurga, Mysore and Raichur. The Malekudiyas speak Tulu which is a dialect spoken by all communities in the region of Dakishna Kannada. The Marathi Naiks and Gowdlu speak Kannada in the Chikmagalur district.
34. Earlier the lands were administered by village elders and there

was no concept of 'exclusive title or possession', within the community, but it was based on mutual respect and recognition to an individual family. See Prabhu, Pradip (2002): 'Land Alienation, Land Reforms and Tribals in Maharashtra', in *Land Reforms in India: Issues of Equity in Madhya Pradesh*, Vol. VII, (ed) Praveen K. Jha, New Delhi, Sage Publications, p. 249.

35. The Government of Assam and Maharashtra obeying the Supreme Court began an eviction drive, whereas the Assam's forest department used elephants to raze huts and homesteads on land recorded as forest. In certain areas however they could be treated as encroachers on forest land owing to "faulty settlement" by state governments. See Akhileshwar, Pathak (1994): "State, Environment and Law", *Economic and Political Weekly*, December 10, pp. 3138-41.
36. Sharachchandra Lele (2011): Rethinking Forest Governance: Towards a Perspective Beyond JFM, the Godavarman and FRA, *The Hindu Survey of the Environment*, pp.95-103.
37. Interview with B.P. Ravi, Koppa Divisional Forest Officer, August 18, 2007, Chikmagalur.
37. Ullas Karanth and Praveen Bhargava (2005): "De-fragmenting Nature", *Seminar* 552, August, pp. 59-62.
39. Rohan D'Souza (2003): 'Environmental Discourses and Environmental Politics' in *The Value of Nature: Ecological Politics in India* (ed) by Smitu Kothari, Imtiaz Ahmad, Helmut Reifeld, Rainbow Publishers, pp. 23-38.
40. Interview with Praveen Bhargava, a Conservationist on December 5, 2006, Bangalore.
41. Asmita Kabra (2013): Conservation-Induced Displacement: The Anatomy of a Win-Win Solution, *Social Change*, 43(4), pp. 533-550.
42. Tiger Task Force (2005): Joining the Dots, Ministry of Environment and Forests, Government of India, New Delhi.
43. Mahesh Rangarajan and Ghazala Shahabuddin (2006): "Displacement and Relocation from Protected Areas: Towards a Biological and Historical Synthesis", *Conservation and Society*, Vol. 4, No. 3, pp. 359-378.
44. Sharad Kulkarni (2000): 'The Plight of the Tribal', *Seminar* No. 492, pp. 37-41.
45. Digvijaya Singh (2005): 'The Real Issues', *Seminar*, 552, Special Issue on Forests and Tribals, New Delhi, pp.20-22.

46. Archana Prasad (2006): "Conservation and Tribal Development in the Forest Rights Bill", *Social Scientist*, Vol. 34, Nos. 7&8, pp. 4-19.
47. Ajith Menon (2007): 'Engaging with the Law on Adivasi Rights', *Economic and Political Weekly*, Vol. XLII, No. 24, June 16-22, pp. 2239-42.
48. In states like West Bengal the share in the final harvest of sal has not been transferred to the forest protection committees. The issue of rights transfer has not translated to real incomes.
49. Sharachchandra Lele and Ajit Menon (2014): Introduction: Forest Governance Beyond Joint Forest Management, Godavarman and Tigers, in *Democratizing Forest Governance in India* (ed), Oxford University Press, pp. 9-11.
50. Sharachchandra Lele (2012): 'Colonial Hangover Persists', *Down to Earth*, June 30.
51. Interview with V.S. Sridhar, KVR Activist on December 7, 2006, Bangalore.
52. 'Naxalites' or 'Maoism' is identified with leftist groups in parts of eastern and central India which have been waging armed struggles for land rights.

6

Naxalite Movement, Democracy and Development

Introduction

The uneven development across the region like the old Hyderabad tended to have lower living standards and infrastructure than the rest of Karnataka causing a high degree of regional imbalance in the state.[1] Inter-regional disparities on many measures of development are substantial. The southern regions of Karnataka consisting of the old Mysore state, Dakshina Kannada, and Uttara Kannada ranked 1, 2, and 7 on human development while the districts of Bellary, Gulburga and Haveri in northern Karnataka are ranked 18, 26 and 20 out of the sample of 27 districts. The level of poverty was wide between the northern and southern regions of the state, while 5.2 per cent was below the poverty line, while in Raichur and Gulburga the figures were 45 and 27 per cent.[2] The various estimates with regard to poverty in the rural sector are estimated at 26.6 per cent for year 2004-05 and another estimate shows at 13.7 per cent. The planning commission's official estimates put rural poverty at 12 per cent.[3] The varying estimates are due to the income and expenditure survey and the price estimation of the price levels of goods and services in the rural and urban sectors. The 'crisis of governability' takes multiple forms like unstable government, frequent elections, weakening law and order, insurgency, growing corruption and the failure of the governments at the centre and state to provide effective governance. In spite of all their weaknesses the political system and its institutions have proved to be quite resilient and have managed to function, even though inadequately. They have also retained legitimacy because of the much greater participation by the people in the political process, through elections.[4]

Prominent Social Movements in Karnataka

The state also witnessed a few new social movements compared to north India, but the prominent ones are the Farmers and Dalit Movements.[5] The democratic aspects of representation and participation were taken care of by the reservations in government jobs and educational institutions led to shift in articulating their experiences of exploitation which subsequently led to the autonomous Dalit politics and identity in states like Maharashtra, Karnataka, Andhra Pradesh who articulated the Dalit identity through literature and other cultural forms.[6] The emergence of the Dalit Movement of the 1970s and 80s 'Dalit' is proposed as a term for the untouchable castes as a whole. This led to integrate the untouchables into a single community and mark their difference from caste Hindus and held the idea of caste annihilation to create a democratic society.

In Karnataka the Dalit movement was marked by three significant developments.

(i) Dalits breaking away from the alliance and stronghold of the Congress-based politics.

(ii) The different political streams coming together, namely from Marxism, Ambedkarism and Lohiaism to form a United Dalit Sangharsh Samiti (DSS).

(iii) The emergence of 'bandaya' or protest literature, which both challenged the mainstream Kannada literature in Brahmanical literature and carved out a distinctive identity and character of its own.

(iv) The invoking of "Boosa" where Kannada literature was equated with cattle fodder. In Chikmagalur the issues of "Bagar Hukum" land destruction of property by the dominant caste controlling common grazing of "gomal" lands created conditions for the Dalit movement to grow. The lack of homogeneity, unity and integrity among the various Dalit communities prevented them from forming an alternative political force of their own in the state.[7] But these movements which had a fine social base have gradually eroded and presently the forces are divided and dispersed. The technological change in the rural economies has reduced the work of the agricultural labourers with the increase in tractors, harvesters; the services of many caste communities were no longer required.

The concern for environment issues like the Appiko movement, social forestry, massive industrialization, pollution and other issues created conditions for social movement in the Western Ghats of Karnataka in 1970-80. Karnataka has witnessed movements like the Appiko movement (hug the trees) in Uttara Kannada district in Sirsi taluk when the Forest Department policy of felling trees for commercial purposes, a number of protests, agitations enveloped the region under the leadership of Panduranga Hegde. The 'Apiko' movement in Karnataka, like the Chipko movement helped create better awareness of the adverse environmental costs of development, commercialization and industrial utilization of forest resources. In Karnataka the focus of private capital into natural resources management began first through the social forestry projects. The Forest Department took over 'wastelands', used as commons for grazing and collection of fuel wood by the rural people to raise commercial plantations to meet the raw material needs of industries. The state leased 28,350 hectares of degraded and forest land in the Kusnur cluster of villages for forty years to the Karnataka Pulpwood Limited, a joint sector company formed on November 14, 1984 by the Government of Karnataka and Birla owned Harihar Polyfibre Company to grow eucalyptus saplings. The venture overlooked the claims of the local villages that depended on these lands to meet the basic needs. The issue was taken up by the local villagers and NGOs like the Samaja Parivantha Samudya with other organizations and eminent personalities like Shivaram Karnath, Justie D.M. Chandrashekar and Kadilal Manjappa took up the cause of peasants who were displaced and rendered unemployed. In December 1986, a public interest litigation case was filed in the Supreme Court by Shivaram Karanth, Anil Agarwal and others. The Supreme Court issued a stay order on March 24, 1987 to maintain the status quo with regard to the possession of land. Meanwhile, the people of Kunsur and the surrounding villages launched a satyagraha on November 14, 1987, which is now popularly known as the Kunsur satyagraha. This led to the famous Kittiko Hattiko Chalavali or 'pluck and plant' in Kusnur in Dharwad district. Due to a sustained struggle for over seven years, 72 legislators from various political parties brought effective pressure on the government to close the KPL.[8] The history of the left movements has been weak in Karnataka as communist parties did try to have its influence in Dakshina Kannada and Socialists in the Shimoga district,[9] but were co-opted by the Congress Party. Dams like Bedthi and Silent Valley have already stopped because of strong people's protest from the Kerala Sastra Sahitya Parishad had a long acrimonious battle over the pollution of the Chiliyar river in Kerala by a rayon mill. These movements have used institutional mechanisms to redress for grievances, but there are non-institutional methods like violence in the large picture of social movements like the Naxalbari Movement. The Naxalites resort to violence as the decisive tool of socio-economic transformation. The crux of the Naxal stand on violence is that violence is imposed by the ruling class like landlords and the state administration which keep violence on their agenda. In such a situation the option left to Naxals is either to surrender to the violence let loose by the state or to counter it by violence.

History of Naxal Movement

In India the Communist Party of India (CPI) was in the forefront in the formation of the communist party from 1920-35 was influenced by the international communist movement during this period.

The inner party struggle would continue and finally led to the split in the communist movement with the Communist Party of India (CPI) and Communist Party of India (Marxist) in

1964 can be traced to the disagreement over how to understand the class nature of the Indian state and the relationship of the left to the Congress. The Communist Party of India (which favoured accommodation to the role of Moscow and the Congress), but on the other hand, the CPI (Marxist) believed in the growth of an independent communist identity, since the Congress had yoked itself to the dominant classes in the country). The differences have weakened the organizational front but have closely aligned in the left front and drew closer to each other.

The frustration with the bourgeois institutions ran right through large sections of the CPI (M) in the 1970s. The younger generation who joined the movement was against the democratic centralism of CPI (Marxist) who had their strengths but their relationships with democratic institutions were unwieldy and unwilling to submit to the needs of the people. In 1967 leaders like Kanu Sanyal and Jangal Santhal, then CPI (Marxist) leaders in Darjeeling district led the tea estate workers and peasants. The area landlords and Congress leader Ishwar Tirkey dismissed a landless farm worker, Bhigul Kisan who started the conflict when Kanu Sanyal and Santhal, who decided that a detachment of the Krishak Sabha would go and seize Trikey's land–peasant leaders also joined in the struggle. The influence of police violence led Charu Majumdar, Sanyal and others to depart from the CPI (Marxist) line and attacked the policy of land reforms of the United Front Government in Bengal. Charu Mazumdar emphasized the peasant struggle by fighting revisionism and believed that land reform in the peasant interest is possible only when we are able to put an end to the sway of feudal classes over the rural areas. He developed a clear cut proletariat framework or armed struggle, to extensively propagate the total politics of seizure of power and build concentrated areas of an anti-feudal peasant movement, establish the leadership of landless and poor peasants as the vehicle of proletarian leadership over the peasant struggle, and rely on them rather than the party organizers from petty bourgeois backgrounds for unleashing a militant peasant movement. He also cautioned against the dangers of mass isolation from the masses due to the base areas to be built in mountainous or forest areas and drew attention to the need of feasibility of developing bases in the plains. He was also keen to develop the distinct features of the Indian path of revolution and emphasized the fight against anarchist ideas and practices such as militarism and infatuation with 'actions'. The 'annihilation of class enemies' emerged as a new form of struggle in the Srikakulam peasant movement in Andhra Pradesh as it sought to combine armed struggle with broad mass mobilizations. The initial success led to the movement in Bhojpur and neighbouring regions in central Bihar and Jana Pratirodh Sangharsh Manch of the Maoist Communist Centre (MCC), which evolved out of the *Dakshin Desh* group all of whom had different styles and different kind of social base.[10] But in many areas annihilation was wrongly conducted as a 'campaign' with a lot of indiscriminate and unnecessary killings leading to the isolation from the peasant class struggle. The annihilation of class enemy had its limitations with the total setback of 1971-72.[11] The third offshoot was that of the Andhra revolutionary communists, mainly represented by T. Nagi Reddy and a group of communist revolutionaries led by Parimal Das Gupta on the one hand, and All-India Coordination Committee of Communist Revolutionaries (ALCCCR), most of whose adherents later formed the CPI (ML), on the other. The differences among Naxalities after the death of Mazumdar in July 1972 and the organization were crippled by mutual slandering among its leaders. The ideological disagreement led to the differences between the Bengal and the Andhra Pradesh units. The Andhra movement stressed the combination of legal and extra-legal activities, whereas the Bengal unit rejected legal and mass work and insisted on immediate armed struggle. The revolutionary movements in Naxalbari, Srikakulam and Bhojpur were the results of a series of struggles and not a sudden outburst of scattered violence. Thus the lack of ideological coherence and the absence of general consensus over tactical lines ultimately led the movement to fragmentation after fragmentation. In Jehanabad in Bihar, Bhumihar landlords were attacked and in turn they built their own forces and started killing Naxals.

The Naxalite movement drew inspiration from the tactical line of CPI (ML) stated in its political resolution of 1969: The basic tactic of struggle of the revolutionary peasantry led by working class is guerrilla warfare. The guerrilla warfare in the struggle of Srikakulam showed that the peasants would carry on protracted war only through guerrilla warfare by relying on the poor and landless peasants, it could be developed. The differences with the tactical line of Mao's emphasis on armed struggle did by no means exclude various forms of mass organization and mass movement. The Naxalities were to rely solely on poor and landless peasants as the CPI (ML) was more attached to Mazumdar's line than Mao. The critique against the Mazumdar line was that those actions were not aimed at the armed component of state power, as their sole targets were individual *jotedars* and landlords.[12] Mazumdar was expelled from the party and the new general secretary Satya Narayan Singh, who was elected the new general secretary, described his line as 'individual terrorism'.[13]

During the period from 1971-80 three distinct trends developed within the CPI (ML). The first was a continuation of the left line of 'annihilation of class enemies'. The second groups like the Second Central Committee and the Mahdev Mukherjee groups criticized the tactical line of the CPI (ML) and once again sought participation to elections. The factions led by Satyanarayan Singh, Kanu Sanyal, Ashim Chatterjee, and Souren Bose came closer towards the CPI (Marxist) Party. The third trends were particularly represented by the Central Organizing Committee which upheld the essence of the CPI (ML) line seeking to rectify the Left errors.

In Andhra Pradesh the CPI (ML) (People's War) founded by Kondapalli Sitaramaya in 1980 set up a number of mass organizations for democratic struggles relying on poor and landless peasants, middle peasants, and urban intellectuals. The organization relied on work in tandem with underground organizations such as Jana Natya Mandli of the People's War group.[14] Most of the Marxist-Leninist groups would subscribe to the need of armed struggle for revolution, but there are disagreements on the relation between mass work and armed struggle and mass work and electoral mobilization. The various lines with regard to personality differences like Charu Majumdar's slogan "expand anywhere and everywhere"- led to the CPI (ML) breaking into many fragments squabbling over the correct line. Kanu Sanyal became the defender of peasant power during the struggle but after some time came closer to the CPI (M).[15] The CPI (ML) (Janashakti) sought to combine an underground party organization with electoral politics which started with the peasant movement in Karimnagar and Adilabad districts of Andhra Pradesh after the Emergency was lifted.[16] The unequal land distribution and upper caste land owners like Velamas led to the rise of Naxalism in Kariamnagar-bordering Warangal and Nizamabad in Telangana and Bastar in Chhattisgarh became a Naxal nerve centre in the 1970s. Several top leaders like Muppala Lakshmana Rao (alias Ganapathy), Mallojula Koteshwara Rao (alias Kishenji) and Sande Rajamouli alias Prasad were born in Karimnagar.

The revised programme of setting up mass organizations and carrying forward the agrarian revolution, CPI (ML) formed the Radical Students Union in 1974 and the other organization named Radical Youth League was also formed in 1975. The two organizations as well as the party were then used to go to rural areas to study the existing socio-economic political structure and build a strong peasant movement. The peasant issues were those of land, wages, and vicious forms of caste oppression which were taken along with the emphasis on the agricultural labourers' union or Raytha Coolie Sangham. The widespread movement between 1978 and 1985 gradually spread to neighbouring districts. The widespread repression by the new regime of the N.T. Rama Rao government realized that Naxalities were seen as the real opposition and wanted to crush with all its might. The Terrorist and Disruptive Activities (Prevention) Act was widely and indiscriminately used and hundreds of Naxalitie sympathizers were arrested without trial. The repression between 1985-89 were relaxed when the opposition Congress Party promised to relax the repression and allow democratic rights to the people in general and the

Naxalities in particular led to the defeat of the Telugu Desam Party. The new regime between 1990 and 1992 initially allowed democratic activity and it was the Naxalite mass organizations that used the relaxed atmosphere the fullest. The popular face of the Naxalite movement like Gaddar who was underground during this period came out openly in support of Naxalitie politics. In 1992 the government announced the ban on the CPI (ML) (People's War) along with the Radical Students Union, Radical Youth League, Raithu Cooli Sangham, Singareni Karmika Samakhya, All India Revolutionary Students Federation, and Viplava Karmika Samakhya. This was the first ban on a political organization as well as mass organizations of students, youth and mine workers in the state. In 1992, the People's War group split owing to differences between Seetharamaiah and Ganapathy, who wanted to make it more militant. The surrender of Seetharamaiah to the police led to the elite strike force called the Greyhounds; commandos hunted the Naxalities and eventually drove them out of undivided Andhra Pradesh. The PWG operations had a large influence in building the movement in Karnataka as some of its members were part of it and wanted to enlarge the movement by making inroads into the Western Ghats as targeted areas.

CPI (ML) Operations in Karnataka

The CPI (ML) People's War, also known as the People's War Group (PWG) organization took a keen interest in organizing the suppressed peasants of the Raichur region in northern Karnataka and attempted to mobilize them against native landlords and their collaborators.[17] The social bases of these organizations have become unstable due to repression, surrenders and voluntary withdrawals. The setbacks to the movement owing to the arrest of its cadres in the Kolar-Tumkur-Raichur region of the state in 1999 and 2001 led to shifting its base to the Western Ghats.

The KVR opposed the formation of the Kudremukh National Park as it would lead to selling biodiversity products to multinational companies, commercial tourism resorts and the eviction of tribals without any compensation from the government.[18] The leader of the Kudremukh Rashtriya Virodhi Okkuta (KRUVO), Vittal Hegde stated that the government had not given sufficient attention to the tribal problem and the adamant attitude of D.D. Chandre Gowda[19] led to the genesis of Naxalism.[20]

The decade -long struggle by various organizations against the eviction of tribal people from the national park was taken up by the Naxalites under the banner of 'Maoist' when the Forest Department served eviction notices to them. The Naxalites tried to establish a base in and around Kudremukh National Park and spread over the forests of Sringeri, Beltahangady and Karkala *taluks* through its links with KRUVO.[21] In November 2004 with the merger of the People's War Group in parts of Andhra Pradesh, Odisha, Chhattisgarh and Maharashtra and Maoist Communist Centre (MCC) two major Naxalite formations in the country, the party changed its name to Communist Party of India (Maoist)[22] which accepts Marxism-Leninism-Maoism as its guiding ideology and is committed to 'new democratic revolution' in India by overthrowing imperialism, feudalism, and comprador bureaucratic capitalism only through the Protracted People's War which will establish the people's democratic dictatorship of the proletariat.[23] The Maoist threat has been seen as the biggest threat and this has been used as an excuse to crush and suppress democratically organized protest.[24]

Maoism

The current strategy of closing our forests to tribal communities is leading to immense alienation and the rise of extremist movements in forested districts with the slogan of Jal, Jangal, Zamin Hamara (Fight for Water, Forest and Land and Life).[25] The New Democratic Revolution will be accomplished through armed agrarian revolutionary war or the Protracted People's War through area-wise seizure of power.[26] This will be followed by encircling of the cities from the countryside and finally capturing them. They have come together to establish the guerilla zones and the base areas which are strategically favourable areas where they can organize and arm the vast peasant masses on the basic slogan of 'revolution' directed against imperialism, feudalism, and comprador bureaucratic capitalism. Unlike the first phase of the Naxalite movement, the new base of today's Maoist movement is no longer the small and marginalized peasantry or landless labour but among tribal and indigenous populations. The CPI (Maoist) believes in capturing political power through protracted armed struggle by building up bases in rural and remote areas where the people have been exploited by the government or landlords. The commitment of the Maoists to their cause is unquestionable for they sacrifice their lives in the most difficult circumstances in pursuit of a successful 'revolution'.[27]

The Maoist Party understands Indian society as a semi-colonial, semi-feudal social order under a neo-colonial form of indirect rule, exploitation and control. The Maoist Party does not believe in parliamentary democracy and is based on the principle of democratic centralism. The Constitution defines Democratic Centralism based on inner party democracy under centralized leadership. The Party Cell is the basic unit of the party which acts as the nucleus for day-to-day activities and can be formed area-wise. The highest body of the party is the Central Committee and there are other major committees like Special Area Committee/Special Zonal Committee/State Committee, Regional Committee, Zonal Committee/ District/ Divisional Committee, Sub-zonal/Sub-divisional Committee, Area Committee, local level committees such as village/*basti*/ factory/college party committee. Social movements repeatedly split over whether to use armed struggle or not, but it has severe limitations in the formation of movements because uncertainty reigns and the state gains psychological advantage for repression and turn non-violent sympathizers away from the movement.[28] The first instance of Naxalities were noticed in 2003 in the village of Edu in Karkala *taluk* where Parvathi and Hajima were killed in a police encounter which highlighted the basic issues of tribals and Naxalites.

Peace Talks with the Government

In the Westetrn Ghats Saketh Rajan,[29] State Secretary of the CPI

(Maoist) Party, and Murthy, District Secretary, invited a team of journalists and spoke on ideological and political matters.[30] Their main demands, conveyed through the media, were that the government must stop the eviction of tribal people from the Kudremukh National Park, and call a halt to combing operations and encounters. Their main demands were:

(a) Kudremukh National Park should be abolished.
(b) All activities incidental to the national park should be stopped immediately.
(c) Tribals should be given the right to self-determinism.
(d) All forest encroachments should be regularized and title deeds issued.
(e) Rural development programmes should be restored to full-scale.
(f) All cases booked against their supporters should be withdrawn.
(g) Locals should be given full rights and authority over the forests and other natural resources, the government should not interfere in any way.[31]

The police-led operations only intensified, and each encounter was followed by a retaliatory strike. The biggest loss to the party was the killing of Saketh Rajan,[32] who was the main architect of the political and organizational growth of the party, and his associate Shivalingu[33] (Arun) in Menisinahadiya of Chikmagalur district.[34] The counter offensive by the Maoists led to gunning down six policemen at Venkatammanhalli in Pavagada *taluk* of Tumkur district by an Andhra Pradesh-based team was for a different reason. The Central Committee was bent on linking it to the killing of Saketh Rajan by the police which resulted in excessive state oppression of the revolutionaries in the Malnad region. The Citizens Initiative for Peace (CIP), human rights and democratic organizations has strongly condemned the killing as an alleged "encounter". The CIP has demanded a judicial inquiry into the alleged encounter, and immediate suspension of the police officials involved in the killing and ends the combing operations in the Western Ghats. In the background the peace talks between the Government of Andhra Pradesh and People's War Group in 2004 failed because of the repression unleashed by the state. The Maoist insistence on resistance, armed if necessary, to counter the violence of the oppressors has appealed to a large section of the oppressed to fight both class exploitation and caste oppression. The struggles in Dandakaranya and Jharkand combine class demands against both the business-state nexus and the regressive traditional authority in villages, with that of self-identity, dignity and autonomy for the marginalized minority nationalities. The emergence of Adivasi peasantry, Dalits, backward castes and labouring classes as an independent and powerful political force, freed from the influence of affluent landowning classes is a great step forward in democratizing society.[35]

The Government of Karnataka views the Maoist movement as not merely a struggle of the poor but it is also a 'war' to overthrow the existing state power with the use of violence challenging state sovereignty.[36] The response of the then N. Dharam Singh government[37], announced a Rs 60 crore special package in the districts of Chikmagalur, Udupi and Dakshina Kannada, which have witnessed Naxal activity. This will enable the state to facilitate voluntary resettlement of the families living inside the Kudremukh National Park. These measures have failed to inspire confidence among the people. It has led to the growing influence of Naxalite groups in tribal areas who thrive on the dissatisfaction of the marginalized. The Naxalite movements have expanded due to the failure of the institutional mechanisms and frameworks to deliver socio-economic justice. The tribals continue to live in fear of both the police and the Naxals and the Karnataka police released a list of people who are sympathetic to the cause of the tribals. Social activists have alleged that the government has been using the 'Naxal' label to suppress the tribal agitation. "Most tribals have little or no faith in the government, will protect them, and over time may see little alternative but to turn to the Maoists as the best of a bad set of choices."[38] The government has made it difficult or impossible for anyone from outside to visit these affected areas. The human rights and individual observers are harassed and chased away repeatedly. In this background there is no chance that Naxalities could threaten the Indian state and the Government of India is unlikely to eradicate Naxalism through police action. The most likely prospect is a continuing and bloody stalemate".[39] The question of Maosim has led the state to polarize the debate and reduce the whole issue to simplistic good versus evil situation in which the government appears to firmly stand on the side of the good. The support in favour of the Maoists from civil society groups, non-governmental organizations, intellectual and the general public has led the state to use action under the Unlawful Activities (Prevention) Act, 1967. It warned that under Section 39 of the Act "any person who commits the offence of supporting such a terrorist organization with inter alia intention to further the activities of such groups would be liable to be punished with imprisonment for a term not exceeding ten years or with fine or with both". The resistance against these policies has resulted in numerous means, while some have resorted to violence, others have taken to movements and struggles. The state responded through the Anti-Naxalite Force, a force reconstituted from the Special Task Force and the police-led operations only intensified, and each encounter was followed by a retaliatory strike.[40]

Anti-Naxal Squad

The Anti-Naxal Squads Force (with 543 officers and men), was a special force reconstituted from the Special Task Force[41] to apprehend the sandalwood smuggler Veerappan.[42] The Naxalite movement in spite of the sacrifices did not translate into mass movement in the region and there is a fear among people to raise their voices against the state. To counter the Maoist movement the state has created a group called 'Salwa Judum' (Peace Hunt) in the state of Chhattisgarh in central India. Young tribal boys are trained with sophisticated guns to fight the Maoists because of the atrocities committed against them. The government claimed that the movement was spontaneous and the battle between the Maoists and the central government continued through its Operation Green Hunt. The operations were carried out in Dantewada where the 'Maoist liberated zone' were established to provide a safe military base to leaders and cadres from the neighbouring state of Andhra Pradesh. After the exclusion of tribal people from the present model of development, the Maoists have found new recruits who believe that armed rebellion against the state is the only way to break the hold of corporations and foreign capital who are in the nexus with the state. The Maoists are committed to the land rights and rights of the tribals to control their land.

Split in the Karnataka Maoist Party

The issues taken up by Maoists is being criticized on the basis that when compared to the dry areas of Andhra Pradesh, the socio-economic situation is different in the Malanad areas of Dakshina Kannada, Udipi and Chikmagalur. The Naxalites have entered the Western Ghats from Andhra Pradesh as a safe haven in the dense forest because it is difficult to access, particularly during the monsoons.[43] The Maoist strategy has come under severe criticism from within for not having mass action in any form and the use of violence as the first option, but without any evidence that the masses politicized in any genuine revolutionary strategy. The split in the party unit of the Western Ghats disagreed with the party's line in respect of Indian society being semi-colonial and semi-feudal in nature despite it being freed from foreign rule and area -wise capture of power — that the revolution would start from forest areas, spread to semi-forest areas and then to villages, towns and to cities gradually. The inner party struggle in the CPI (Maoist) internally has debated around a whole range of ideological, political and organizational issues. The ideological differences revolve around the static, mechanical or dogmatic conceptions in the party related to the overall conditions and contradictions in Indian society. The political differences were primarily focused on the narrow, sectarian and empirical outlook on many aspects including the overemphasis on armed struggle as against open-broad based mass struggle, secret organization as against open mass organizations and rural work at the cost of urban work.

The Maoist strategy has been criticized within the party

by members like Noor Zulfikar and Shirimane Nagraj who came out of the CPI (Maoist) because the party refused to adapt itself to changed realities. The major disagreement over the Maoist strategy initially started with Noor Zulfikar who was chosen by the central committee of CPI (Maoist) as State Secretary of Karnataka. However, he refused the post owing to his differences with the Maoists' strategy of area-wise seizure of power which led to a split in the CPI (Maoist) in Karnataka. Therefore this resulted in the formation of the Karnataka Maowadi Swatantra Kendra in July 2006 which culminated in the founding of the Revolutionary Communist Party (RCP) in September 2007. The RCP believes that there is a need for a bold, strong and broad-based mass movement, and not an armed struggle in Karnataka. Even though the intention of both schools of thought was to build a strong revolutionary movement, with the aim of creating an egalitarian society, the paths advocated were different.

Critique of the Naxalite Movement

The commitment of the Maoists to their cause is unquestionable for sacrificing their lives in the most difficult circumstances in pursuit of a successful 'revolution'. The issues taken up by Maoists is being criticized on the basis that when compared to the dry areas of Andhra Pradesh, the socio-economic situation is different in the Malanad areas of Dakshina Kannada, Udipi and Chikmagalur. The daily wage offered to farm workers is around ₹ 247 and the literacy levels in some of these areas are very high. The Maoists' movements have been criticized as "left adventurist in nature" because they have been executed without considering the specifics of the region and readiness of the people.[44] The concept of 'protracted people's war' is not suited to the conditions of India, and intensifying guerrilla warfare when people lack readiness for the struggle is bound to fail. The CPI (Maoist) Party avoids responding to these ideological observations or critiques and accuses the RCP members of individualism, degeneration and betrayal. The Maoist movement has excluded the big landlords and rich coffee planters in their struggle as they have focused on tribals. The hierarchies and inequalities were addressed by the political leaders through accommodative politics which offered something to the disadvantaged groups. The caste hierarchies have eroded, but it has undermined the mutual interdependence against the uncertainties.

The left forces with their one-sided emphasis on class and base by and large are limited to struggles and thus do not try to address the specific issues pertaining to castes within it, campaign or struggle against it, which is considered as divisive, and against class unity to do so. The mutually contemplating role of exploiting classes and oppressing castes in promoting and preserving the caste system in all its cruel forms is undermined in the process. The fight against caste is a complex one as described by Arundhati Roy: "Philosophically speaking, subordinated castes have to take pride in their identity and have to assert that pride to fight caste oppression. But then there comes a tipping point at which the radical positioning is used against itself, in order to promote a kind of isolation, and it suits the privileged to keep that going". The undermining of caste by the left parties by terming 'caste is class' has failed to intellectually deal with the issue and made it irrelevant. The left forces with emphasis on class and base by and large limited struggles in this direction considering it as divisive, dangerous and against class unity.

The criticism against CPI (Marxist) is that it does not want to intensify the struggle for the poor and has reverted to bourgeois rule with its limited support base. It has not been able to broaden or improve working class political activity. The declining electoral presence of the left parties is due to the vast changes in the deeper economic and political changes which has posed a deeper challenge to the conventional forms of trade union mobilizing and organizing workforce that formed the traditional base of left parties. The economic disparities have been growing and the parliamentary communist parties are contesting the correct line and complexities involved in applying the abstract to the concrete. The linking of neo-liberalism and the rise of the Hindu right in Adivasi regions should have made some kind of alliance between the social movements and the Indian Left. The CPI (Marxist) with its limited presence in Karnataka have criticized the Maoists for misinterpreting realities, whereas the regional communal forces have taken advantage of the presence of Maoists in the Western Ghats and the Naxal issue to attack secular forces. The CPI (M) has urged the government to drop the idea of evicting people from the Kudremukh National Park area and grant *pattas* for the settlement.[45] The Communist Party of India (CPI) has been a major force through its trade union, All India Trade Union Congress (AITUC) working for the plantation labourers from the 1980s led by the late B.K. Sundaresh who organized several movements against estate owners and brought a significant change in the relationship between owners and labourers. The reinforcing of caste and market has been able to adapt themselves whereas the market thrives on capital and profit and the upper castes with enormous opportunities. The neoliberal market reforms have brought internal contradictions. The dominant caste has appropriated the greater benefits and has socially excluded low castes like Scheduled Castes, Scheduled Tribes and women. In the recent decades, 'caste' denotes difference more than hierarchy. But it has undermined the limited sense of interdependence and mutuality which offered much protection against uncertainties. The spaces left over by the left parties and the coffee labourers comprising Dalits and the tribal people constitute the major force from the plantation labour force; have joined the Sangh Parivar when it came to religious mobilization against Bababudan Dargah. The marginalization of social movements has been taken advantage of by the Hindutva forces creating a Hindu nation in alliance with the state which wants to consolidate and expand its bases to make way in Indian politics. The identity politics has become prominent in the last few years like rise of low castes, religious identities, linguistic groups and ethnic conflicts have contributed to the significance of identity politics in India.

Bababudan Dargah

The Hindus worship the place as Datta Peeta and the Muslims revere it as the holy abode of Bababudangiri, as a Fakir has threatened the inter-community relations in Karnataka.[46] The annual Urs festival held in March attracts thousands of devotees from both communities. Both Baba and Datta represent the common people's tradition that rebelled against narrow religious boundaries and orthodox dogma.[47] The controversy is centred on the issue of the ownership and control of the shrine, between the two administrative bodies. The control of the shrine which was under the Muzrai Department, that administers a large number of almost exclusively Hindu shrines in Karnataka was contested by the Karnataka Waqf Board who issued a notification claiming the *dargah* as under its jurisdiction. But this was disputed by the Muzrai department on the grounds that the dargah was not exclusively of the Muslim shrine as it belongs to both Hindus and Muslims.[48] The support also came from the *Sajjada nashins* (were given certain privileges on par with the heads of some leading Hindu shrines) supported the Muzari department's stand arguing against the Waqf Board. The battle in the courts led the jurisdiction of the dargah under the direction of the Muzrai department and not the Waqf Board that the Muslim *Sajjada nashin* is the sole administrator of the *dargah*.

In the backdrop of the Hindu Nationalist Movement in the 1990s to demolish the Babri Masjid at Ayodhya the Karnataka unit of the Vishwa Hindu Parishad (VHP) also tried to liberate the dargah of Dada Hayat.[49] The Datta Peetha Samrakshana Samiti for the first time organized a puja which was conducted by a group of Brahmins. This resulted in various other programmes of the Sangh Parivar with two more programmes: Datta Mala and Shobha Yatra.[50]

The identity politics has become prominent in the last few years like rise of low castes, religious identities, linguistic groups and ethnic conflicts contributing to the significance of identity politics in India. The other means of identity are violence and terror by professing allegiance to a particular faith. The Hindutva forces were keen to make an experimental lab for furthering its policies with its numerous organizations like Sri Rama Sene, Hindu Jagaran Vedike, Hindi Janajagruti Samiiti, Sanatan Sanstha, etc. leading to the increasing violence in democracy.[51] The religious identity becomes a means to the members of a particular religion to share, to mobilize, compete effectively in the majoritarian public sphere claiming a moral basis to their understanding of 'evil' and the ways to tackle it. The religious identities are garnered for the political benefit and create a vote bank among different religious communities and target some communities in order to emerge as a champion of one community.[52] Thus inter-religious clashes are in fact, inter-political clashes as in Chikmaglur, Hubli, and Mangalore where the Jan Sangh is trying to get a hold in politics through the coastal belt where the Hindutva ideology is popularized by the Bharatiya Janata Party (BJP). The democratic deficit has led to political violence and clashes in many states in relation to land acquisition for industrialization as part of the economic reform agenda based on a competitive basis unleashing a new trend of development in Indian democracy.[53]

Democracy and Development: The Challenges

The Karnataka state with its capital city Bangalaru (Bangalore) is known for its Information Technology (IT) sector with companies like Wipro and Infosys that were set up specializing in computer systems and software production. The boom in the IT sectors have liberalized the real estate and infrastructure sectors leading to increase in land prices and rapidly increasing construction of infrastructure leaving the door open for speculative land prices.[54] The Karnataka model of development with spectacular technology has led to growth on the one hand and the challenges and contradictions that are faced by the state with regard to peasant suicides, gender inequity and regional disparities. The major shift with the neoliberal reforms is to attract major investors, for which concessions and incentives are offered by the state government in the neoliberal polity. The earlier growth model has been reformist with welfare, pro-poor orientation, land reforms, positive discrimination or reservations for the Scheduled Castes and Tribes. The exclusion of tribal people from the present model of development, the Maoists have found new recruits who believe that armed rebellion against the state is the only way to break the hold of corporations and foreign capital who are in the nexus with the state. The Maoists are committed to the land rights and rights of the tribals to control their land. The neoliberal economy tends to keep the people fractured, disunited and engaged in a mutual struggle of livelihood, rather than in a common struggle to recover their democratic rights and pursue an alternative economic strategy. The numerous non-governmental organizations also raise the questions of accountability, democracy and representation. It is far from clear as they are open structures in shaping the development of privatizing dynamics that remain unaccountable.[55] The focus on the local-global nexus becomes more compelling given the interconnections between environmental issues and those pertaining to rights. Despite the decentralized initiatives through constitutional amendments, the decision-making process is with the prerogative of the privileged few. This has led to the absence of equity and is relegated to a secondary position, particularly in the era of quick success of consumerism. These two forces are moving in opposite directions without any concerted attempt by the political parties at a reconciliation or mediation.[56]

Conclusion

The relatively equitable distribution of land (the former princely state of Mysore) has given many lower groups in the caste hierarchy at least a modest stake in the existing order. The unique feature of the old Mysore area is the irrigation system which was widely regarded to be the best in India. The social order across most of the state was less oppressive than in other parts of India, the accommodative and inclusive politics has also reduced the discontent among the people. The transformation of Karnataka state from welfare policies like land reforms and poverty reduction has witnessed a further shift towards the capitalist mode of development that has resulted in the drastic social fallout due to its neoliberal policy priorities by protecting certain financially affluent sections and leaving the majority of the population on the crossroads. Many of the social movements have been accommodated in politics by actively co-opting a number of movements and their leadership and drawing them into its funding schemes, academic programmes and award ceremonies, uplifting a small section of various exploited classes and oppressed communities into its fold, providing a place for them in local power structures, etc. As a result, several social movements taken up by various social groups on the one hand and the Maoist movement on the other have questioned the prosperity of the state. The state on the contrary, has been suppressing these movements, questioning its supremacy over the authority of the state. The assumption with regard to the neoliberal policies by the state that the development squeezed from the neoliberal policies would include the excluded in the mainstream over a period of time; however the real time practices are quite disastrous. The Maoist movement has not able to forge an alliance with the broader united front with various other struggles and this is due to the ideological, strategic and organizational orientation which does not have clarity as to how far they need to go. There is insecurity about diluting the 'core focuses' of armed struggle with relation to other political movements.

References

1. Harish Ramaswamy, S.S. Patagundi and S.H. Patel (2007): *Karnataka Government and Politics*, Concept Publishing Company, New Delhi.
2. V.N. Balasubramanyam and Ahalya Balasubramanyam (2012): 'Karnataka and Andhra Pradesh: The Disparate Twins' in *Growth, Development and Diversity: India's Record Since Liberalization*, Oxford University Press, p. 31.
3. Ibid., p. 30
4. Nivedita Menon and Aditya Nigam (2007): *Power and Contestation: India Since 1989*, Hyderabad, Oriental Longman Private Limited, pp. 1-15.
5. The Dalit question had subsumed under the nationalist agenda for development. The growth model has been reformist with welfare, pro-poor orientation, positive discrimination or reservation of the Scheduled Castes and Tribes. The reservations in government jobs and educational institutions led to the shift in articulating their experiences

of exploitation. This led to the autonomous Dalit politics and identity was confined to a few states like Maharashtra and Karnataka, Andhra Pradesh who articulated the Dalit identity through literature and other cultural forms.

6. Gail Omvedt (1994): 'We Want the Return for Our Sweat: The New Peasant Movement and Formation of a New Agricultural Policy', *Journal of Peasant Studies*, Vol. 21, No. 3&4, April/May, pp. 253-279.
7. Manohar Yadav (1998): 'Carrier of Dalit Movement in Karnataka', *Journal of Social and Economic Development*, Vol. I, January-June, pp. 111-16.
8. Sadanand Kanwalli (1993): 'Quest for Justice', *Samaj Parivartana Samudaya*, Dharwad, Karnataka, pp. 1-30.
9. The Kogaodu satyagraha in Shimoga led by the socialist leaders like Gopal Gowda and others were inspired by Ram Manohar Lohia. The region had a strong base for the socialist party as the first socialist party legislator in the Karnataka assembly. In the 1970s, socialist leaders like J.H. Patel moved to the Janata Party after the socialists merged with it in 1977, while S.Bangarappa and Kogadau Thimmapa shifted to Congress. See Rajashekera, G (1980): *Kogodu Satyagraha*, Sagar, Akshara Prakashan, Shimoga (in Kannada).
10. Valerian Rodrigues (2006): 'The Communist Parties in India', in *Indian Political Parties* (Ed) by Peter Ronald de Souza and E.Sridharan, Sage Publications, pp. 237-38.
11. Arindam Sen (2010): Anarchism or Revolutionary Marxism? *Seminar*, 607, pp. 1-10.
12. Tarun Kumar Banerjee (2010): The Naxalite Movement: Currents and Cross Currents, Kolkata, Progressive Publishers, p. 472.
13. Nirmalangshu Mukherji (2013): *The Maoists in India: Tribals Under Siege*, Amaryllis, New Delhi, pp. 140-82.
14. The famous ballad singer Gaddar (Gummadi Vithal Rao), the Dalit singer, poet and performer who through this performance propagated the ideology of the CPI (ML) People's War and was the secretary of the party's cultural wing. See S.V. Srinivas (2015): Maoism to Mass Culture: Notes on Telangana's Cultural Turn, *Bio Scope*, Vol. 6, Number 2, July, pp. 187-205.
15. Vijay Prashad (2015): *No Free Left: The Future of Indian Communism*, Leftword Books, New Delhi, pp. 161-65.
16. Aditya Nigam (2010): The Rumour of Maoism, *Seminar*, pp. 1-13.

17. Vijay Poonacha, Thambanda (2004): *Conflicting Identities in Karnataka: Separate State and Anti-Separate Movements in Coorg,* Published by Kannada University, Hampi, pp. 16-17.
18. Interview with G.V. Kempegowda, District President of the Sri Durga Parameshwari Yuvaka Sangaha, Menasinahadya, on November 15, 2006.
19. D.B. Chandre Gowda was then Minister for Law and Parliamentary Affairs, Government of Karnataka.
20. Interview with Vittal Hedge President of the Kudremukh Rashtriya Virodhi Okkuta on December 28, 2006, Sringeri.
21. Niren Jain (2005): 'Note on Possible Infiltration of Naxalite Activity into Kudremukh National Park', Kudremukh Wildlife Division, Mangalore.
22. In November 2004 the CPI (Maoist), programme jointly drafted by the erstwhile People's War Group in parts of Andhra Pradesh, Odisha, Chhattisgarh and Maharashtra and Maoist Communist Centre (MCC) which was once known as the Maoist Centre of Communist Revolutionaries. They have come together to establish the guerilla zones and the base area in strategically favourable areas where they can organize and arm the vast peasant masses on the basic slogan of "revolution" directed against imperialism, feudalism, and comprador bureaucratic capitalism. After the merger of the two major Naxalite formations in the country, the party changed its name to Communist Party of India (Maoist) which accepts Marxism-Leninism-Maoism as its guiding ideology and is committed to "new democratic revolution" in India before passing on to achieve its socialist goal. Ramachandra Guha (2007): "Adivasis, Naxalites and Indian Democracy", *Economic and Political Weekly,* August 11, Vol. XLII, No. 32, pp. 3305-12.
23. The "Maoist" and "Naxalite" are used interchangeably.
24. Prabhat Patnaik (2014): 'Neoliberalism and Democracy', *Economic and Political Weekly,* April 12, Vol. XLIX, No. 15, pp. 39-44.
25. Amarnath Mohanty (2011): *Justice, Democracy and State in India: Reflections on Structure, Dynamics and Ambivalence,* Routledge, New Delhi, p. 266.
26. Sumanta Banerjee (2006): 'Maoist Movement in India: Beyond Naxalbari', *Economic and Political Weekly,* Vol. XL, No. 29, pp. 3159-62.

27. In a major public relation exercise, in 2004 when negotiations were underway between the Andhra Pradesh Government and CPI (ML) (People's War) came into prominence, due to a drastic change in government policy that regarded the Naxalite movement from a socio-politico-economic standpoint rather from the law and order issue. The main demands during the talks were land distribution, the right of tribals over forest lands, scrapping of World Bank dictated policies that are causing mass retrenchment of workers and draining out people's resources, and formation of Telangana state.
28. Interview with K.G. Sridhar on November 14, 2006, Thirathahalli, Shimoga.
29. Com. Saketh Rajan (Prem) hailed from Mysore and since his student days was imbedded with the ideology of Marxism-Leninism-Maoism and inspiration for advancement of the revolutionary movement in Andhra Pradesh, had turned him into a dedicated revolutionary from 1983. In 1987 he was elected to the state committee in the first state conference of Karnataka and in the fourth state conference in 2000, elected as the state secretary. He was the delegate to the 9th All India Congress of the erstwhile CPI (ML) (Peoples War) and was elected to the CC as an alternate member. His contribution to the Indian revolution was with others he pioneered the initiation of armed struggle under communist leadership in the Western Ghats of Karnataka. He has also written the history of Karnataka in two volumes of "making history" tracing the history of the Kannadaiga nationality from the earliest of times of 1857. His study of the plight of the people in plantations and in the Kudremukh National Park area in nearly 100 villages has been a major factor in extending the Naxalite movement to the Malnad area. See Saket Rajan (2005): 'Voice of the Indian Revolution', *People's March*, Vol. 6, No. 3, March, Kerala, pp. 18-19.
30. In Andhra Pradesh due to the efforts of the Committee of Concerned Citizens (CCC), the talks between the emissaries of the CPI (ML) (People's War) and the Government of Andhra Pradesh. The talks would materialize only if encounter killings are stopped and a proper trial is assured for the arrested activists in 2001. There were major compulsions for the state because of the World Bank dictated reforms and

inviting multinational companies to come to the state. N. Venugopal (2013): *Understanding Maoists: Notes of a Participant Observer from Andhra Pradesh*, Setu Prakashani, pp. 75-102.

31. Anita Arekal (2003): 'Revised management Plan for Kudremukh National Park', Kudremukh Wildlife Division, Karnataka Forest Department.
32. Saket Rajan was inspired by the anti-colonial revolutionary theorist Frantz Fanon on "Violence as a cleansing force. It frees the native from his inferiority complexes, and from his despair and inaction, it makes him fearless and restores his self-respect". Through violence the colonized transcended fear of the colonizer and reclaimed their humanity. See Fanon, Frantz (1968): *The Wretched of the Earth*, Trans. Constance Farrington, New York, p. 94.
33. Comrade Shivalingu (Arun) hailed from a middle peasant background in Sindhanur taluk of Raichur district and was inspired by the revolutionary peasant movement in Raichur in 1988.
34. In a swift and brutal retaliation, armed Naxalite squads from Andhra Pradesh struck at a police station in Pavagada in Tumkur district.
35. Pamphlet of Democratic Students Union (2007): 'What is Really the Question, Law and Order or Justice?' Jawaharlal Nehru University, dated 31st.
36. Saroj Giri (2009): The Maoist "Problem" and the Democratic Left in India, *Journal of Contemporary Asia*, Vol. 39, No. 3, August, pp. 463-474.
37. The Congress and the Janata Dal (Secular) allied to form the government with the Congress Dharam Singh as Chief Minister from 2004 to 2006. The alliance was broken when Kumaraswamy, JD(S) leader withdrew support along with the party's MLAs.
38. *The Hindu*, March 24, 2011.
39. Ambrose Pinto (2014): *From Democratic Socialism to Neoliberalism: The Story of India's Democracy*, Indian Institute of Advanced Study, Rashtrapati Nivas, Shimla, p. 209.
40. Awasthi Kirtiman (2008): 'Many Takers of a Park', *Down to Earth*, Vol. 16, No. 23, April 16-30, pp. 23-27.
41. The Tamil Nadu and Karnataka governments formed the special task force in the 1990s to apprehend Veerappan and in the last fifteen years there were many encounters between the STF and

Veerappan group. Even after accomplishing the task of hunting Veerappan, the STF is not disbanded; instead the government has announced that STF operations in the forest area. See Ravindran (2005): 'Veerappan: A Bandit who Turned as a Rebel Against the State', *People's March Voice of the Indian Revolution,* Vol. 6, No. 1, January, pp. 18-21.

42. Awasthi Kirtiman (2008): 'Many Takers of a Park', *Down to Earth,* Vol. 16, No. 23, April 16-30, pp. 22.
43. Interview with Girjashankar, Editor of *Janmitra Magazine,* January 27, 2007, Chikmagalur.
44. In Odisha Sabyasachi Panda joined the Naxalite movement in 1991 and revived it in 1996 giving the call for a full-scale armed struggle against the establishment. The practice of killing comrades or common people after branding them 'informers' has led to his expulsion from the Maoist Party. In 2004 he formed a new party called Odisha Maoist Party (OMP) to strengthen the movement.
45. Interview with G.N. Nagraj, General Secretary of CPI (Marxist), on March 16, 2007, Bangalore.
46. The construction of histories or lineages by the Sangh Parivar as a moral booster for legitimacy is to link up the present aspirations with the past has been a standard feature of modern political mobilizations. The 'specific kind of history' that goes back to medieval discourse by mythical struggle of Hindus against the Muslims with Mahmud of Ghazni and coming of the Muslims. Savarkar begins with the claim that 'Hindutva is not a word but a history—a history in full'. The linkage between *pitribhumi* and *punyabhumi* (fatherland and holy land) is equated with the land of the origin of one's religion and culture and the major argument is clearly directed against the Indian Muslims and Christians who might not like to be termed as Hindu. See Sumit Sarkar (2002): *Beyond Nationalist Frames; Relocating Postmodernism, Hindutva, History,* Permanent Black, New Delhi, pp. 242-262.
47. Muzzaffar Assadi (1998): 'Saffronisation with Upper Castes Support', *Economic and Political Weekly,* March 21, p. 627.
48. Yoginder Sikand (2006): *Muslims in India: Contemporary Social and Political Discourses,* Hope India Publications, Gurgaon, p. 269.
49. Thomas Blom Hansen (2015): Communalism, Democracy and

Indian Capitalism, *Seminar*, 674, October, pp. 40-43.

50. Parvathi Menon (2003): 'A Communal Campaign', *Frontline,* Vol. 20, Issue-25, December 6-19, pp. 41-3.
51. Badri Narayan (2015): 'Democracy and Identity Politics in India: Is it a Snake or Rope?' *Economic and Political Weekly,* April 18, Vol. L, No. 16, pp. 61-65.
52. Sitharaman, Sudha (2010): 'Conflict Over Worship: A Study of the Sri Guru Dattatreya Swami Bababudhan Dargah in South India', Institute for Social and Economic Change, Bangalore, p. 12.
53. Atul Kohli (1990): Democracy and Discontent: India's Growing Crisis of Governability, Cambridge: Cambridge University Press, pp. 1-19.
54. Gopal K. Kadekodi, Ravi Kanbur and Vijendra Rao (2008): *Development in Karnataka: Challenges of Governance, Equity and Empowerment* (ed), Academic Foundation, New Delhi, p. 17.
55. Ramachandra, Guha and J. Martinez-Alier (1997): *Varieties of Environmentalism: Essays North and South,* EarthScan Publications, London, pp. 96-7.
56. Zoya Hasan (2009): 'Indian Democracy and Social Inequalities' in *Challenges to Democracy in India* (ed) by Rajesh M. Basrur, Oxford University Press, pp. 127-45.

Conclusion

The interface of coffee economy, mining and conservation conflicts in the rural Chikmagalur district illustrate that the very concept of land must be re-imagined as ecology rather than land. These include forests, fields, minerals, water and animals on the one hand and specific modes of habitation and relation to such land on the other. Social movements have a general orientation to bring about (or prevent) change. These features are not constant; it may change over the course of a social movement life.[1] It is unclear whether the alternative proposed are genuine alternatives as the rifts among decision-makers at different levels have to understand the regional diversity of the Western Ghats.

Regional Diversity

The Western Ghats form a highly heterogeneous region with heavy rainfall and has variation in elevation and geology. Consequently there is substantial state-to-state variation in ecological endowments and sensitivity. The Western Ghats region occupies (52,950 square kilometres) 27.8 per cent of Karnataka's area, hosting 23.4 per cent of its population. In Chikmagalur Arabica coffee is grown under shade in contrast with Robusta. The other major difference is pest resistance and large-scale development of irrigation systems for Arabica with Robusta requires less pesticides. Due to the long gestation between replanting of coffee saplings and production of cherries, many cultivators are forced to supplement their income by harvesting timber from their estates. Although the loss of native trees is being compensated by planting a greater number of trees, including the fast-growing exotic silver oak has resulted in a decrease in canopy cover and the population of native tree species. The shift towards the Silver Oak makes a shift from poly-cultures to monocultures primarily for economic benefits derived from harvesting of timber. Although the shifts in coffee agro forests in Karnataka were evolved over time, they still retain strong traditional roots. The coffee agro-forest systems can aid in effectively reducing the intensity of physical damages to the ecosystem services generally provided by natural forests, including prevention of soil erosion, water sequestration, wildlife corridors, carbon sequestration and livelihoods for the poor. The harmony between the plantations and people has been acknowledged by the Western Ghats Ecology Experts Panel which had recommended that large-scale efforts such as regenerating forests where plantations were no longer profitable. This was distorted to allege that WGEEP had recommended that coffee plantations be converted to forests, created a panic among plantation owners in Kodagu.[2] The other concerns are with the suitable infrastructure and high cost of treatment, coffee growers have failed to adopt suitable pollution control measures leading to water pollution. Clearly, a uniform set of regulations cannot be promulgated for the Western Ghats regions, a graded approach, has been prescribed by Dr. Madhav Gadigil as regions of high, moderate and low sensitivity.

The environmental questions were linked to democratic possibilities and were tied centrally to efforts at evolving sustainable livelihood strategies[3] which frequently used 'advocacy' or Public Interest Litigation. It was intended to ensure legal rights to people who could not reach the court due to various reasons because of poverty, helplessness or disability or socially or economically disadvantaged position. This made it possible for citizens to approach the Supreme Court on grounds of violations of fundamental rights sometimes on behalf of public interest, and not only when they were themselves the aggrieved party.

The growing influence of Public Interest Litigation (PIL) has led to petitions on behalf of parties who are not directly affected but are questioning with regard to nature and wildlife affected by pollution.[4] The initial judgments in the public interest litigation were expanded to include other concerns like bonded labour, child labour, rights of the poor to education, shelter and other essential amenities which would enable them to lead a life of dignity. In the last two decades a number of cases heard in the Supreme Court judgments have been insensitive towards the rights of the poor and disadvantaged sections of society such as recent cases like BALCO Employees Union vs. Union of India[5], Narmada Bachao Andolan, Tehri Dam Case and Forest Conservation Cases and Delhi air pollution. The Narmada Bachao Andolan gathered a huge support from global civil society organizations such as Environmental Defence and Oxfam. The limitations of civil society working in different areas are that they have not been able to address the inequality in society because they lack the power, responsibility and accountability of the state. The case of KIOCL illustrates the increasing incidence of judicial activism which reflects the growing insensitivity of the government to the problems of those who do not have a strong political voice. It also reflects the inability of institutional processes to resolve conflicts in society. The perception that the political decision-making process works on partisan interests and the judicial process is neutral and transparent has grown over the years. The self-image of law and adjudication as apolitical provides an ideological cover for the pursuit of private, partisan ends, in the name of 'public interest'. The NGOs have resorted to Public Interest Litigation in the Supreme Court to close down the company. The trade unions in the era of globalization have relied more on the welfare state, labour legislation, wage agreements which are deeply rooted in the nation-state, whereas capitalist forces operate freely in a deregulated world market.

The management of the KIOCL defended the mining on the plank that check-dams like Lakya dam were constructed before the commencement of the project operations to store tailings and allow clean water to the plant for recycling. The closure of industries has attracted criticism from the workers union as it neither heard all the affected workmen before passing the order.

The environmentalists believe that without state intervention, deforestation and wildlife depletion would be accelerated, given the pressures on forests from local communities and also from industrial, commercial and development projects on the other. This has led to the stringent legislations such as the Wildlife Protection Act (1972) and (1991), the Forest Conservation Act (1980) and the Environment Protection Act (1986). The environmentalists of the poor are dependent on the middle class which has relied on public interest litigation for the closure of industries. The role of the state as the owner of natural resources has created a dual problem where it imposed the British legal order based on customary usage and norms guided by ecological parameters. On the other hand it paved a way for a Western model of conservation inherently established on the duality of man and nature. The state's monopoly of forest regimes has led to treating the erstwhile owners and rights holders as 'encroachers'. The issue of encroachers has asked questions of economy, ecology and polity playing out to our disadvantage, as demonstrated in the recent debates around the Scheduled Tribes and Other Traditional Forest Dwellers (Recognition of Forest Act) Act 2006. There are various questions which require further explorations with regard to the impact this new act has on the KNP tribals. The conflicting interests of green thought in India and their core concerns may lead to the conclusion that they may not be able to resolve their differences. But there are instances where organizations have come together like Tarun Bharat Sangh, in the Aravalli hills of western India, has revived water sources and illegal mining. The other initiative of scientists, sholaga Adivasis, and Viekananda Girijana Kalyana Kendra in the BR Hills Reserve in Karnataka have proved to be successful.[6]

Conservation Beyond National Park

The conservation biologist as a tradition defined includes activities as preservation (as in protected areas) sustainable harvesting (as in fisheries) and control or regulation of organisms harmful to human interests (man-eating tigers or crop-raiding elephants). It gained impetus for setting up parks came from a class of ex-hunters turned conservationist belonging from the erstwhile princely states and representatives of international agencies, such as the World Wild Fund (WWF) and International Union for Conservation of Nature and Natural Resources (IUCN). This group of environmentalists successfully brought pressure on the government to create a network of national parks and sanctuaries all over India to protect endangered wildlife, overlooking the claims of the local residents. During this period the number of parks went from 19 to 52 and central law favouring drastic measures for wildlife conservation was strengthened. The national parks and wildlife sanctuaries form only 3% of our country's land area and within these areas we have human habitations, roads, dams, mines, power plants and other activities which have been the biggest threats to forests and wildlife have caused habitat fragmentation. The government strategies have been seriously questioned for their top-down, non-participatory character by the grass root activists and the failure to recognize the social roots of environmental use and abuse.

The 'biodiversity conservation' movement argues that the resources must be set aside and 'protected' from the people. Biological conservation must be based on science but scientific investigation is not the only output required for effective conservation and even when there is substantial information, prudent conservation policies are not assured. It can never be proven in a relatively short period of time that human-related activities have been the cause of species extinctions. The sustainable use approach of biological resources succeeds in rising local interest and involvement in conservation of widespread and non-charismatic forms of biological biodiversity of human use. But devoid of any definition has resulted anything they want it to mean.[8] The major criticism against sustainable use is based on untested assumption on conservation and the integration of global markets has altered the traditional subsistence cropping to market-oriented crop. Ullas Karnath, Director of Wildlife First, has argued that the pragmatic conservationist[9] model has worked well with certain fragile groups of animals like tiger, lion-tailed macaques or hornbills for survival of such animals.[10] The strength of the preservationist approach lies in its recognition that certain forms of biological diversity are nearly impossible to conserve in the context of human density and extractive use and need inviolate areas. Biodiversity conservation initiatives do not acknowledge the important role that tribal communities play in conservation. The knowledge of the various tribal people is often on the side of conservation and clean environment even though they do not claim to be environmentalists. This is because they have been treated as enemies, and not as partners in conservation efforts which are pursued as a bureaucratic effort. But over the years it has taken over the state and interpreting conservation as a task to be performed by force of arms keeping the tribal and livestock away. Added to this the biologists have focused on the human impact on ecosystems like hunting, poaching and forest fire.[11] On the other hand, the social scientists in contrast argue more in favour of equity and justice from the sociological and historical perspective. The conservation approach to biodiversity should not be a uniform policy as it has been followed in India for all the national parks. The Western Ghats Ecology Experts panel that was dumped by the central government with the widespread protest against its implementation, had shrunk to only about 37 per cent of the total area, as against about 64 per cent in the Western Ghats Ecology Exerpts panel.[12] The Western Ghats cover six states of Gujarat, Maharashtra, Goa, Karnataka, Kerala and Tamil Nadu. The ESA was reduced to 60,000 square kilometre as against original 1.29 lakh sq kms identified in the Gadgil report. The high-level working group headed by space scientist Kasturirangan, in its report declared 4,156 villages—2,159 in Maharashtra, 1,576 in Karnataka, 135 in Tamil Nadu, 123 in Kerala, 99 in Goa and 64 in Gujarat—as ESA villages and the states were asked to carry out a 'physical verification'. The Karnataka government in its reply dated April 24, 2015 has mentioned 'public outrage' as the reason for dropping more villages from the ESA list.[13]

The centralized system has resulted in a centralized response with regard to the Forest Rights Act or amendments to the Wildlife Protection Act or Forest Conservation Act 1980 in the name of national interests which have been insensitive to the local context and history. These laws date back to 1864 when the Forest Department was created and the institutions are the product of imperial legislation and practice and remaking them to suit a democratic order is a challenging task. The intervention of the Supreme Court in the forest governance and definition of forest has led to simple categories of forest and non-forest. The anomalies have to be addressed as forest generate, a range of benefits like coffee plantation labours a significant amount of biodiversity, but on the other hand, monoculture timber under FCA, provide much lower biodiversity benefits. There is a need for change in the forest governance which has to address these complexities and push for more local-specific, democratic forms of governance with varied interests of all the stakeholders like environmentalists, social activists, local communities and the corporate sector. In Kudremukh the communities are largely non-tribal and the economy is relatively prosperous and where substantial forest rights were granted to forest-dependent households at the individual rather than community level but in a discriminatory manner (landed versus landless). In the Western Ghats the tribal question was never fully addressed by the representational aspect of democracy, for the simple reason that the very small population of tribes made them ineffectual in the electoral process of democracy. The ongoing struggle of land acquisition, forest appropriation and minerals extraction and forced displacement by development projects establishes the autonomy question as constitutive of democracy. The majority of the populations living in rural areas where land is not only the main source of livelihoods but also the basis of social stratification, power structure, and family organization and belief systems. The report of the Government of India, Development Challenges in Extremist Affected Areas looked at the Naxalite movement in the historical context of the "development paradigm pursued since independence" which they assert, has "aggravated the prevailing discontent among marginalized sections of society". The report also highlights the "directional shift in governmental policies towards modernization and mechanization, export orientation, diversification to produce for the market, withdrawal of various subsidy regimes and exposure to global trade". These factors have led the Naxalities to exploit the situation for their own political gain by giving the affected people an element of relief or response.

References

1. Prathama Banaerjee (2016): Writing the Adivasi: Some Historiographical Notes, *The Indian Economic and Social History Review*, 53, 1, pp. 131-153.
2. Madhav Gadgil (2014): 'Western Ghats Ecology Expert Panel: A Play in Five Acts', *Economic and Political Weekly*, Vol. XLIX, No. 18, May 3, p. 48.
3. A. Agrarwal and Sunil Narain (1996): *The State of India's Environment 1984-85: A Second Citizens Report*, New Delhi, Centre for Science and Environment.
4. Kuldeep Mathur (2004): 'Battling for Clean Environment: Supreme Court, Technocrats and Populist Politics in Delhi', Centre for the Study for Law and Governance, Jawaharlal Nehru University, Working paper series, p. 8.
5. The employees union had challenged the company to sell off the Public Sector Unit on the grounds of arbitrary and non-fixation of its reserve price in a non-transparent and arbitrary valuation conducted by the company.
6. Interview with Deputy Conservator of Forests, A.M. Annaiah on October 9, 2007, Bangalore.
7. T.P. Sreedharan (2004): 'Biodiversity Diversity of Kerala: A Survey of Kalliasseri Panchayat, Kannur District', Discussion Paper No. 62, *Kerala* Research Programme on Local Level Development, Thiruvanthapuram, p. 11.
8. M.D. Madhusudan, and Shankar Raman, T.R. (2003): 'Conservation as if Biological Diversity Matters: Preservation versus Sustainable Use in India', *Conservation and Society*, Issue 1, Sage Publications, New Delhi, pp. 49-57.
9. The pragmatic conservationist comprising scientists and forest managers who concentrated on getting the bureaucracy to extend protected areas and stringent police action. See Mahesh Rangarajan, (1996): 'The Politics of Ecology: The Debate on Wildlife and People in India', 1970-85, *Economic and Political Weekly*, Special Number, September, pp. 2391-2409.
10. Ramachadra Guha, (2003): 'The Authoritarian Biologist and

the Arrogance of Anti-humanism: Wildlife Conservation in the Third World', in *Battles of Nature: Science and the Politics of Conservation* (ed) Vasanth K. Saberwal and Mahesh Rangarajan, Permanent Black, Delhi, pp. 139-158.

11. Mahesh Rangarajan and Ghazala Shahabuddin (2006): 'Relocation from Protected Areas: Towards a Historical and Biological Synthesis', *Conservation and Society*, Vol. 1-4, No. 3. September, pp. 360-361.
12. Kanchan Chopra (2014): 'Conservation and Development in the Western Ghats: A Tale of Two Committees and More', *Economic and Political Weekly*, Vol. XLIX, No. 11, pp. 12-14.
13. A.K. Verma (2015): 'Importance of Preserving Karnataka's Western Ghats' Tigers', *Deccan Herald*, April 30.

APPENDIX-I (A)

Environmental Costs – Capital Expenditure

S. No.	Item	Year of Completion	Expen-diture	Cumulative (Rs. Lakhs)
1.	Lakhya Tailings Dam (a) First Stage, 65 m height (b) Second Stage, 100 m height **Total**	 1978-79 1991-94	 1300 9900	12000
2.	Pollution Control Dams (2 nos) (a) First Stage (b) Second Stage **Total**	 1979-80 1995	 246 70	316
3.	Diversion Channel for Kudremukh Holey	1980	----	13
4.	(a) Dump Ponds (2 nos) for containing beneficiation plant discharge (b) Pump House for recycling **Total**	1980 1980	50 15	**65**

S. No.	Item	Year of Completion	Expen-diture	Cumulative (Rs. Lakhs)
5.	Sewage Treatment Plant			
	(a) In Township	1980	16	
	(b) Two at Beneficiation plant and shop area	1980	05	
	Total			12
6.	Industrial effluent treatment plant	1980		05
7.	Equipment for desilting of dam			890
	Grand Total			**12600**

APPENDIX-I (B)

Concern for Neighbourhood

S.No.	Project Scheme
A	**Drinking water supply** (1) Water supply scheme to Kalasa (2) Water supply to Samse village (3) Bore wells at Nellibeedu (4) Drinking water supply to Jamble village (5) Drinking water to Vinobha Nagar
B	**Health and Medical Facilities** (1) Clinic to provide medical facilities for Vinobha Nagar residents at Kudremukh (2) Clinic at Nellibeedu for the people in and around Nellibeedu village (3) Donation to Chief Minister's Medical Relief Fund (4) Donation to Spastic Society of Karnataka for setting up a diagnostic centre (5) Donation to Chinmaya Mission Hospital for building (6) Donation of incubator to Dhanvantri Hospital, Sringeri (7) Donation of dialysis machine to Wenolock Hospital, Mangalore (8) Donation of emergency generator to Artificial Limb Centre, Mangalore (i) Donation for improvement of Dhanvantari Hospital, Sringeri

C	**Assistance to Educational Institutions** (1) Donation of books to Government Junior College, Kudremukh, Government High School, Kudremukh, Girijyothi Convent, Kudremukh, St. Alosyius College, Canara College, Sharada School, and Central School all at Mangalore. (2) Institution of a Professor's Chair at KREC, Surathkal, Mangalore (3) Electrification of Jamble Village Schools (4) Construction of Government High School building at Kudremukh (5) Playground at Kalasa, Samse, Hirebyle, Banakal, Mettigere, Gabgal, Niduvale, Jannapura, Jenubyle, Kuduvalli, Aldur Junior College, Muttigepura, Angadi, Balahole, Balehonnur, Karkala (Kudubettu), Sringeri. (6) Donation of construction of a school building at Kulur, Mangalore
D	**Environment** (1) (a) Financial assistance to Forest Department, Government of Karnataka for development of wildlife at Kudremukh National Park (1994-1998) (b) Financial assistance to Wildlife Wing of Government of Karnataka (1999-2000) Rs. 2 crores each year for 10 years (2) MOU with Mangalore University for research and identification of local species to be grown in degraded land for a period of 5 years (3) MOU with National Environment Engineering Research Institute (NEERI), Nagpur for development of bio-fertilizer to support the soil nutrients for natural vegetation. (4) Construction of panther enclosure in Pilikula Biological Park at Pilikula Nisarga Dhama, Mangalore

E	**Assistance for the Poor and Downtrodden** (1) Construction of Community Hall at Vinobhanagar in association with NAC, Kudremukh, construction materials were supplied (2) Provision of houses for the homeless at Vinobhanagar in association with Lion's Club (3) Construction of roads and drains at Vinobhanagar (4) Provision of street lights and TV network at Vinobhanagar (5) Construction of suspension bridge across Bhadra near Nellibeedu (6) Construction of RCC bridge across Bhadra near Koteholey, Kalasa (Financial assistance to Zilla Panchayat, Chikmagalur)
F	**Agriculture** Supply of water for irrigation to sugarcane fields near Mangalore (project is yet be implemented – pipes have been purchased).
G	**Rehabilitation** (1) 63 families were rehabilitated with alternate land, compensation and housing with all basic facilities like roads, water supply, electricity and TV network. (2) 63 persons form all the 32 displaced families were provided with employment in the company.

H	**Other Welfare Measures** (1) Electronic traffic signal at Hanumanthappa Circle, Chikmagalur (2) Contribution to Kala Mandir at Chikmagalur (3) Provision of a traffic island at Kavoor, Mangalore (4) Creation of a Police Parade Ground at Chikmagalur (5) Suspension bridge across river Bhadra at Nellibeedu (6) Construction of bridges across river Bhadra near Kudremukh (7) Towards maintenance of roads – contribution to the Mangalore City Corporation (8) Making a road along Gurupur River from Kulur Bridge to Airport Road (9) Donation to Lions Club of Bangalore Airport City, Bangalore for construction of hospital (10) Financial assistance to M/s. Age-Care India, New Delhi, for nodal project for Age-Care Complex at New Delhi (11) Donation for construction of 3 storeyed guest house by Sri Aurobindo Complex Trust, Bangalore.

APPENDIX-I (C)

The Rating of the Kudremukh Iron Ore Company

Year	Total sales	Foreign Exchange Earnings (In million dollars)	Dividend Paid (Rs. Crores)	MoU Rating
2001-2002	721.69	150.884	22.0	Excellent
2000-2001	583.00	127.000	22.0	Excellent
1999-2000	620.46	142.980	22.21	Excellent
1998-99	547.76	129.698	15.86	Very Good
1997-98	593.91	158.402	22.21	Excellent
1996-97	492.59	138.355	20.62	Excellent
1995-96	478.48	143.245	20.62	Excellent
1994-95	369.34	117.639	19.04	Excellent
1993-94	416.69	132.976	19.04	Excellent
1992-93	313.90	101.951	19.04	Very Good
1991-92	392.81	151.711	----	Very Good

APPENDIX-I (D)

Details of Contract of KIOCI with Other Countries

Country	Quantity	Nature & Duration of Contract	Value in US Dollars	Value in INR/Year	Remarks
Conce-ntrate					
Japan	500000 to 1000000	Long-Term upto 2005	17250000	807300000	
Iran	1500000	Long-Term upto 2006	31260000	1462968000	Contract provides for penalty for non-delivery upto 15.5% i.e. US $ 4.8 million (in INR 22.68 crores)
China	300000 to 600000	MOU annual basis	11550000	540540000	

Pellet					
China	2100000 to 2400000	Annual Basis	76190400	3565710720	
Taiwan	600000	Long-Term upto 2005	18183600	880476480	KIOCL has participated in tender period is likely to extend by two more years
Japan	80000 to 120000	Long-Term upto 2002	3730320	174578976	
Pellet Fines					
Japan	60000	Long-Term upto 2002	1042200	48774960	
Vessel accepted till September 2001 and its impact	Demurrage/cancellation charges US $ 1.0 million per month in case mining lease is not extended.				

APPENDIX-I (E)

Loss of Revenue Per Year to Government of India and Government of Karnataka

S. No.	Agency	Amount (Rs. Crores/annum)
1.	Port Charges to New Mangalore Port	20.00
2.	Land Rent to New Mangalore Port Trust	2.50
3.	Dividend Payment to Government of India	22.00
4.	Loss of Foreign Exchange to Govt. of India	600.00 (US $ 150 million)
5.	Total Loss to Port and Government of India	644.50

Loss of Revenue to Government of Karnataka Per Year

S.no.	Agency	Amount (Rs. Crores/annum)
1.	Karnataka State Electricity Board (KPTCL)	220.00
2.	Royalty to Mines and Geology	1.50
3.	Payment of Taxes, i.e. Sales Tax, Entry Tax, etc.	8.00
4.	Total Loss to State Government	299.50

APPENDIX-II

List of Scheduled Tribes As Per the 1991 Census of Karnataka

S. No.	Names of the Tribes
1.	Adiyan
2.	Barda
3.	Bavacha, Bamcha
4.	Bhil, Bhil Garasia, Dholi Bhil Rawal Bhil, Tadvi Bhil, Vasave
5.	Chenchu, Chenchwar
6.	Chodhara
7.	Dubla, Talavia, Halpati
8.	Gamit, Gamta, Gavit, Mavachi, Padvi valvi
9.	Gond, Naikpod, Rajgond
10.	Gowdalu
11.	Happipikki
12.	Hasalaru
13.	Irular
14.	Iruliga
15.	Jenu Kuruba
16.	Kadu Kuruba
17.	Kammara (in South Kanara District and Kollegal Taluk of Mysore District)
18.	-
19.	Kathodi, Katkari, Dhor Kathodi, Dhor
20.	-

21.	-
22.	Konda Kapus
23.	-
24.	Koraga
25.	Kota
26.	Koya, Bhine Koya
27.	Kudiya, Melakudi
28.	Kuruba (in Coorg District)
29.	Kurumans
30.	Maha Malasar
31.	Malaikudi
32.	Malasar
33.	-
34.	-
35.	-
36.	Marati (in South Canara district)
37.	Meda
38.	Naikda, Nayaka, Cholivala Nayaka, Nana Nayaka
39.	Palliyan
40.	Paniyan
41.	Paradhi, Advichincher, Phanse Pardhi
42.	Patelia
43.	Rathawa
44.	Sholaga
45.	Soligaru
46.	Toda
47.	Varli
48.	Vitolia, Kotwalia, Barodia
49.	Yerava

APPENDIX-II

Survey Number-wise Forest Areas of Kudremukh National Park

S. No.	Name of the Reserve Forest	Taluk	Village	Notified RF Area/ S. No.	Total RF Area of the Village	S. No. Wise Breakup		Total Area Mutated
						S. No.	Area in Acres	
1	2	3	4	5	6	7	8	9
SRINGERI WILDLIFE RANGE, KEREKATTE								
1.	Tunga Bhadra Reserve Forest	Sringeri	Kere	760.00	2166.16 Or 2166.00	14	470.27	3005.98 Or 3007.45
	Narasimha Parvatha Reserve Forest			1496.16		67 69 66 62 63 61 60	200.00 296.09 149.02 29.16 487.30	

2.	TungaBhadra Reserve Forest Narasimha Parvatha Reserve Forest	Sringeri	Gulaganjimane	2691.06 121.00	2812.06 Or 2812.15	7 24 25 28 32 33 35 12	499.36 707.00 423.06 612.00 300.00 293.30 675.17 242.00	3751.23 Or 3751.58
3.	Tunga Bhadra Reserve Forest	Mudigere	Samse	17015.04	17015.04 Or 17015.10	54/1 55/1 56 57/1 59/1 64/1 73/1 74/1 75/2 120/P2P	1961.35 1955.32 2076.16 1284.28 2220.00 982.00 1500.00 1309.33 1649.07 785.00	15724.78
4.	Tunga Bhadra Reserve Forest	Mudigere	Samse	20914.34	20914.34	25/P21 25/P122 26 27P1 28 29 33	280.00 100.00 22.08 869.33 0.10 3.23 39.28	21465.92

4.						34/1 38 39 40 41 42 43 44 50P2 138/2 141 142/1 143 183/2 104	2169.32 32.36 82.14 52.15 4678.10 2093.12 5.37 2154.03 1469.26 712.00 1011.34 2028.25 1450.11 1600.00 600.00	
VENOOR WILDLIFE RANGE, BELTHANGADI								
1.	Naravi Reserve Forest	Belthangadi	Malavanthige	236/P1 236/P2 236/P3 236/P1P1	10078.60 124.20 191.35 2303.00		12697.20	12697.20

2.	Naravi Reserve Forest	Belthangadi	Navoor	160/5P1 160/5P2 160/5P3	1963.83 23.12 10570.00		12556.95	12556.95
3.	Naravi Reserve Forest	Belthangadi	Nada	115/1P1 115/1P16 115/1P55	1316.50 60.00 62.08		1438.58	1438.58
4.	Naravi Reserve Forest	Belthangadi	Laila	158/1P6 158/1P63 158/1AP64	51.30 180.61 127.00		358.91	358.91
5.	Naravi Reserve Forest	Belthangadi	Sulkeremogru	64/1	3310.34		3310.34	3310.34
6.	Naravi Reserve Forest	Belthangadi	Shirlal	69/1	4366.36		4366.36	4366.36
7.	Naravi Reserve Forest	Belthangadi	Navara	41/1P1	475.70		475.70	475.70
8.	Naravi Reserve Forest	Belthangadi	Savanal	81/1P1	3058.87		3058.87	3058.87

9.	Naravi Reserve Forest	Belthangadi	Kuthloor	96/1	4437.23		4437.23	4437.23
10.	Naravi Reserve Forest	Belthangadi	Naravi	170/P1 242/P1	20.35 3064.30		3084.65	3084.65
11.	Naravi Reserve Forest	Belthangadi	Mittabagilu	184 184/P2	5.20 33.26		38.46	38.46
12.	Naravi Reserve Forest	Belthangadi	Badaga Karandoor	25/2	0.33		0.33	0.33
VENOOR WILDLIFE RANGE, BELTHANGADI								
1.	Andar Reserve Forest	Karkala	Andar	135	7196.62	135	7196.62	7196.62
2.	Andar Reserve Forest	Karkala	Shirlal	226	214.10	226	214.10	214.10

3.	Andar Reserve Forest	Karkala	Shirlal	101	3260.00	101	3260.00	3260.00
4.	Andar Reserve Forest	Karkala	Kervase	175	6032.00	175	6032.00	6032.00
5.	Andar Reserve Forest	Karkala	Marne	376	244.83	376	244.83	244.83
6.	Andar Reserve Forest	Karkala	Marne	349	0.92	349	0.92	0.92
7.	Andar Reserve Forest	Karkala	Marne	482	0.52	482	0.52	0.52
8.	Andar Reserve Forest	Karkala	Marne	543	2.42	543	2.42	2.42

9.	Andar Reserve Forest	Karkala	Kabbinale	103	4456.67	103	4456.67	-
10.	Andar Reserve Forest	Karkala	Mudradi	195	581.95	195	581.95	-
11.	Andar Reserve Forest	Karkala	Varanga	20	29.83	20	29.83	-
12.	Andar Reserve Forest	Karkala	Varanga	23	128.30	23	128.30	-
13.	Andar Reserve Forest	Karkala	Mala	237	5722.94	237	5722.94	-
14.	Andar Reserve Forest	Karkala	Mala	222	228.17	222	228.17	-

15.	Andar Reserve Forest	Karkala	Idu	209	3440.18	209	3440.18	-
16.	Andar Reserve Forest	Karkala	Idu	120/1	1.23	120/1	1.23	-
17.	Andar Reserve Forest	Karkala	Idu	120/2	0.69	120/2	0.69	-
18.	Andar Reserve Forest	Karkala	Idu	120/3	0.10	120/3	0.10	-
19.	Andar Reserve Forest	Karkala	Idu	120/4	0.12	120/4	0.12	-
20.	Andar Reserve Forest	Karkala	Idu	119/1	0.93	119/1	0.93	-
21.	Andar Reserve Forest	Karkala	Idu	119/2	2.90	119/2	2.90	-

22.	Andar Reserve Forest	Karkala	Idu	199/3	0.19	119/3	0.19	-
23.	Andar Reserve Forest	Karkala	Idu	118/1	1.38	118/1	1.38	-
24.	Andar Reserve Forest	Karkala	Idu	118/2	0.73	118/2	.73	-
25.	Andar Reserve Forest	Karkala	Idu	118/3	0.11	118/3	0.11	-
26.	Andar Reserve Forest	Karkala	Nooralbettu	123/1	1840.62	123/1	1840.62	-
27.	Andar Reserve Forest	Karkala	Nooralbettu	122/1	194.64	122/1	194.64	-
Serial Number-wise break up of areas is subject to confirmation by Revenue Authorities.								

APPENDIX-III (A)

Demographics of Buffer Villages within 5 Km Radius

S. No.	Village Name	Area of the village (in ha.)				Total (3+4+5+6)	Village Population (in no.)				Total (8+9+10+ 11)	Cattle Popul-ation (in nos.)	People Residing Within Forest Area, if any
		Revenue Land	Degraded Forest Land	Good Forest	Other Land		SC	ST	OBC	Gen-eral			
1	2	3	4	5	6	7	8	9	10.	11.	12.	13.	14.
	KARKALA WILDLIFE RANGE, KARKALA												
1.	Kervase	882.22	1012.13	2014.44	301.51	4210.30	290	216	2006	380	2892	1968	11
2.	Shirlal	768.57	744.07	1292.52	846.53	3681.69	89	270	1966	218	2543	1645	-
3.	Andar	437.25	1263.45	1867.23	590.17	4158.10	107	326	1623	154	2210	1433	766
4.	Kabbinale	390.56	236.85	1938.7	28.85	2594.96	61	263	1247	-	1571	534	168
5.	Mala	1347-.9	394.72	2452.75	506.08	4701.45	908	1089	1906	1034	4937	3408	28
6.	Eedu	1017.79	497.46	862.49	615.31	2993.05	365	742	1584	1326	4017	3174	5
7.	Nuralbettu	621.82	286.82	873.46	338.34	2120.44	168	63	795	1074	2100	1160	207
8.	Naravi	895.22	-	1351.78	493.83	2740.83	327	764	1734	2139	4964	2796	69
9.	Kuthloor	528.21	108.07	1921.44	102.6	2660.32	223	251	769	327	1570	839	302
	WILDLIFE RANGE, KEREKATTE												
1.	Navoor	417.12	81.00	5000.73	579.92	6078.77	82	179	250	1844	2355	623	-
2.	Nada	577.61	4.00	20.28	1285	1886.89	129	209	400	1981	2719	1022	-
3.	Malav-anthige	533.61	396.99	4765.45	897.61	6593.66	23	379	550	1646	2598	1545	-
4.	Laila	413.11	45.00	100.25	1300.18	1858.54	743	228	1850	3377	6198	1015	-
5.	Mittabagilu	641.78	2.00	13.56	54.05	711.39	103	59	950	1982	3094	1147	-
6.	Shirlal	389.29	300.00	1509.92	215.23	2414.44	209	255	600	889	1953	1302	-

7.	Savanalu	291.65	100.00	1386.01	183.09	1960.75	162	230	470	629	1491	817	-
8.	Navara	173.98	2.00	15.93	361.23	553.14	108	107	185	344	744	287	-
9.	Sulkerimogru	246.33	100.00	1239.67	648.47	2234.47	95	115	500	508	1218	475	-
10.	B.Karandoor	297.97	0.13	-	178.09	476.19	269	10	150	1414	1843	542	-
11.	Kanyadi	354.92	-	-	568.29	923.21	56	103	779	625	1563	580	-
12.	Kadirudyavara	557.82	-	-	188.99	746.81	174	373	1400	768	2715	1433	-
13.	Indabettu	668.72	-	-	640.45	1309.17	286	98	950	1796	3130	687	-
	Total	5563.91	1031.12	14051.80	7100.60	27747.43	2439	2345	9034	17803	31621	11475	0
WILDLIFE RANGE, KEREKATTE													
1.	K.Masige	-	54.06	621.14	29.14	704.34	23	28	65	241	357	714	-
2.	Yadadalli	-	123.43	499.88	14.67	637.98	180	80	457	350	1067	857	-
3.	Markal	-	406.22	1136.2	5.72	1548.14	198	275	356	596	1425	540	-
4.	Kere	-	-	1298	70.01	1368.01	23	28	65	241	357	26	-
5.	Shirlu	-	-	4076.66	31.97	4108.63	-	217	-	-	217	247	-
6.	Gulganjimane	-	78.42	1525.33	34.03	1637.78	13	26	53	66	158	289	-
7.	Balikadi	-	-	2103.3	46.97	2150.27	35	53	51	48	187	338	-
8.	Karkikan Est.	-	-	73.02	-	73.02	-	-	-	-	0	-	-
9.	Murvalli Est.	-	-	208.92	-	208.92	-	-	-	-	0	-	-
10.	Sunkadamakki	-	-	289.88	-	289.88	40	9	35	39	123	25	-
11.	Hadi	-	-	978.19	16.18	994.37	8	10	9	26	53	205	-
12.	Hadikeruru	-	-	688.36	16.39	704.75	20	69	19	31	139	202	-
13.	Balegere	-	19.09	2978.41	49.37	3046.87	10	185	11	25	231	490	-

14.	Muduba	-	-	2585.09	217.05	2802.14	20	53	40	77	190	205	-
15.	Kallugudde	-	398.08	1174.29	13.09	1585.46	6	201	45	-	252	218	-
16.	Haralane	-	99.15	383.04	10	492.19	5	9	11	-	25	124	-
	Total		1178.45	20619.71	554.59	22352.75	581	1243	1217	1740	4781	4480	0
KUDREMUKH WILDLIFE RANGE, KUDREMUKH													
1.	Samse	3737	6140	9210	373	19460	156	306	9050	950	10462	3200	280
2.	Hornadu	1634	80	120	163	1997	25	15	85	25	150	275	-
3.	Kalkodu	738	820	1230	73	2861	12	25	453	40	530	750	-
4.	Total	6109	7040	10560	609	24318	193	346	9588	1015	11142	4225	280

Glossary

S. No.	Word	Meaning
1.	*Areca nut*	betel nut
2.	*Adivasi*	indigenous people, often associated with tribals
3.	*Bandh*	militant form of agitation-struggle or complete stoppage of work
4.	*Dharna*	picketing
5.	*Gunta*	measure of land (100 *gunta* is one hectare)
6.	*Gheraos*	to surround or lay siege
7.	*Gunta*	measure of land (100 *gunta* is one hectare)
8.	*Jathas*	procession
9.	*Jagirs*	the land and other revenues of a certain area assigned to an individual who is given the power to administer the area in lieu of services rendered as a mark of favour.
10.	*Lingayats and vokkaligas*	peasant caste of South India, particularly in Karnataka (an upwardly mobile, politically powerful group located in the middle of the Hindu caste system).
11.	*Patel*	Hereditary post of village officer meant to serve as tax intermediary during the British period
12.	*Ryotwari*	a form of land settlement in which the peasants pay their land tax directly to the state.

13.	*Ryot*	peasant
14.	*Sufi*	Muslim devotional sect, emphasizing love and reflection of established conventions.
15.	*Scheduled Castes and Scheduled Tribes*	caste groups listed in the Fifth Schedule of the Constitution of India for preferential treatment (positive discrimination) in education and government employment; list renewed/ modified every 10 years by presidential promulgation.
16.	*Taluk*	a unit of revenue and administration, several units constitute a district or zilla

Bibliography

Primary Source

A Fact-Finding Report Escalating Ecocide in the Kudremukh National Park, Nagarika Seva Trust, Gurvayanakere, Dakshina Kannada, Karnataka.

Annual Report of the Kudremukh Iron Ore Company Limited, 1999-2000.

Annual Report of the Kudremukh Iron Ore Company Limited, 2004-2005.

Circular of Kudremukh Shram Shakti Sangathan dated December 26, 2005.

Copy of the letter No. 13-1/90-F.P (1) dated September 18, 1990 from the Joint Secretary to the Government of India, Ministry of Environment and Forests, Department of Environment, Forests and Wildlife, addressed to the Secretary, Forest Department, Bangalore, Karnataka regarding Encroachments on Forest Lands – A Review thereof and Measure for Containment.

Curative Petition for Re-examination of the Order dated October 30, 2002 of this Honorable Court in I.A. No. 670/2001 directing the closure of Kudremukh Iron Ore Mines in Karnataka with effect from December 31, 2005.

Karnataka Growers Association (2006): Letter to Shri Kamal Nath Regarding Relief Package for Coffee Growers, dated May 27, Saklespur, Karnataka.

Karnataka Planters Association (1983): The Development of Malnad, Plantation Industry in Perspective, Published by Karnataka Planters Association, Chikmagalur.

Karnataka State Archives: Enclosure No. 1157/81, Office of the Inspector General of Forests and Plantations in Mysore to the Chief Secretary to the Government of Mysore, dated August 7, 1889, Report of Forests 1868-1900, Bangalore.

Kudremukh Daily Wage Workers Union, Mudigere Taluk, Chikmagalur District: Letter Written to Shri Manmohan Singh, February 9, 2006.

Letter from KIOCL SC/ST Employees Welfare Association, for the Extension of Mining, 2002.

Letter From P. Ganesan, Chairman-Cum-Managing Director of KI-OCL, to then Chief Minister of Karnataka, S.M. Krishana, on February 28, 2003.

Letter From P. Ganesan, Chairman-Cum-Managing Director of KIO-CL, to then Chief Minister of Karnataka Mr. Dharam Singh, on June 25, 2004.

Letter from P. Ganesan, Chairman-Cum-Managing Director of KIO-CL, to then Minister for Industries, P.G.R. Sindhia, on August 28, 2004.

Letter from the Government of Karnataka Addressed to Central Government for Approval for the Renewal of Lease for a period of 20 years, dated July 6, 1999.

Letter from the Principal Conservator of Forests, No. A5 (B1), MNG, CR. 343/92-93, submitted in favour of M/s. Kudremukh Iron Ore Company Limited.

Letter No. C3/CR/30/KNP/99-2000 Office of the Deputy Conservator of Forests, Kudremukh Wildlife Division, Karkala, dated June 30, 2000.

Letter No. 5(B3) GFL.CR. 231/92-93 from the Principal Chief Conservator of Forests to the Principal Secretary to Government, Department of Forests, Ecology and Environment, dated October 17, 1997.

Letter No. 8-50/95-FC, dated May 15, 1996 of the Government of India regarding regularization of encroachment of forest lands that have taken place prior to April 27, 1978 and diversion of 14,848.81 hectares of forest land.

Acquisition and Rehabilitation, Phase-I in Kudremukh National Park, Kudremukh Wildlife Division, Karkala, Karnataka Forest Department, 2004.

Annual Meeting of the Livelihoods of Adivasis Through Multipurpose Societies Lamp Sahakara Sangha (LAMPS) Registered, Koopa Taluk, Chikmagalur 2007.

Letter No. FEE.270.FWL.99, dated June 16, 2001.

Letter Written by Rajan Rao Yedoor of Nagarika Seva Trust to Shri H.K. Patil, Honourable Minister for Medium and Large Irrigation projects, Government of Karnataka, Vidhana Soudha, July 19, 2001.

Letter Written by Rajan Rao Yedoor of Nagarika Seva Trust to the Chief Justice of India, Supreme Court of India, July 19, 1999.

Letter Written by Rajan Rao Yedoor of Nagarika Seva Trust to the Principal Conservator of Forests, Wildlife, July 19, 1999.

Letter written to Shri Atal Behari Vajpayee Former Prime Minister of India, by Srikantappa, D.C. (Member of Parliament) to consider the interests of farmers and tribals, instead of viewing the prospects of KIOCL only, dated April 25, 2001.

Memorandum submitted to Honorable Minister, Mr. Vidya Sagar Rao Minister of State for Commerce and Industry, on behalf of Coffee Growers of Karnataka, Kerala and Tamil Nadu, Government of India, July 2, 2003.

Memorandum submitted by Kudremukh Employees Union to Valmik Thapar to Honourable Chairman and Members of the Central Empowered Committee during his visit to Kudremukh on September 30, 2002.

Memorandum submitted by Kudremukh Mazdoor Sangh to Valmik Thapar to Honourable Chairman and Members of the Central Empowered Committee during his visit to Kudremukh on September 30, 2002.

Memorandum submitted by Kudremukh Officers Association to Valmik Thapar to Honourable Chairman and Members of the Central Empowered Committee during his visit to Kudremukh on September 30, 2002.

Memorandum submitted by Kudremukh Shram Shakti Sanghatan to Valmik Thapar to Honorable Chairman and Members of the Central Empowered Committee during his visit to Kudremukh on September 30, 2002.

Minutes of the meeting held under the Chairmanship of Ministry of Commerce and Industry, Department of Commerce, to consider the implementation of SCTL package for coffee growers and other financial problems of coffee sector, July 7, New Delhi, 2003.

Opening Remarks of Chairperson, Coffee Board at the 174th Meeting of the Board on December 6, 2004.

Rajya Sabha: Unstarred Question No.1107, answered on March 3, 2003, by Minister of Commerce and Industry Shri Rajiv Pratap Rudy.

Recommendations of the Central Empowered Committee in I.A. No. 670 of 2001 in Writ Petition (Civil) No. 202 of 1995.

Report of the First Convention: Mines, Minerals and People: *Our Land, Our Minerals, Our Rights*, from April 28 to May 1, 2000,

Hyderabad, Andhra Pradesh.

Report of the BNHS titled 'Representative Sample filed Survey of Flora and fauna in Kudremukh Mine Area', 1998.

Report of the Indian Institute of Science titled 'Impact of Iron Ore Mining on Flora and Fauna of Kudremukh National Park and Environment—A Rapid Assessment' in 2001.

Report of the Mangalore University titled 'Studies on Conservation of Plant Biodiversity and Eco-restoration of Abandoned Mines of Kudremukh Iron Ore Company Limited' 1996.

Report of the NEERI titled 'Comprehensive Environment Impact Assessment of Kudremukh Iron Ore Mines', 2001.

Report on the forest Violation by the Kudremukh Iron Ore Company Limited, Deputy Conservator of Forests, Kudremukh Wildlife Division, Karkala, 2002.

The Coffee Guide: Central Coffee Research Institute, (CCRI) Coffee Research Station, Chikmagalur District Karnataka, 1997.

Tiger Task Force (2005): Joining the Dots, Ministry of Environment and Forests.

Task Force for Recovery of Public Land and its protection (2011): Greed and Convenience, Government of Karnataka.

Interviews (Arranged by Date)

G.V. Kempegowda, District President of the Sri Durga Parameshwari Yuvaka Sangaha, Menasinahadya, Affiliated to Kudremukh Rashtriya Udyana Virodhi Okkouta, November 15, 2006.

Kulki Vittal Hedge President of the Kudremukh Rashtriya Virodhi Okkuta, December 28, 2006.

K.G. Sridhar, Activist Spearheaded Tunga Ulisi, November 14, 2006.

Sundar, a former KVR activist, November 28, 2006.

Praveen Bhargava, A Conservationist, December 5, 2006.

V.S. Sreedhar, KVR activist, December 7, 2006.

Girjashankar, Editor of *Janmitra Magazine*, January 27, 2007.

Vijay Ranjan Singh, Deputy Conservator of Forests, January 29, 2007.

Anwar Pasha, Member of Kudremukh Employees Union affiliated to Indian National Trade Union Congress (INTUC), January 29, 2007.

S. Venkatraya, General Secretary of Kudremukh Shram Shakti Sanghatan, affiliated to H.M.S., January 31, 2007.

Rajan Rao Yedoor, Trustee of Nagrika Seva Trust, March 5, 2007.

Subhash Kharbare, Member of H.M.S, Bangalore, March 10, 2007.

B.G. Kushalappa, Industrial Relation Officer of Karnataka Planters Association, February 13, 2007.

K.S. Kashinath, General Manager (CP&TS) Kudremukh Iron Ore Company, March 15, 2007.

G.N. Nagraj, General Secretary of CPI(Marxist) March 16, 2007.

Ashish Kothari, Kalpavriskh, September 10, 2007.

T. Veeranna, Secretary Kudremukh Employees Union affiliated to Indian National Trade Union Congress (INTUC), September 14, 2007.

B.P. Ravi, Divisional Forest Officer, Koppa division, September 18, 2007.

G.H. Onkarappa, Deputy Director (Extension), Coffee Board, September 19, 2007.

Periyaswamy, Secretary of the Kuduremukh Daily Wage Workers Union Affiliated to AITUC, on September 25, 2007.

Kalavathi, Former Employee as Daily Wage, September 26, 2007.

Kulkarni, Member of BMS, Kudremukh, September 26, 2007.

Ramesh, a Taxi driver in, Jamble, Kudremukh, September 27, 2007.

Saathi Sundaresh, Zilla Parishad Member of CPI, October 5, 2007.

A.M. Annaiah, Deputy Conservator of Forests, October 9, 2007.

B.P. Ravi, District Forest Officer, Koppa Division, October 18, 2007.

Gunashekaran, General Secretary of United Plantation Workers Union, October 19, 2007.

B.S. Jayaram, President of Karnataka Growers Federation, June 17, 2015.

George Austin, Taluk Secretary of Coffee Labour Union, Communist Party of India, June 20, 2015.

Prasanna, Gram Panchayat Member, Shirivase Village, June 21, 2015

P. Ramesh Kumar, Deputy Conservator of Forests, Kudremukh Wildlife Division Karkala, June 24, 2015.

Secondary Sources

Alavi, Seema (2003): *The Eighteenth Century in India* (ed), Oxford University Press, New Delhi.

Appaiya, M.M. (1993): *Coffee: The Consolidated Story*, United Planters Association, Connore.

Assadi, Muzzaffar (1997): *Peasant Movement in Karnataka 1980-94*, Shipra Publications, Delhi.

Baden Powel, B.H. (1974): *The Land Systems of British India*, Oriental Publishers, New Delhi.

Bhaduri, Amit and D. Nayyar (1996): *The Intelligent Persons Guide to Liberalization*, Penguin Books, New Delhi.

Banarjee, Sumanta (1980): *In the Wake of Naxalbari: A History of the Naxalite Movement in India*, Subarnarekha, Calcutta.

Basrur, M. Rajesh (2009): Challenges to Democracy in India (ed), Oxford University Press, New Delhi.

Bayly (1983) *Townsmen and Bazaars: North Indian Society in the Age of British Expansion*, 1770-1870, Cambridge University Press.

Beauchamp, Joan (1934): *British Imperialism in India*, Martin Lawrence Ltd., London.

Beckford, G.L. (1972): *Persistent Poverty: Underdevelopment in Plantation Economies of the Third World*, Oxford University Press, London.

Beteille, Andre (1966): *Caste, Class, and Power: Changing Patterns of Stratification in a Tanjore Village*, Oxford University Press, New Delhi.

Bjorn, Hettne (1978): *Political Economy of Indirect Rule: Mysore -1881-1947*, Curzon Press, London.

Boralingaiah, H.C and N. Huchappa Master (2002): *Kagodu Chalavali: Suvarna Samputa: A Golden Jubilee Volume on Peasant Movements in Kagodu* (ed), Published by Malendadu Janapada Loka, Shimoga Karnataka.

Buchanan, Francis (1807): *A Journey from Madras, Through the Countries of Mysore, Malabar and Canara*, Vol. I and Vol. II, Blumar and Co. London.

Baviskar, Amita and Raka Ray (2011): *Elite and Everyman: The Cultural Politics of the Indian Middle Classes* (ed), Routledge Publishing.

Bayly, C.A. (1988): *Indian Society and the Making of the British Empire*, Vol. 2, New Cambridge History of India, Cambridge.

Bardhan, Pranab (1984): *The Political Economy of Development in India*, New Delhi, Oxford University Press, New Delhi.

Banerjee, Tarun Kumar (2010): *The Naxalite Movement: Currents and Cross Currents*, Progressive Publishers, Kolkata.

Chandrasekhar, C.P. and Jayati Ghosh (2002): *The Market That Failed: A Decade of Neoliberal Economic Reforms in India*, LeftWord Publications, New Delhi.

Coffee Guide (2014): *A Manual of Coffee Cultivation*, Published by Coffee Research Station, Chikmagalur District, Karnataka.

Chandrasekhar, S (1985): *Dimensions of Socio-Political Change in Mysore, 1918-80*, Ashish Publishing House, New Delhi.

Cassen, Robert and Vijay Joshi (1995): *India: The Future of Economic Reform* (eds), Oxford University Press, Delhi.

Chakravorty, Sanjoy (2013): *The Price of Land: Acquisition Conflict Consequence*, Oxford University Press, New Delhi.

Chandrashekar, S (1995): *Colonialism, Conflict and Nationalism South India: 1857-1947*, Wishwa Prakashan, Bangalore.

Chandrashekar, S. (2004): *Peoples Movements in the Princely States* (ed) by V. Vaikuntham, Manohar Publishers, New Delhi.

Chatterjee, Pratap and Matthias Finger (1994): *The Earth Brokers: Power, Politics and World Development*, Routledge, London.

D'Souza, Rohan (2006): *Drowned and Dammed: Colonial Capitalism and Flood Control in Eastern India*, Oxford University Press, New Delhi.

Damle, C.B. (1993): *Land Reforms and Changing Agrarian Relations*, Rawat Publications, New Delhi.

Dutta, Ritwick and Bhupender Yadav (2011): *Supreme Court on Forest Conservation*, Universal Law Publishing Company, New Delhi.

Della Porta, D. and M. Diani (1999): *Social Movements*, Blackwell Publishers.

Nash, June (2005): *Social Movements: An Anthropological Reader* (ed) by June Nash, Blackwell Publishing.

Oommen, T.K. (1990): *Protest and Change: Studies in Social Movements*, Sage Publications, New Delhi.

Elliot, H. Elliot (1894): *Gold, Sport and Coffee Planting in Mysore*, London.

Enrlich, P.R. and Enrlich (1968): *The Population Bomb Linking*, New York.

Fernandes, Leena (2006): *Liberalization, Democracy and Middle Class Politics*, Oxford University Press, New Delhi.

Fernandes, Walter and Sharad Kulkarni (1983): *Towards a New Forest Policy: People's Right and Environment Needs*, Indian Social Institute, New Delhi.

Francine, R. Frankel, Zoya Hasan, Rajeev Bhargava and Balveer Arora (2000): *Transforming India: Social and Political Dynamics of Democracy*, Oxford University Press, New Delhi.

Frykenberg (1977): *Land Tenure and Peasants in South Asia*, Orient Longman, New Delhi.

Gadgil, Madhav and R. Guha (1995): *Ecology and Equity: The Use and Abuse of Nature in Contemporary India*, Penguin Books, New Delhi.

Glyan and Emma Mawdsley (2006): "India's Evolving Political Ecologies" in *Colonial and Post-colonial Geographies of India* (ed) by Saraswati Raju, M. Satish Kumar, and Stuart Corbridge, Sage Publications.

Gopal, M.H. (1960): *The Finances of the Mysore State* 1799-1831.

Gopal, M.H. (1993): *British Sources of the Economic, Political and Social History of Mysore State*, Vol. I, Popular Prakashan, Bombay.

Gudavarthy, Ajay (2014): *Maoism, Democracy and Globalization: Cross Currents in Indian Politics*, Sage Publications, New Delhi.

Guha, Ramachandra (1989): *The Unquiet Woods: Ecological Change and Peasant Resistance in the Himalayas*, Oxford University Press, Delhi.

Guha, Ramachandra and Juar Martinez Alien (1997): *Varieties of Environmental: Essays on North and South*, Earth Scan Publications Ltd.

Guha, Ramachandra (2003): *The Last Liberal and Other Essays*, Permanent Black, New Delhi.

Gudavarthy, Ajay (2015): *Cultural Politics of Modern India*, Aakar Books, New Delhi.

Halappa, G.S. and Krishna Rao, M.V. (1962): *History of Freedom Movement* (Ed), Vol. I, Bangalore.

Hasan, Zoya (2000): *Politics and the State in India* (ed), Sage Publications, New Delhi.

Harddin, Garrett and John Baden (1977): *Managing the Commons* (ed), W.H. Freeman and Company, San Francisco.

Jayal, Niraja Gopal and Pratap Bhanu Mehta (2011): *The Oxford Companion to Politics in India* (Ed), Oxford University Press, New Delhi.

Jogdand, P.G. and S.M. Michael (2003): *Globalization and Social Movements: Struggle for a Humane Society*, (ed), Rawat Publications, Jaipur.

Jenkins, Rob (1999): *Democratic Politics and Economic Reform in India*, Cambridge University Press.

Kanawalli, Sadanand (1993): *Quest for Justice*, Samaj Parivartana Samudaya, Dharwad.

Khilnani, Sunil (1997): *The Idea of India*, Penguin Books, New Delhi.

Kumar, Dharma (1982): *The Cambridge Economic History of India: 1757-1990*, Cambridge University Press, New Delhi.

Kumar, Deepak (1995): *Science and the Raj: A Study of British India*, Oxford University Press, New Delhi.

Kothari, Ashish (1997): *Understanding Biodiversity: Life Sustainability and Equity*, Orient Longman, New Delhi.

Kothari, Smitu, Imtiaz Ahmad and Helmut Reifeld (2003): *Ecological Politics in India: The Value of Nature* (ed), Rainbow Publishers, New Delhi.

Kohli, Atul (1987): *The State and Poverty in India*, Cambridge, Cambridge University Press.

Kadekodi, K. Gopal, Ravi Kanbur and Vijendra Rao (2008): *Development in Karnataka: Challenges of Governance, Equity and Empowerment* (ed), Academic Foundation, New Delhi.

Krishnamurti, Y.G. (1941): *Sir M. Visvesvaraya: A Study*, Popular Book Depot, Bombay.

Muthiah, S. (1993): *A Planting Century: The First Hundred Years of the United Planters Association of South India 1883-1993*, Bangalore.

Menon, Nivedita and Aditya Nigam (2007): *Power and Contestation India Since 1989*, Orient Longman Private Limited, Hyderabad.

Mohanty, Amarnath (2011): *Justice, Democracy and State in India: Reflections on Structure, Dynamics and Ambivalence*, Routledge Publications, New Delhi.

Mukherji, Nirmalangshu (2013): *The Maoists in India: Tribals Under Siege*, New Delhi, Amaryllis Publications.

Lele, Shaarachchandra and Ajit Menon (2014): *Democratizing Forest Governance in India* (ed), Oxford University Press, New Delhi.

Nadkarni, M.V. and Syed Ajmal Pasha (1989): *Political Economy of Forest Use and Management*, Sage Publications, New Delhi.

Nage Gowda, H.L (1969): *Bettadinda Battalige* (From the Mountain to the Cup), Published by Sahitya Sadana, Arasikere, Manipal (in Kannada).

Nair, Janaki (1998): *Miners and Mill Hands: Work, Culture and Politics in Princely Mysore*, Sage Publications, New Delhi.

Neginhal, S.G. (2011): *Forest Trees of the Western Ghats (includes Eastern Ghats and Deccan Plateau)*, Bangalore.

Omvedt, Gail (1994) *Reinventing Revolution: New Social Movements and Socialist Tradition in India*, New York.

Oommen, T.K (1990): *Protest and Change: Studies in Social Movements*, Sage Publications, New Delhi.

Patnaik, Utsa and Manjari Dingwaney (1985): *Chains of Servitude, Bondage and Slavery in India* (ed), Sangam Books, Madras.

Pinto, Ambrose (2014): *From Democratic Socialism to Neoliberalism: The Story of India's Democracy*, Indian Institute of Advanced Study, Shimla.

Prabhu, Pradip (2002): "Land Alienation, Land Reforms and Tribals in Maharashtra", in *Land Reforms in India: Issues of Equity in Madhya Pradesh*, Vol. VII (ed) Praveen K. Jha, Sage Publications, New Delhi.

Prasad, Archana (2004): *Environmentalism and the Left*, Leftword Books, New Delhi.

Prasad, Vijay (2015): *No Free Left: The Future of Indian Communism*, Left Word Books, New Delhi.

Pushpangadan, K. and V.N. Balasubramanyam (2012): *Growth, Development, and Diversity: India's Record Since Liberalization*, Oxford University Press, New Delhi.

Radhakrishnan, B.P. (1996): *Mineral Resources of Karnataka*, Geological Society of India, Bangalore.

Rajan, M.A.S. (1979): *The Land Reforms Law in Karnataka*, Government Press, Bangalore.

Rajan, S. Saket (2004): *Making History Karnataka's People and Their Past*, Vol. II, Vimukthi Prakashana, Bangalore.

Rajashekera, G. (1980): *Kagodu Satyagraha*, Sagar, Akshara Prakashan, (in Kannada).

Ramachandra (2003): *The Last Liberal and Other Essays*, Permanent Black, New Delhi.

Rao, C. Hayavadana, (1927): *History of Mysore (1399-1799)* Compiled for Mysore Gazetteer, Vol. I, New Edition, Bangalore.

Rao, Shama (1936): *Modern Mysore from the Beginning to 1868*, Higginbotham, Bangalore.

Rudolph, Lloyd I. and Sussanne Hoebaer Rudolph (1987): *In Pursuit of Lakshmi: The Political Economy of the Indian State*, Orient Longman, New Delhi.

Raghavan, E. and James Manor (2009): *Broadening and Deepening Democracy: Political Innovation in Karnataka*, Routledge, New Delhi.

Ramaswamy, Harish, S.S. Patagundi and S.H. Patel (2007): *Karnataka Government and Politics*, Concept Publishing Company, New Delhi.

Ray, Raka and Mary Fainsod Farzenstein (2005): Farmers' Movements and the Debate on Poverty and Economic Reforms in India, in *Poverty, Power and Politics* (ed), Rowman Littlefield Publishers.

Saberwal, K. Vasanth and Mahesh Rangarajan (2003): *Battles of Nature: Science and the Politics of Conservation*, Permanent Black, New Delhi.

Sachs, J.D, Ashutosh Varshney and Nirupam Bajpai (1999): *India in the Era of Economic Reforms*, Oxford University Press, New Delhi.

Sahu, Geetanjoy (2014): *Environmental Jurisprudence and the Supreme Court Litigation, Interpretation, Implementation*, Orient Blackswan, New Delhi.

Samaddar, Ranabir and Suhit K. Sen (2012): *Political Transition and Development Imperatives in India* (ed), Routledge Publications, New Delhi.

Sarkar, Sumit (2002): *Beyond Nationalist Frames: Relocating Post Modernism, Hindutva, History*, Permanent Black, New Delhi.

Sathe, S.P. (2002): *Judicial Activism in India: Transgressing Borders and Enforcing Limits*, Oxford University Press, New Delhi.

Savyasaachi and Ravi Kumar (2014): *Social Movements: Transformative Shifts and Turning Points* (ed), Routledge Publications, New Delhi.

Scott, John (2001): *Power*, Polity Press, Cambridge.

Sengupta and Stuart Corbridge (2010): *Democracy, Development and Decentralisation in India* (ed), Routledge Publications, New Delhi.

Shah, Esha (2003): *Social Designs: Tank Irrigation Technology and Agrarian Transformation in Karnataka, South India*, Orient Longman, New Delhi.

Shrivastava, Aseem and Ashish Kothari (2002): *Churning the Earth: The Making of Global India*, Penguin, New Delhi.

Sikand, Yoginder (2006): *Muslims in India: Contemporary Social and Political Discourses*, Hope India Publications, Gurgaon.

Singh, Rajendra (2001): *Social Movements Old and New: A Post-Modernist Critique*, Sage Publications, New Delhi.

Sinha, Aseema (2005): *The Regional Roots of Developmental Politics in India*, Indiana University Press, Bloomington.

Speer, S.G. (1953): *UPASI 1853-1953*, Association of South India, Coonor.

Sridharan, E. and Peter Ronald D'Souza (2006): *Indian Political Parties*, (ed), Sage Publications, New Delhi.

Stein, Burton (1990): *Thomas Munro: The Origins of the Colonial State and His Visions of Empire*, Oxford University Press, Delhi.

Swaminathan, Madhura (2002): *Weakening Welfare: The Public Distribution of Food in India*, Leftword, New Delhi.

Swamy, Siddalinga (1997): *Agrarian Relations in Mysore, 1799-1881*, Nation Builders Booksellers, Bangalore.

Thambanda, Vijay Poonacha (2004): *Conflicting Identities in Karnataka: Separate State and Anti-Separate Movements in Coorg*, Kannada University, Hampi.

Thapar, Valimik (2003): *Battling for Survival: India's Wilderness Over*

Two Centuries (ed), Oxford University Press, New Delhi.

Tucker, Richard P. (2012): *A Forest History of India*, Sage Publications, New Delhi.

Vanaik, Achin and Rajeev Bhargava (2010): *Understanding Contemporary India, Critical Perespectives*, Orient BlackSwan.

Varma, Pavan K. (1998): *The Great Indian Middle Class*, Penguin Books, New Delhi.

Vasant, Saberwal, Mahesh Rangarajan and Ashish Kothari (2001): *People, Parks and Wildlife: Towards Coexistence*, Oriental Longman.

Venugopal, N. (2013): *Understanding Maoists: Notes of a Participant Observer from Andhra Pradesh*, Setu Prakashani, Kolkata.

Watts, Michael and Richard Peets (1996): *Liberation Ecologies: Environment, Development, Social Movements*, Routledge Publications, London.

Wignaraja, Poona (1993): *New Social Movements in the South: Empowering the People* (ed), Vistaar Publications, New Delhi.

Articles

Assadi, Muzaffar (1998): 'Saffronization with Upper Castes Support', *Economic and Political Weekly*, March 21, pp. 626-28.

Assadi, Muzzaffar (1998): 'The State and Tribal Rights Confrontation Over Land Question', *Economic and Political Weekly*, August 15-22, 1998, pp. 2210-2212.

Assadi, Muzzaffar (2004): 'Forest Encroachments, Left Adventurism and Hindutva', *Economic and Political Weekly*, February 26, Vol. 39, No. 9, pp. 882-885.

Assadi, Muzaffar (2006): 'Agrarian Crisis and Farmers' Suicide in India: Dimension, Nature and Response of the State in Karnataka', *The Indian Journal of Labour Economics*, Vol. 49, No. 4, pp. 791-811.

Awasthi, Kirtiman (2008): 'Many Takers of a Park', *Down to Earth*, Vol. 16, No. 23, April 16-30, pp. 23-27.

Bahl, Vinay (1994): 'The Emergence of Large-Scale Steel Industry in India Under British Colonial Rule, 1880-1907', *The Indian Economic and Social History Review*, Vol. 31, No. 4, pp. 410-460.

Balakrishnan, Rajagopal (2004): 'Limits of Law in Counter-Hegemonic Globalization: The Indian Supreme Court and the Narmada Valley Struggle', *Working Paper Series*, Centre for the Study of Law and Governance, Jawaharlal Nehru University.

Banaji, Jairus (1996): 'Globalization and Restructuring the Indian Food Industry', *Journal of Peasant Studies*, Vol. 24, No. 1&2, October, pp. 191-210.

Banerjee, Prathama (2016): 'Writing the Adivasis: Some Historiogrpahical Notes', *The Indian Economic and Social History Review*, 53, 1, pp. 131-153.

Banerjee, Sumanta (2006): 'Maoist Movement in India: Beyond Naxalbari', *Economic and Political Weekly*, Vol. XL, No. 29, pp. 3159-62.

Baumann, Pari (1998): 'The Persistence of Populism in Forest Policy', *Journal of Peasant Studies*, Vol. 25, No. 4, July, pp. 96-123.

Baviskar, Amita (2003): 'Between Violence and Desire: Space, Power and Identity in the Making of Metropolitan Delhi', *International Social Science*, Journal, pp. 89-98.

Bebbington, Anthony (2007): 'Social Movements and the Politicization of Chronic Poverty', *Development and Change*, Vol. 38, No. 5, pp. 739-816.

Bellamy, Foster J. and Brett Clark (2008): 'Rachel Carson's Ecological Critique', *Analytical Monthly Review*, Vol. 5, No. 11, pp. 1-5.

Betellie, Andre (2007): 'Classes and Communities', *Economic and Political Weekly*, Vol. XLII, No. 11, pp. 945-952.

Bhargava, Praveen and Niren Jain (2004): 'Battle For Kudremukh', *The Hindu*, January 4.

Bhattacharya, Bhaswati (2014): 'Local History of a Global Commodity: Production of Coffee in Mysore and Coorg in the Nineteenth Century', *Indian Historical Review*, 41 (1), pp. 67-86.

Brockington, Dan (2000): 'Community Conservation, Inequality and Injustice', *Conservation and Society*, 2, pp. 411-32.

Chandra, Navin (2002): 'Organizing Labour: The Question of Form and Content', *The Indian Journal of Labour Economics*, Vol. 45, No. 4, pp. 1329-37.

Chatterjee, Partha (2008): 'Democracy and Economic Transformation in India', *Economic and Political Weekly*, 43 (16), April 19, pp. 53-62.

Chopra, Kanchan (2014): 'Conservation and Development in the Western Ghats: A Tale of Two Committees and More', *Economic and Political Weekly*, Vol. XLIX, No. 11, pp. 12-14.

Coffee (2001): 'Hard Times', *Economic and Political Weekly*, September 1, pp. 3332-33.

Coffee Industry on the Verge of Collapse: KPA, *Deccan Herald*, November 11, 2002.

Das, Raju (2007): 'Looking, But Not Seeing: The State and/as Class in Rural India', *Journal of Peasant Studies*, Vol. 34, No. 3&4, July-October, pp. 408-40.

David, Stephen (2007): 'Environment: Forest Encroachment', *India*

Today, May 21, pp. 75, 78.

Deshpande, Rajeshwari (2014): 'Seeking OBC Status: Political Strategies of Two Dominant Castes', *Studies in Indian Politics*, 2 (2), New Delhi, Sage Publications, pp. 169-183.

Diani Mario (1992): 'The Concept of Social Movement', *Sociological Review*, 40, pp. 1-25.

Divyabhanusinh (1998): 'A Princely Bequest', *Seminar 466*, June, pp. 40-46.

Dutta, Ritwick (2003): 'Courts and Environmental Justice: Critical Issues', *Social Change*, Vol. 33, No. 2&3, June-September, pp. 24-5.

Environment in Karnataka (1999): 'A Status Report, Ecological Economics Unit, Institute for Social and Economic Change, Bangalore', *Economic and Political Weekly*, Vol. XXXIV, No. 38, September 18, pp. 2735-2744.

Foster, John Bellamy (2002): 'Capitalism and Ecology: The Nature of the Contradiction', *Monthly Review*, Vol. 54, No. 4, pp. 6-16.

Foster, John Bellamy (2007): The Ecology of Destruction, Analytical *Monthly Review*, February, Vol. 4, No. 11, pp. 1-13.

Gadgil, Madhav (1991): 'Restoring India's Forest Wealth', *Nature and Resources*, Vol. 27, No. 2, pp. 12-20.

Gadgil, Madhav (1992): 'Can Conserving India's Biodiversity be Turned into a People's Movement?', Background paper prepared for the expert groups consultation on conservation of biological diversity, *India International Centre*, December 3, New Delhi.

Gadgil, Madhav (2014): 'Western Ghats Ecology Expert Panel: A Play in Five Acts', *Economic and Political Weekly*, Vol. XLIX, No. 48, May 3, pp.

Gadgil, Madhav 2000: 'Conservation: Taking Care of All Life', *The Hindu Survey of the Environment*, pp. 69-75.

Gadgil, Madhav and Ramachandra Guha (1994): 'Ecological Conflicts and the Environment Movement in India', *Development and Change*, Vol. 25, pp. 100-135.

George, Jose and P. Krishnaprasad (2006): 'Agrarian Distress and Farmers' Suicides in the Tribal District of Wayanad', *Social Scientist*, Nos. 7-8, July-August, pp. 70-85

George, P.T. (1970): 'Land System and Laws in Mysore State', March-June Vol. 12, No. 1&2, *Artha Vijana*, Poona, pp. 1-74.

Giri, Saroj (2009): 'The Maoist "Problem" and the Democratic Left in India', *Journal of Contemporary Asia*, Vol. 39, No. 3, Routledge Publications, August, pp. 463-474.

Giri, Saroj (2009): Maoists and the Poor: Against Democracy? *Economic and Political Weekly*, Vol. XLIV, No. 49, December 5, pp. 17-21.

Guha, Ramachandra (1983) 'Forest in British and Post-British India: A Historical Analysis', *Economic and Political Weekly*, Vol. 18 (44), October 29, pp. 1882-96.

Guha, Ramachandra (2007) "Adivasis, Naxalities and Indian Democracy", *Economic and Political Weekly*, August 11, Vol. XLII, No. 32, pp. 3305-12.

Guha, Ramachandra and Madhav, Gadgil (1989) 'State Forestry and Social Conflict in British India', *Past and Present, A Journal of Historical Studies*, Number 123, pp. 141-177.

Hensman, Rohini (2012): 'Workers, Union and the Left: Responding to Global Crisis', Working Paper, Nehru Memorial Museum and Library, New Delhi.

Hoque, Ridwanul (2006): 'Taking Justice Seriously: Judicial Public Interest and Constitutional Activism in Bangladesh', *Contemporary South Asia*, 15 (4), December, pp. 399-422.

Indira, M. (1995): 'What Brought Depooling?' Published by Indian Coffee Board, Bangalore, pp. 5-6.

Jain, Niren (2003): 'The Kudremukh Experience', Sanctuary Asia, Vol. XXIII, No. 4, pp. 18-29.

Joseph, Sarah (2007): 'Neoliberal Reforms and Democracy', *Economic and Political Weekly*, Vol. XLII, No. 31, August 4th, pp. 3213-3218.

Joy, C.V. (2004): 'Small Coffee Growers of Sulthan Bathery, Wayanad', Centre for Development Studies, Kerala.

Kabra, Asmita (2013): Conservation Induced Displacement: The Anatomy of a Win-Win Situation, Social Change, 43, 4, pp. 553-550.

Karanth, Ullas (1985): 'The Primate Conservation: The Newsletter and Journal of the IUCN/SSC', Primate Specialist Group, Number 6, July, pp. 73-84.

Karanth, Ullas and Praveen Bhargava (2005): 'Defragmenting Nature', *Seminar*, No. 552, pp. 5-62.

Karat, Prakash (1984): 'Action Groups, Voluntary Organizations: A Factor in Imperialist Strategy', *The Marxist*, Vol. 2, April-June, pp. 19-54.

Karnaik, Kusum (2003): 'Where are the People'? January 15, *Down to Earth*.

Kaviraj, Sudipto (1989): 'A Critique of the Passive Revolution', *Economic and Political Weekly*, XXIII, No. 45-47, pp. 2429-44.

Klein, Ira (1984): 'When the Rains Failed: Famine, Relief and Mortality in British India', *The Indian Economic and Social History Review*, 21,

2, pp. 184-214.

Kooiman, Dick (1992): 'Plantations in Southern Asia: Indigenous Plants and Foreign Implantations', *South Asia*, Vol. XV, No. 1, pp. 59-73.

Kothari, Ashish, Solani Suri, and Neena Singh (1995): 'Conservation in India: A New Direction', *Economic and Political Weekly*, 28 October, pp. 2755-2766.

Kudremukh Mining: Reality and Myth (2001): A Report by the Fact-Finding Team of Democratic Youth Federation of India (DYFI) Udupi District Committee, Published by Pragathipara Janasamudaya Prakashana, Mangalore. (Booklet in Kannada).

Kudremukha Ganigarike Pancghamahaa Sullugalu: A Collection of articles by Tunga-Bhadra Joint Struggle Forum, Published by Nama Nadu, Shimoga (in Kannada).

Kulkarni, Sharad (2000): 'The Plight of the Tribal', *Seminar* No. 492, pp. 37-41.

Kulkarni, Sharad (2005): 'UPA-Promises to Keep': Background paper prepared for the workshop on 'Tribals, Forests and Related Issues: People Oriented Natural Resource Policies and Legislations', on October 19-20 at Gandhi Peace Foundation, New Delhi, organized by National Committee for Protection of Natural Resources (NCPNR).

Kummitha, Rama Krishna Reddy (2015): 'Social Exclusion: The European Context for Indian Social Reality', *Social Change*, March 45 (1), pp. 15-18.

Labour file (2006): 'Bonded Labour: It's Not Over, But it's All Over!" *A Bimonthly Journal of Labour and Economic Affairs*, Vol. 4, No. 3, May-June, pp. 1-64.

Lele, Sharachchandra (2002): 'A Defining Moment for Forests', *Economic and Political Weekly*, June 23, pp. 2380-2384.

Lele, Sharachchandra (2011): Rethinking Forest Governance: Towards a Perspective Beyond JFM, the Godavarman and FRA, *The Hindu Survey of the Environment*, New Delhi.

Lokesh, P.V. (2001): 'An Open Letter from the Coffee Growers to Different Associations, People's Representatives and State Government', published by Siravase Coffee Belegara (Growers) Sangha, Chikmagalur (in Kannada).

Macdonald, Kate (2007): 'Globalizing Justice within Coffee Supply Chains; Fair Trade, Starbucks and the Transformation of Supply Chain Governance', *Third World Quarterly*, Vol. 28, No. 4, pp. 793-812.

Madhusudan , M.D. and Rohan Arthur (2007): 'Succeeding Poorly or Failing Better' *Seminar* No. 577, pp. 74-78.

Madhusudan, M.D. and Shankar Raman, T.R. (2003): 'Conservation as if Biological Diversity Matters: Preservation versus Sustainable Use in India', *Conservation and Society,* 1, pp. 49-57.

Mann, Michael (1995): 'A Permanent Settlement for the Ceded and Conquered Provinces: Revenue Administration in North India', 1801-1833', *The Indian Economic and Social History Review,* 32, 2, pp. 245-69.

Manor, James (1980): 'Pragmatic Progressive in Regional Politics: The Case of Devraj Urs', *Economic and Political Weekly,* Annual Number, February, pp. 210-213.

Mathur, Kuldeep (2004): 'Battling for Clean Environment: Supreme Court, Technocrats and Populist Politics in Delhi', Centre for the Study for Law and Governance, Jawaharlal Nehru University, Working Paper Series.

Mawdsley, E.E. (2004): 'India's Middle Class and the Environment', *Development and Change,* 35 (1), pp. 79-103.

Mazumdar, Surajit (2012): 'Industrialization, Dirigisme and Capitalists: Indian Big Buisness from Independence to Liberalization', Nehru Memorial Museum and Library, *Occasional Paper,* New Delhi.

McGregor, Andrew (2007): 'Development, Foreign Aid and Post-Development in Timor-Leste', *Third World Quarterly,* Vol. 28, No. 1, pp. 155-170.

Mendiratta, Uttara and Nupur Dhingra (2002): 'A Win-Win Situation for People and Wildlife', *Sanctuary Asia,* pp. 28-31.

Menon, Parvathi (2002): 'The Cup of Woes', Frontline, March 16, Vol. 19, Issue 6, pp. 49-51.

Menon, Parvathi (2003): 'A Communal Campaign', *Frontline,* Vol. 20, Issue-25, December 6-19, pp. 41-2.

Menon, Parvathi (2003): 'Karnataka's Agenda', *Frontline,* January 17, pp. 17-18.

Mukul (1997): 'Tribal Areas: Transition to Self-Governance', *Economic and Political Weekly,* Vol. XXXII, No. 18, May 3, pp. 928-29.

Mustafa, Mohammed (2007): 'The Shaping of Land Revenue Policy in Madras Presidency: Revenue Experiments: The Case of Chittor District', *The Indian Economic and Social History Review,* 44, 2, pp. 213-36.

Naganna, N. (1999): 'A Structural Analysis of India's Mining Sector in the Context of Development Planning', *Indian Journal of Economics,* Vol. LXIX, Part III, No. 274, pp. 279-30.

Narayan, Badri (2015): Democracy and Identity Politics in India: Is it a Snake or Rope? *Economic and Political Weekly*, Vol. 1, No. 16, April 18, pp. 18-51.

Narayana, M.S. (2014): 'Size Distribution of Estates, Inequlaity and Poverty: Evidence for India's Household Coffee Farmers', *Journal of Asian Policy*, Vol. 7, No. 1, Routledge, pp. 18-40.

Nigam, Aditya (2010): 'The Rumour of Maoism', Seminar, pp. 1-13.

Omvedt, Gail (1980): 'Migration in Colonial India: The Articulation of Feudalism and Capitalism by the Colonial State' *The Journal of Peasant Studies*, pp. 180-212.

Panchu, Sriram (1997): 'In the Public Interest', *Seminar*, 451, pp. 55-8.

Pani, Narendar (1988): 'Political Economy of Karnataka 1950-1955: An Overview', *Journal of Social and Economic Development*, Vol. I, No. I, January-June, pp. 64-84.

Pasha, Syed Ajmal (1994): 'Uncultivated Lands: Institutional Aspects of Their Use and Management in Karnataka', Institute for Social and Economic Change (ISEC), Bangalore.

Pathak, Akhileshwar (1994): 'State, Environment and Law', *Economic and Political Weekly*, December 10, Vol. XXIX, No. 50, pp. 3138-41.

Patnaik, Prabhat (2014): 'Neoliberalism and Democracy', *Economic and Political Weekly*, Vol. XLIX, No. 15, April 12, pp. 39-44.

Patnaik, Utsa (1996): 'Export-Oriented Agriculture and Food Security in Developing Countries', *Economic and Political Weekly*, Vol. XXXI, No. 35, 36, Special Number, September, pp. 2429-49.

Perlin, F. (1978): 'Of White Whales and Countrymen in the Eighteenth Century Maratha Deccan', *Journal of Peasant Studies*, Vol. 5, pp. 172-237.

Petras, James and Henry Veltmeyer (2007): 'The 'Development State' in Latin America: Whose Development, Whose State?', *Journal of Peasant Studies*, Vol. 34, No. 3&4, July-October, pp. 371-407.

Ponte, Stefano (2001): 'Behind the Coffee Crisis', *Economic and Political Weekly*, November 24, Vol. XXXVI, No. 46 and 47, pp. 4410-4417.

Prasad, Archana (2003): 'Forest Encroachments: Guidelines and Implications of Recent Orders', *People's Democracy*, Vol. XXVI, No. 1, January 5.

Prasad, P. Krishna (2004): 'Farmers form Platform for Resistance', *People's Democracy, Weekly Organ of the Communist Party of India* (Marxist) Vol. XXVI, No. 36, September.

Rajagopal, Balakrishnan (2004): 'Limits of law in Counter-Hegemonic Globalization: The Indian Supreme Court and the Narmada Valley Struggle', *Working Paper Series*, Centre for the Study of

Law and Governance, Jawaharlal Nehru University.

Raji (2004): 'Bitter Coffee, Crisis of the Indian and Global Coffee Industry', published by Vimukthi Prakashana, Bangalore.

Ramesh, P. Babu (2007): 'Optional or Imposed / An Ex-Post Evaluation of Voluntary Retirement Scheme in BALCO', *Economic and Political Weekly*, Vol. XLII, No. 21, May 26, pp. 1934-41.

Rangarajan, Mahesh (1994): 'Imperial Agendas and Indian Forests: The Early History of Indian Forestry, 1800-1878', *The Indian Economic and Social History Review*, Vol. 31, No. 2, pp. 147-167.

Rangarajan, Mahesh (1996): 'The Politics of Ecology: The Debate on Wildlife and People in India', *Economic and Political Weekly*, Special Number, September, pp. 2391-2409.

Rangarajan, Mahesh and Ghazala Shahabuddin (2006): 'Relocation from Protected Areas: Towards a Historical and Biological Synthesis', *Conservation and Society*, Vol. 1-4, No. 3, September, pp. 360-361.

Rodrigues, Valerian (2014): Political Power and Democratic Enablement: Devaraj Urs and Lower Caste Mobilizations in Karnataka, *Economic and Political Weekly*, Vol. XLIX, No. 25, pp. 62-70.

Rosencranz, Armin, Edward Boenig and Brinda Dutta (2007): 'The Godavarman Case: The Indian Supreme Court's Breach of Constitutional Boundaries in Managing India's Forest', *ELR News and Analysis*, 37, Washingtion, pp. 10032-42.

Roy, A.K. (1997): 'Can Courts Run the Country?', *Economic and Political Weekly*, October 11, pp. 2579-81.

Roy, Dunu (2003): 'Emerging Paradigms in Environmental Conservation and Management', *Social Change*, Vol. 33, No. 2&3, June-September, pp. 1-15.

Roy, Kaushik (2004): 'A Military Revolution in Mysore', Vol. 3. No. 4, July-September, *Contemporary India*, New Delhi, pp. 19-37.

Saravanan, Velayutham (2004): 'Colonialism and Coffee Plantations: Decline of Environment and Tribals in Madras Presidency During the 19th Century', *The Indian Economic and Social History Review*, 41, 4, pp. 440-75.

Sarin, Madhu (2002): 'Who is Encroaching on Whose Land?', *Seminar* No. 519, pp. 1-10.

Sarkar, Sahotra (2003): 'Conservation Area Networks', *Conservation and Society*, 1, 2, pp. 1-3.

Sen, Arindam (2010): 'Anarchism or Revolutionary Marxism', *Seminar*, 607, pp. 1-10.

Seth, D.L (1984): 'Grass Roots Initiatives in India', *Economic and Political Weekly*, 19 (16), pp. 1-24.

Sethi, Harsh (2001): 'Movements and Mediators', *Economic and Political Weekly*, January 27, Vol. XXXVI, No. 4, pp. 269-270.

Shahabuddin, Ghazala, Ravi Kumar, Manish Shrivastava (2007): 'Creation of 'Inviolate Space': Lives, Livelihoods and Conflict in Sariska Tiger Reserve', *Economic and Political Weekly*, May 19, pp. 1855-62.

Shaker, Dattari (2007): 'Wildlife Films, Do They Have a Future in India?', *Sanctuary Asia*, Vol. XXVII, No. 1, Mumbai, pp. 18-29.

Sharma, Ravi (2003): 'Eating Up Forest Land', March 28, Vol. 20, No. 6, *Frontline*, pp. 50-54.

Sharma, Ravi (2006): 'Waiting for a Miracle', Volume 23, Issue 01, *Frontline*, January 14-27, pp. 32-35.

Shivaramakrishnan, K. (1995): 'Imagining the Past in Present Politics: Colonialism and Forestry in India', *Comparative Studies in Society and History*, Vol. 37, pp. 3-40.

Singh, Digvijay (2005): 'The Real Issues', *Seminar*, 522, Special Issue on Forests and Tribals, pp. 20-22.

Sitharaman, Sudha (2010): 'Conflict Over Worship: A Study of Sri Guru Dattatreya Swami Babadudan Dargah in South India', *Working Paper*, Institute for Social and Economic Change, Bangalore.

Sreedhara,V.S. (2004): 'Street Fighting Years: Karnataka Komu Souharda Vedike (Karnataka Communal Harmony Forum)', *Communalism Combat*, Cover Story, September No. 118.

Sreedharan, T.P. (2004): 'Biodiversity of Kerala: A Survey of Kalliasseri Panchayat, Kannur District', *Discussion Paper No. 62*, Kerala Research Programme on Local Level Development, Thiruvanthapuram, Kerala.

Srinidhi, A.S. and S. Lele (2001): "Forest Tenure Regimes in the Karnataka, Western Ghats: A Compendium" *Working Paper*, Institute for Social and Economic Change, Bangalore.

Srinivas, M.N. and M.N. Pannini (1984): 'Politics and Society in Karnataka', *Economic and Political Weekly*, Vol. 19(2), January 14, pp. 70-71.

Srinivas, S.V. (2015): 'Maoism to Mass Culture: Notes on Telangana's Cultural Turn', *Bioscope*, Vol. 16, No. 2, July, pp. 187-205.

Srinivasan, Janaki (2010): 'The World Social Forum and the Debate on the Alternative Development in India', *Critical Engagement*, CSCIM Occasional Publications, New Delhi.

Stein, Burton (1989): 'State Formation Reconsidered', *Modern Asian*

Studies, Vol. 19, pp. 415-81.

Subrahmanyam, Sanjay (1989): 'Welfare and State Finance in Wodeyar Mysore, 1724-25: A Missionary Perspective', *Indian Economic and Social History Review*, Vol. 26, No. 2, pp. 204-7, 226-7.

Taneja, Nalini (2006): 'The Ongoing Communalism in Karnataka', *People's Democracy*, Weekly Organ of the Communist Party of India (Marxist), Vol. XXX, No. 46, November 12.

Vagholikar, Neeraj, Kaustabh. A. Moghe and Ritwick Dutta (2003): Undermining India: Impacts of Mining on Ecologically Sensitive Areas, Kalpavriksh (NGO), Pune.

Venkatachalam, Lakshmi (2004): 'Global Coffee Crisis and the Quest for Sustainable Solutions', Vol. LXVIII, No. 9, September 6, Coffee Board, Bangalore, pp. 4-7.

Venkatachalapathy, A.R. (2002): 'In Those Days There was No Coffee: Coffee-Drinking and Middle-Class Culture in Colonial Tamil Nadu', *The Indian Economic and Social History Review*, 39, 2&3, Sage Publications, pp. 301-316.

Verma, A.K. (2015): 'Importance of Preserving Karnataka's Western Ghats' Tigers', *Deccan Herald*, April 30.

Vicziany, Marika (1986): 'Imperialism, Botany and Statistics in Early Nineteenth Century India: The Surveys of Francis Buchanan (1762-1829)', *Modern Asian Studies*, Vol. 20, pp. 625-660.

Vijayalakshmi,V. (2003): 'Scheduled Tribes and Gender: Development Perceptions from Karnataka', Working Paper No. 128, *The Institute for Social and Economic Change*, Bangalore, pp. 1-25.

Vittalahedge, Kalkuli (2002): 'Kadu Kirukula' (Collection of Columns), Nammanaadu Prakashana, Shimoga, Karnataka (in Kannada).

Williamson, John (2003): 'The Washington Consensus and Beyond', *Economic and Political Weekly*, April 12, Vol. 38, pp. 1475-81.

Yadav, Manohar (1998): 'Carrier of Dalit Movement in Karnataka', *Journal of Social and Economic Development*, Vol. I, January-June, pp. 111-16.

Newspapers, Websites and Compact Discs

The Hindu

Deccan Herald

The Indian Express

The Times of India

www.oxfam.org.uk

www.iisc.ernet.in/nias/bidar.htm